Table of Contents

SQL
IN A NUTSHELL
A Desktop Quick Reference

Kevin Kline with Daniel Kline

O'REILLY®

Beijing · Cambridge · Farnham · Köln · Paris · Sebastopol · Taipei · Tokyo

SQL in a Nutshell

by Kevin Kline with Daniel Kline

Copyright © 2001 O'Reilly & Associates, Inc. All rights reserved.
Printed in the United States of America.

Published by O'Reilly & Associates, Inc., 101 Morris Street, Sebastopol, CA 95472.

Editor: Gigi Estabrook

Production Editor: Mary Sheehan

Cover Designer: Ellie Volckhausen

Printing History:

    January 2001:   First Edition.

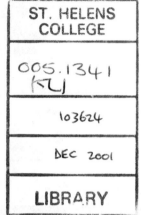
Library of Congress Cataloging-in-Publication Data

Kline, Kevin E., 1966-
    SQL in a nutshell : a desktop quick reference/Kevin Kline with Daniel Kline.
      p. cm.
    Includes index.
    ISBN 1-56592-744-3
    1. SQL server 2. SQL (Computer program language) 3. Client/server computing.
      I. Kline, Daniel.

QA76.73.S67 K55 2000
005.75'85--dc21   00-065206

ISBN: 1-56592-744-3   [6/01]
[M]

Preface

The explosive growth of the information technology industry and the constantly growing need to compile, store, access, and manipulate increasingly larger masses of data have required the development of ever more sophisticated database management tools.

Since its first incarnation in the 1970s, Structured Query Language (SQL) has been developed hand in hand with the information boom, and as a result, is the most widely used database manipulation language in business and industry. A number of different software companies and program developers, including those in the open source movement, have concurrently developed their own SQL dialects in response to specific needs. All the while, standards bodies have developed a growing list of common features.

SQL in a Nutshell identifies the differences between the various vendor implementations of SQL. Readers will find a concise explanation of the Relational Database Management System (RDBMS) model, a clear-cut explanation of foundational RDBMS concepts, and thorough coverage of basic SQL syntax and commands. Most importantly, programmers and developers who use *SQL in a Nutshell* will find a concise guide both to the most popular commercial database packages on the market (Microsoft SQL Server and Oracle8*i*), and to two of the best known open source (*http://www.opensource.org*) database products (MySQL and PostgreSQL). *SQL in a Nutshell's* attention to open source SQL products is an affirmation of the growing importance of the open source movement within the computing community.

As a result, *SQL in a Nutshell* benefits several distinct groups of users: the knowledgeable programmer who requires a concise and handy reference tool, the developer who needs to migrate from one SQL dialect to another, and the user who comes to SQL from another programming language and wants to learn the basics of SQL programming.

How This Book Is Organized

This book is divided into five chapters and one appendix:

Chapter 1, *SQL, Vendor Implementations, and Some History*
> This chapter discusses the Relational Database Model, describes the current and previous SQL standards, and introduces the SQL vendor implementations covered in this book.

Chapter 2, *Foundational Concepts*
> This chapter describes the fundamental concepts necessary for understanding relational databases and SQL commands.

Chapter 3, *SQL Statements Command Reference*
> This chapter is an alphabetical command reference. It details each SQL99 command, as well as the implementations of each command by Oracle, Microsoft SQL Server, MySQL, and PostgreSQL.

Chapter 4, *SQL Functions*
> This chapter is an alphabetical reference of the SQL99 functions, describing vendor implementations of these functions and vendor extensions.

Chapter 5, *Unimplemented SQL99 Commands*
> This chapter lists commands that are included in the SQL standards, but have not yet been implemented by any of the vendors.

Appendix, *SQL99 and Vendor-Specific Keywords*
> The appendix provides a table that displays keywords declared in SQL99 and by the various database vendors.

Conventions Used in This Book

Constant Width
> Used to indicate programming syntax, code fragments, and examples.

Italic
> Used to introduce new terms, for emphasis, and to indicate commands or user-specified file and directory names.

Bold
> Used to display the names of database objects, such as tables, columns, and stored procedures.

UPPERCASE
> Used to indicate SQL keywords.

 The owl icon indicates a tip, suggestion, or general note.

The turkey icon indicates a warning or caution.

How to Contact Us

The information in this book has been tested and verified, but you may find that features have changed (or you may even find mistakes!). Please let us know about any errors you find, as well as your suggestions for future editions, by writing to:

O'Reilly & Associates, Inc.
101 Morris Street
Sebastopol, CA 95472
(800) 998-9938 (in the United States or Canada)
(707) 829-0515 (international/local)
(707) 829-0104 (fax)

There is a web page for this book, which lists errata and any additional information. You can access this page at:

http://www.oreilly.com/catalog/sqlnut/

To comment or ask technical questions about this book, send email to:

bookquestions@oreilly.com

For more information about books, conferences, software, Resource Centers, and the O'Reilly Network, see the O'Reilly web site at:

http://www.oreilly.com

Resources

The following web sites provide additional information about the various vendors covered in this book:

MySQL
> The corporate resource for MySQL is *http://www.tcx.se*. A great developer resource with lots of useful tips is Devshed.com: see *http://www.devshed.com/Server_Side/MySQL/* for MySQL-specific information.

Microsoft SQL Server
> The official Microsoft SQL Server web site is *http://www.microsoft.com/sql/*. Microsoft also hosts a strong technical site for SQL Server at *http://www.microsoft.com/technet/sql/default.htm*. Another good resource is found at the home of the Professional Association for SQL Server (PASS) at *http://www.sqlpass.org*.

PostgreSQL

The home for this open source database is located at *http://www.postgresql.org*. This site contains a great deal of useful information available for download, as well as mailing lists that enable exchanges with other PostgreSQL users. Additional PostgreSQL sites worth investigating are *http://www.pgsql.com* and *http://www.GreatBridge.com*, which offer support for commercial customers.

Oracle

Oracle's cyberspace home is *http://www.oracle.com*. A great resource for hard-core Oracle users is *http://technet.oracle.com*.

Acknowledgments

We'd like to take a moment to thank a few special individuals at O'Reilly & Associates. First, we owe a huge debt of gratitude to Gigi Estabrook, the initial editor of this book, and Robert Denn, the ultimate editor of this book. Gigi's outstanding work and caring attitude were always refreshing and rejuvenating. Robert's attention to detail and exceptional management skills are the reason this book is here today. Thank you both! And of course, thanks to Tim O'Reilly for having a direct hand in the birth of this book.

We also owe a debt to our fine technical reviewers. To Thomas Lockhard (PostgreSQL and SQL99), Matthew Toennies and Jonathan Gennick (Oracle), Baya Pavliachvili and Ron Talmage (Microsoft SQL Server), and George Reese (MySQL): we owe you a hearty thanks! Your contributions have greatly improved the accuracy, readability, and value of this book. Without you, our sections on each of the language extensions would have been on shaky ground.

CHAPTER 1

SQL, Vendor Implementations, and Some History

In the 1970s, IBM developed a product called SEQUEL, or Structured English Query Language, which ultimately became SQL, the *Structured Query Language*.

IBM, along with other relational database vendors, wanted a standardized method for accessing and manipulating data in a relational database. Over the decades, many competing languages have allowed programmers and developers to access and manipulate data. However, few have been as easy to learn and as universally accepted as SQL. Programmers and developers now have the benefit of learning a language that, with minor adjustments, is applicable to a wide variety of database applications and products.

SQL in a Nutshell describes four implementations of the current SQL standard, SQL99 (also known as SQL3): Microsoft's SQL Server, MySQL, Oracle, and PostgreSQL. For those migrating from implementations of the earlier SQL standard, this chapter describes the current SQL standard and the ways in which it differs from the earlier standard. This chapter also provides a bit of history of the standards evolution.

The Relational Database Model

Relational Database Management Systems (RDBMSs), such as SQL Server and Oracle, are the primary engines of information systems worldwide, particularly Internet/Intranet applications and distributed client/server computing systems.

An RDBMS is defined as a system whose users view data as a collection of tables related to each other through common data values. Data is stored in tables, and tables are composed of rows and columns. Tables of independent data can be linked (or *related*) to one another if they each have columns of data (called *keys*) that represent the same data value. This concept is so common as to seem trivial; however, it was not so long ago that achieving and programming a system capable of sustaining the relational model was considered a long shot that would have limited usefulness.

Relational data theory was developed by E. F. Codd in the 1960s. Codd compiled a list of criteria a database product must meet to be considered relational. For those who are curious, Codd's list appears at the end of this chapter.

The Databases Described in This Book

SQL in a Nutshell describes the SQL standard and the vendor implementations of four leading RDBMSs—two that are from leading commercial vendors (Microsoft SQL Server and Oracle) and two that are from the chief open source database projects (MySQL and PostgreSQL):

Microsoft SQL Server
Microsoft SQL Server is a popular RDBMS that runs only on the Windows platform. Its features include ease of use, low cost, and high performance. This book covers Microsoft SQL Server 2000.

MySQL
MySQL is a popular open source Database Management System (DBMS) that is known for its blistering performance. It runs on numerous operating systems, including most Linux variants. To improve performance, it has a slimmer feature set than do many other DBMSs. Its critics point out that it is not a fully relational DBMS since it does not support many key features of relational databases, particularly in how it processes transactions. This book covers MySQL 3.22.9.

Oracle
Oracle is a leading RDBMS in the commercial sector. It runs on a multitude of operating systems and hardware platforms. Its scalable and reliable architecture have made it the platform of choice for many users. Because of their highly tunable nature, Oracle RDBMSs require a well-trained database administrator (DBA). *SQL in a Nutshell* covers Oracle Release 8.1.

PostgreSQL
PostgreSQL is one of the most feature-rich RDBMSs of the open source world. Its compliance with SQL standards is unmatched by other open source RDBMSs. In addition to its rich set of features, PostgreSQL runs on a wide variety of operating systems and hardware platforms. This book covers PostgreSQL 7.0.

The SQL Standard

To bring greater conformity among vendors, the American National Standards Institute (ANSI) published its first SQL standard in 1986 and a second widely adopted standard in 1989. ANSI released updates in 1992, known as SQL92 and SQL2, and again in 1999, termed both SQL99 and SQL3. Each time, ANSI added new features and incorporated new commands and capabilities into the language. Unique to the SQL99 standard is a group of capabilities that handle object-oriented datatype extensions. The International Standards Organization (ISO) has also approved SQL99. An important change from SQL92 is that SQL99 expands on SQL92's *levels of conformance.*

Levels of Conformance

SQL92 first introduced levels of conformance by defining three categories: Entry, Intermediate, and Full. Vendors had to achieve Entry-level conformance to claim ANSI SQL compliance. The U.S. National Institute of Standards and Technology (NIST) later added the Transitional level between the Entry and Intermediate levels. So, NIST's levels of conformance were Entry, Transitional, Intermediate, and Full, while ANSI's were only Entry, Intermediate, and Full. Each higher level of the standard was a superset of the subordinate level, meaning that each higher level of the standard included all the features of the lower level of conformance.

SQL99 altered the base levels of conformance. Gone are the Entry, Intermediate, and Full levels of conformance. With SQL99, vendors must implement all the features of the lowest level of conformance, *Core SQL:1999,* in order to claim (and publish) that they are SQL99 ready. Core SQL:1999—or Core SQL99, for short—includes the old Entry SQL92 feature set, features from other SQL92 levels, and some brand new features. This upgrade to the SQL standard enabled vendors to go quickly from the Entry SQL92 feature set to the Core SQL99 feature set.

Whereas SQL92 featured the Intermediate and Full levels of conformance, SQL99 has *Enhanced SQL:1999.* Any DBMS that supports the Core SQL99 benchmarks, plus one or more of nine additional feature packages, is now said to meet Enhanced SQL:1999 standards defined in SQL99 (also called Enhanced SQL99).

Supplemental Features Packages

The SQL99 standard represents the ideal, but very few vendors immediately meet or exceed the Core SQL99 requirements. The Core SQL99 standard is like the interstate speed limit: some drivers go above, others go below, but few go exactly the speed limit. Similarly, vendor implementations can vary greatly.

Two committees—one within ANSI and the other within ISO—composed of representatives from virtually every RDBMS vendor drafted these definitions. In this collaborative and somewhat political environment, vendors must compromise on exactly which proposed feature and implementation will be incorporated into the new standard. Many times, a new feature in the ANSI standard is derived from an existing product or is the outgrowth of new research and development from the academic community. Consequently, many vendors adopt some features in the standard, and later add still more.

The nine supplemental features packages, representing different subsets of commands, are vendor-optional. Some SQL99 features might show up in multiple packages, while others do not appear in any of the packages. These packages and their features are described in Table 1-1.

Table 1-1: SQL99 Supplemental Features Packages

ID	Name	Features
PKG001	Enhanced datetime facilities	• Interval datatype • Time zone specification • Full datetime • Optional interval qualifier
PKG002	Enhanced integrity management	• Assertions • Referential delete actions • Referential update actions • Constraint management • Subqueries in CHECK constraint • Triggers • FOR EACH STATEMENT triggers • Referential action RESTRICT
PKG003	OLAP capabilities	• CUBE and ROLLUP • INTERSECT operator • Row and table constructs • FULL OUTER JOIN • Scalar subquery values
PKG004	SQL Persistent Stored Modules (PSM)	• A programmatic extension to SQL that makes it suitable for developing more functionally complete applications • The commands CASE, IF, WHILE, REPEAT, LOOP, and FOR • Stored Modules • Computational completeness • INFORMATION_SCHEMA views
PKG005	SQL Call-level Interface (CLI)	• SQL Call-level Interface support: an Application Programming Interface (API) that enables SQL operations to be called that is very similar to the Open Database Connectivity (ODBC) standard
PKG006	Basic object support	• Overloading SQL-invoked functions and procedures • User-defined types with single inheritance; basic SQL routines on user-defined types (including dynamic dispatch) • Reference types • CREATE TABLE • Array support: basic array support, array expressions, array locators, user-datatype (UDT) array support, reference-type array support, SQL routine on arrays • Attribute and field reference • Reference and dereference operations
PKG007	Enhanced object support	• ALTER TABLE, ADD • Enhanced user-defined types (including constructor options, attribute defaults, multiple inheritance, and ordering clause) • SQL functions and type-name resolution • Subtables • ONLY in queries • Type predicate • Subtype treatment • User-defined CAST functions • UDT locators • SQL routines on user-defined types such as identity functions and generalized expressions

Table 1-1: SQL99 Supplemental Features Packages (continued)

ID	Name	Features
PKG008	Active database features	• Triggers
PKG009	SQL Multimedia (MM) support	• Handling for streaming multimedia data and for large and complex audio and video data

Be aware that a DBMS vendor may claim Enhanced SQL99 compliance by meeting Core SQL99 standards *plus only one of nine added packages*; so read the vendor's fine print for a full description of its program features. By understanding what features comprise the nine packages, programmers and developers gain a clear idea of the capabilities of a particular DBMS, and how the various features behave when SQL code is transported to other database products.

The ANSI standards—which cover retrieval, manipulation, and management of data in commands, such as *SELECT, JOIN, ALTER TABLE,* and *DROP*—formalized many SQL behaviors and syntax structures across a variety of products. These standards become even more important as open source database products, such as MySQL, miniSQL, and PostgreSQL, grow in popularity and are developed by virtual teams rather than large corporations.

SQL in a Nutshell explains the SQL implementation of four popular RDBMSs. These vendors do not meet all the SQL99 standards; in fact, all RDBMS vendors play a constant game of tag with the standards bodies. Many times, as soon as vendors close in on the standard, the standards bodies update, refine, or otherwise change the benchmark.

SQL99 Statement Classes

Comparing statement classes further delineates SQL92 and SQL99. In SQL92, SQL statements are grouped into three broad categories: the *Data Manipulation Language* (DML), the *Data Definition Language* (DDL), and the *Data Control Language* (DCL). The DML provides specific data-manipulation commands such as *SELECT, INSERT, UPDATE,* and *DELETE.* The DDL contains commands that handle the accessibility and manipulation of database objects, including *CREATE* and *DROP,* while the DCL contains the permission-related commands *GRANT* and *REVOKE.*

In contrast, SQL99 supplies seven Core categories that provide a general framework for the types of commands available in SQL. These statement "classes" are slightly different than the SQL92 statement classes, since they attempt to identify the statements within each class more accurately and logically. Furthermore, because SQL is constantly under development, new features and commands enter the standard and may necessitate new statement classes. So, to accommodate future growth, SQL99 developed new sets of statement classes, making them somewhat more comprehensible and logical. Additionally, the new statement classes now allow some "orphaned" statements—which did not fit well into any of the old categories—to be properly classified.

Table 1-2 identifies the SQL99 statement classes and lists a few commands in each class, each of which is fully discussed later. At this point, the key is to remember the statement class title.

Table 1-2: SQL Statement Classes

Class	Description	Example Commands
SQL Connection Statements	Start and end a client connection	*CONNECT, DISCONNECT*
SQL Control Statements	Control the execution of a set of SQL statements	*CALL, RETURN*
SQL Data Statements	Have a persistent and enduring effect upon data	*SELECT, INSERT, UPDATE, DELETE*
SQL Diagnostic Statements	Provide diagnostic information and raise exceptions and errors	*GET DIAGNOSTICS*
SQL Schema Statements	Have a persistent and enduring effect on a database schema and objects within that schema	*ALTER, CREATE, DROP*
SQL Session Statements	Control default behavior and other parameters for a session	*SET*
SQL Transaction Statements	Set the starting and ending point of a transaction	*COMMIT, ROLLBACK*

Those who work with SQL regularly should become familiar with both the old (SQL92) and the new (SQL99) statement classes, since many programmers and developers still use the old nomenclature to refer to current SQL features.

Dialects of SQL

The constantly evolving nature of the SQL standard has given rise to a number of SQL *dialects* among the various vendors and products. These dialects most commonly evolved because the user community of a given database vendor required capabilities in the database before the ANSI committee created a standard. Occasionally though, a new feature is introduced by the academic or research communities due to competitive pressures from competing technologies. For example, many database vendors are augmenting their current programmatic offerings with Java (as is the case with Oracle and Sybase) or VBScript (as Microsoft is doing). In the future, programmers and developers will use these programming languages in concert with SQL to build SQL programs.

Nonetheless, each of these dialects includes conditional processing (such as that controlled through *IF . . . THEN* statements), control-of-flow functions (such as *WHILE* loops), variables, and error handling. Because ANSI had not yet developed a standard for these important features, RDBMS developers and vendors were free to create their own commands and syntax. In fact, some of the earliest vendors from the 1980s have variances in the most elementary commands, such as *SELECT,* because their implementations predate the standards. (ANSI is now refining standards that address these shortcomings.)

Some of these dialects have introduced procedural commands to support the functionality of a much more complete programming language. For example, these procedural implementations contain error-handling commands, control-of-flow language, conditional commands, variable handling, arrays, and many other extensions. Although these are technically divergent procedural implementations, they are called *dialects* here.

Some popular dialects of SQL include:

PL/SQL
> Found in Oracle. PL/SQL stands for Procedural Language/SQL and contains many similarities to the language Ada.

Transact-SQL
> Uses both Microsoft SQL Server and Sybase Adaptive Server. As Microsoft and Sybase have moved away from the common platform they shared early in the 1990s, their implementations of Transact-SQL have also diverged.

PL/pgSQL
> The name of the SQL dialect and extensions implemented in PostgreSQL. The acronym stands for Procedural Language/postgreSQL.

However, even if a vendor conforms to the SQL99 standards, its commands differ from other DBMSs because SQL statements may be parsed, compiled, and executed in different ways, especially if differing *binding styles* are used. There are three common binding styles:

SQL Module Language
> Causes the SQL statements to be prepared when the module is created, and executed when the module is called (like a stored procedure).

Embedded SQL Syntax
> Allows the SQL statements to be prepared when the host language program is precompiled, and executed when the host program is called (like PRO*C or PRO*Fortran).

Direct SQL Invocation
> Causes a static SQL statement to be prepared then immediately executed.

Therefore, differences in binding style may be one more reason DBMSs function differently. Binding styles go deep into the heart of the database code. In general, the SQL commands discussed in this book utilize the Direct SQL Invocation binding style. However, when the situation warrants, other relevant binding styles are discussed within the command reference of each specific command.

Principles of Relational Databases

Following are E.F. Codd's Twelve Principles of Relational Databases. These principles continue to be the litmus test used to validate the "relational" characteristics of a database product; a database product that does not meet all of these rules is not fully relational. These rules do not apply to applications development, but they do determine whether the database engine itself can be considered truly "relational." Currently, most RDBMSs pass Codd's test, including all of the databases discussed in this book, except MySQL. (MySQL does not currently support views or atomic transactions. Therefore, it does not qualify as a true relational DBMS under Codd's rules.)

Codd's Rules for a Truly Relational Database System

Codd's criteria provide the benchmarks for defining RDBs. Knowing and understanding these principles will help you develop and design RDBs:

1. Information is represented logically in tables.
2. Data must be logically accessible by table, primary key, and column.
3. Null values must be uniformly treated as "missing information," not as empty strings, blanks, or zeros.
4. Metadata (data about the database) must be stored in the database just as regular data is.
5. A single language must be able to define data, views, integrity constraints, authorization, transactions, and data manipulation.
6. Views must show the updates of their base tables and vice versa.
7. A single operation must be able to retrieve, insert, update, or delete data.
8. Batch and end-user operations are logically separate from physical storage and access methods.
9. Batch and end-user operations can change the database schema without having to recreate it or the applications built upon it.
10. Integrity constraints must be available and stored in the RDB metadata, not in an application program.
11. The data manipulation language of the relational system should not care where or how the physical data is distributed and should not require alteration if the physical data is centralized or distributed.
12. Any row processing done in the system must obey the same integrity rules and constraints that set-processing operations do.

Knowing and understanding these principles assists programmers and developers in the proper development and design of Relational Databases (RDBs).

CHAPTER 2

Foundational Concepts

SQL provides an easy, intuitive way to interact with a database. The SQL99 standard does not define the concept of a "database," but it does define all the functions and concepts needed for a user to create, retrieve, update, and delete data. It is important to review a few of the concepts upon which the SQL standard is based.

Row Processing Versus Set Processing

Other database manipulation languages, such as Xbase or Visual Basic, perform their data operations quite differently from SQL. These languages require the programmer to tell the program exactly how to treat the data, one record at a time. Since the program cycles down through a list of records, performing its logic on one record after another, this style of programming is frequently called *row processing* or *procedural programming*.

SQL programs operate in logical *sets* of data. Set theory is applied when the *FROM* clause is used, as in the *SELECT* statement. In effect, data is selected from a set called a table. Unlike the row processing style, *set processing* allows a programmer to tell the database simply *what* is required, not *how* each individual piece of data should be handled. Sometimes set processing is referred to as *declarative processing*, since a programmer declares only what data is necessary, as in "Give me all employees in the southern region who earn more than $70,000 per year," rather than describes the exact procedure used to manipulate the data.

 Set theory was the brainchild of Russian mathematician Georg Cantor, who developed it at the end of the nineteenth century. At the time, set theory (and his theory of the infinite) was quite controversial; today, set theory is such a common part of life that it is learned in elementary school.

Examples of set theory in conjunction with relational databases are detailed in the following section.

The Relational Model

Effective SQL programming requires that the programmer think in terms of sets of data, rather than of individual rows. The RDBS model follows a linguistic protocol to define the hierarchy of data sets within the SQL99 standard.

Figure 2-1 is a description of the SQL99 terminology used to describe the hierarchical working sets used by a relational database—clusters contain sets of catalogs; catalogs contain sets of schemas; schemas contain sets of objects, such as tables and views; and tables and views are composed of sets of records.

In the relational model, data is shown logically as a two-dimensional *table* that describes a single entity (for example, business expenses). Data in the table is displayed in *columns* and *rows*. Each column of the table describes a specific attribute of the entity. For example, in a **Business_Expense** table, a column called **Expense_Date** might show when the expense was incurred. Each record in the table describes a specific entity; in this case, everything that makes up a business expense (when it happened, how much it cost, who incurred the expense, what it was for, and so on). The specific values of each attribute are supposed to be *atomic*; that is, they are supposed to contain one, and only one, value. If a table is constructed in which the intersection of a row and column can contain more than one distinct value, then one of SQL's primary design guidelines has been violated.

There are rules of behavior specified for column values. Foremost is that the column values must share a common *domain*, better known as a *datatype*. For example, the value 'ELMER' should not be placed into the **Expense_Date** field. The **Expense_Date** field should contain only dates; therefore, this column would be defined as having a date datatype. In addition, SQL99 further controls the values of such a field through the application of *rules*. A SQL rule might limit **Expense_Date** to expenses less than a year old.

Additionally, data access for all individuals and computer processes is controlled at the schema level by an *<AuthorizationID>* or *user*. Permissions to specific sets of data may be granted or restricted to each user.

Moreover, SQL databases also employ *character sets* and *collations*. Character sets are the "symbols" used by the "language" of the data. Character sets can contain multiple collations. A collation is the basic set of rules that define how SQL sorts the data. For example, an American English character set might be sorted either by character-order, case-insensitive, or by character-order, case-sensitive.

SQL99 and Vendor-Specific Datatypes

The previous section mentioned that a table could contain one or many columns, each with a single defining datatype. In real world applications, datatypes provide some control and efficiency as to how tables are defined. Using specific datatypes enables better, more understandable queries and controls the integrity of data.

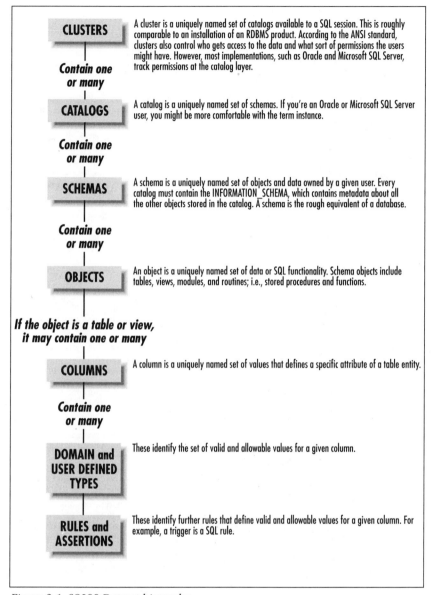

CLUSTERS

A cluster is a uniquely named set of catalogs available to a SQL session. This is roughly comparable to an installation of an RDBMS product. According to the ANSI standard, clusters also control who gets access to the data and what sort of permissions the users might have. However, most implementations, such as Oracle and Microsoft SQL Server, track permissions at the catalog layer.

Contain one or many

CATALOGS

A catalog is a uniquely named set of schemas. If you're an Oracle or Microsoft SQL Server user, you might be more comfortable with the term instance.

Contain one or many

SCHEMAS

A schema is a uniquely named set of objects and data owned by a given user. Every catalog must contain the INFORMATION_SCHEMA, which contains metadata about all the other objects stored in the catalog. A schema is the rough equivalent of a database.

Contain one or many

OBJECTS

An object is a uniquely named set of data or SQL functionality. Schema objects include tables, views, modules, and routines; i.e., stored procedures and functions.

If the object is a table or view, it may contain one or many

COLUMNS

A column is a uniquely named set of values that defines a specific attribute of a table entity.

Contain one or many

DOMAIN and USER DEFINED TYPES

These identify the set of valid and allowable values for a given column.

RULES and ASSERTIONS

These identify further rules that define valid and allowable values for a given column. For example, a trigger is a SQL rule.

Figure 2-1: SQL99 Dataset hierarchy

The tricky thing about SQL99 datatypes is that they do not map directly to an identical implementation in a given vendor's product. Although the vendors provide "datatypes" that correspond to the SQL99 datatypes, these vendor-specific datatypes are not true SQL99 datatypes. Nonetheless, each vendor's datatypes are close enough to the standard to be both easily understandable and job-ready.

The official SQL99 datatypes (as opposed to vendor-specific) fall into the general categories described in Table 2-1.

Table 2-1: SQL99 Datatypes

Category	Example Datatypes and Abbreviations	Description
binary	binary large object (BLOB)	This datatype stores binary string values in hexadecimal format.
bit string	bit bit varying	These datatypes store either binary or hexadecimal data. *BIT* has a fixed length, while *BIT VARYING* has a variable length.
boolean	boolean	This datatype stores truth values —either *TRUE, FALSE,* or *UNKNOWN.*
character	char character varying (VARCHAR) national character (NCHAR) national character varying (NVARCHAR) character large object (CLOB) national character large object (NCLOB)	These datatypes can store any combination of characters from the applicable character set. The varying datatypes allow variable lengths, while the other datatypes allow only fixed lengths. Also, the variable-length datatypes automatically trim trailing spaces, while the other datatypes pad all open space.
numeric	integer (INT) smallint numeric decimal (DEC) float(p,s) real double precision	These datatypes store exact numeric values (integers or decimals) or approximate (floating point) values. *INT* and *SMALLINT* store exact numeric values with a predefined precision and a scale of zero. *NUMERIC* and *DEC* store exact numeric values with a predefined precision and a definable scale. *FLOAT* stores approximate numeric values with a definable scale, while *REAL* and *DOUBLE PRECISION* have predefined precisions. You may define a precision (p) and scale (s) for a float to indicate the total number of allowed digits in the floating point number and the number of decimal places, respectively.
temporal	date time time with time zone timestamp timestamp with time zone interval	These datatypes handle values related to time. *DATE* and *TIME* are self-explanatory. Datatypes with the *WITH TIME ZONE* suffix also include a time zone offset. The *TIMESTAMP* datatypes store values that are calculated at current machine runtime. *INTERVAL* specifies a value or increment of time.

Table 2-2 through Table 2-5 map the SQL99 datatypes onto the various vendor-implemented datatypes. Descriptions are provided for non-SQL99 datatypes.

Microsoft SQL Server Datatypes

Table 2-2 shows that Microsoft SQL Server supports most SQL99 datatypes. It also supports additional datatypes used to uniquely identify rows of data within a table and across multiple servers hosting the same databases. These datatypes support Microsoft's hardware philosophy of deploying on many Intel-based servers, rather than deploying on huge, high-end Unix servers.

Table 2-2: Microsoft SQL Server Datatypes

Microsoft SQL Server Datatype	SQL92 or SQL99 Datatype	Description
bigint		Stores signed or unsigned integers between −9223372036854775808 and 9223372036854775807.
binary	binary	Describes a fixed-length binary value up to 8000 bytes in size.
bit	bit	Stores 1 or 0 value.
char(n)	character	Holds fixed-length character data up to 8000 characters in length.
cursor		Describes a cursor.
datetime		Holds date and time data within the range of 1753-01-01 00:00:00 through 9999-12-31 23:59:59.
decimal(p,s)	decimal	Stores precision and scale values up to 38 digits long.
float	float	Holds floating precision numbers of −1.79E + 308 through 1.79E + 308.
image		Describes a variable-length binary value up to 2147483647 bytes in length.
int	integer	Stores signed or unsigned integers between −2147483648 and 2147483647.
money		Stores monetary values within the range of -922337203685477.5808 and −922337203685477.5807.
nchar(n)	national character	Holds fixed-length Unicode data up to 4000 characters in length.
ntext		Holds Unicode text passages up to 1,073,741,823 characters in length.
numeric(p,s)		A synonym for decimal.
nvarchar(n)	national character varying	Holds variable-length Unicode data up to 4000 characters in length.
real		Holds floating precision numbers of −3.40E + 38 through 3.40 + 38.
rowversion		A unique number within a database that is updated whenever a row is updated. Called "timestamp" in earlier versions.
smalldatetime		Holds data and time data within the range of 1900-01-01 00:00:00 through 2079-12-31 23:59:59.
smallint	smallint	Stores signed or unsigned integers between −32768 and 32767.
smallmoney		Stores monetary values within the range of −214748.3648 and 214748.3647.
sql_variant		Stores values of other SQL Server–supported datatypes, except text, ntext, rowversion, and other sql_variants.
table		Stores a result set for a later process.

Table 2-2: Microsoft SQL Server Datatypes (continued)

Microsoft SQL Server Datatype	SQL92 or SQL99 Datatype	Description
text		Stores very large passages of text up to 2147483647 characters in length.
tinyint		Stores signed or unsigned integers between 0 and 255.
unique-identifier		Represents a value that is unique across all databases and all servers.
varbinary	binary varying	Describes a variable-length binary value up to 8000 bytes in size.
varchar(n)	character varying	Holds fixed-length character data up to 8000 characters in length.

Notice that Microsoft SQL Server supports dates starting with the year 1752. This is because the English-speaking world used the Julian calendar prior to September 1752 and refiguring dates prior to that time is an inconvenience.

MySQL Datatypes

Table 2-3 shows that MySQL supports most of the SQL99 datatypes, plus several additional datatypes used to contain lists of values, as well as datatypes used for BLOBs.

Table 2-3: MySQL Datatypes

MySQL Datatype	SQL92 or SQL99 Datatype	Description
bigint		Stores signed or unsigned integers within the range of −9223372036854775808 to 9223372036854775807.
char(n) [binary]	character(n)	Contains a fixed-length character string of 1 to 255 characters in length, but trims spaces as *varchar* does. The BINARY option allows binary searches rather than dictionary-order, case-insensitive searches.
datetime	datetime	Stores data and time values within the range of 1000-01-01 00:00:00 to 9999-12-31 23:59:59.
decimal	decimal(precision, scale)	Stores exact numeric values.
double(p,s), double precision	double precision	Holds double-precision numeric values.
enum("val1," "val2," . . . n)		Is a char datatype whose value must be one of those contained in the list of values. Up to 65535 distinct values are allowed.
float	float(p)	Stores floating-point numbers with a precision of 8 or less.
int, integer	int, integer	Stores signed or unsigned integers within the range of −2147483548 to 2147483547.
longblob, longtext	binary large object	Stores BLOB or TEXT data up to 4294967295 characters in length.

Table 2-3: MySQL Datatypes (continued)

MySQL Datatype	SQL92 or SQL99 Datatype	Description
mediumblob, mediumtext		Stores BLOB or TEXT data up to 65535 characters in length.
mediumint		Stores signed or unsigned integers within the range of –8388608 to 8388607.
nchar(n) [binary]	national character	Holds Unicode character strings, but is otherwise the same as char.
numeric(p,s)	numeric(p,s)	A synonym of decimal.
nvarchar(n) [binary]	nvarchar	Holds Unicode variable length character strings up to 255 characters in length.
real(p,s)	double precision	Is a synonym of double precision.
set("val1," "val2," . . . n)		Is a char datatype whose value must be equal to zero or more values specified in the list of values. Up to 64 items are allowed in the list of values.
smallint	smallint	Stores signed or unsigned integers within the range of –32758 to 32757.
times-tamp(size)	timestamp	Stores the date and time within the range of 1970-01-01 00:00:00 to 2037-12-31 23:59:59.
tinyblob, tinytext		Is a BLOB or TEXT column of 255 characters or less.
tinyint		Stores signed or unsigned integers within the range of –128 to 127.
varchar(n)	character varying(n)	Stores variable-length character strings trimmed up to 255 characters in length.
year(2, 4)		Stores either 2 or 4 year values, in the range of (19)70–(20)69 for 2-year format and 0000, 1901–2155 in 4-year format.

In general, MySQL supports many of the SQL99 datatypes, but provides added datatypes for *BLOB* and *TEXT* fields.

Oracle Datatypes

As shown in Table 2-4, Oracle supports a rich variety of datatypes, including most of the SQL99 datatypes. Oracle includes unique datatypes that write directly to the filesystem or handle extremely large files.

Table 2-4: Oracle Datatypes

Oracle Datatype	SQL92 or SQL99 Datatype	Description
bfile		Holds a value for a BLOB stored outside the database of up to 4 GB in size. The database streams input (but not output) access to the external BLOB.
BLOB		Holds a binary large object (BLOB) value up to 4 GB in size.
char(n), character(n)	character	Holds fixed-length character data up to 2000 bytes in length.

Table 2-4: Oracle Datatypes (continued)

Oracle Datatype	SQL92 or SQL99 Datatype	Description
CLOB		Stores a character large object (CLOB) of either fixed-width or variable-width char character sets. It may be up to 4 gigabytes in size.
date	date	Stores a valid date and time within the range of 4712BC-01-01 00:00:00 to 9999AD-12-31 23:59:59.
decimal	decimal	A synonym of *NUM* that accepts precision or scale arguments.
double precision	double precision	Stores *NUM* values with double precision, the same as *FLOAT(126)*.
float (n)	float	Stores floating-point numeric values with a precision of up to 126.
integer(n)	integer	Stores signed and unsigned integer values with a precision of up to 38. It does not accept decimals (scale) as an argument.
long		Stores variable-length character data up to 2 gigabytes in size.
long raw		Stores raw variable-length binary data up to 2 gigabytes in size.
national character varying (n), national char varying (n), nchar varying (n)	national character varying	The same as NVARCHAR2.
nchar(n), national character(n), national char(n)	national character	Holds fixed-length standard and UNICODE character data up to 2000 bytes in length.
nclob		Represents a CLOB that supports multibyte and UNICODE characters.
number (p,s), numeric (p,s)	numeric	May have a precision of 1 to 38 and a scale of -84 to 127.
nvarchar2(n)		Represents Oracle's preferred Unicode variable-length character datatype. It can hold up to 4000 bytes.
raw(n)		Stores raw binary data up to 2000 bytes in size.
real	real	The same as FLOAT.
rowID		Represents a unique hexadecimal identifier for each row in a table, often used in conjunction with the ROWID pseudocolumn.
smallint	smallint	The same as INT.
urowid [(n)]		Stores a hexadecimal value showing the logical address of the row in its index. It defaults to 4000 bytes in size, but you may optionally specify its size.

Table 2-4: Oracle Datatypes (continued)

Oracle Datatype	SQL92 or SQL99 Datatype	Description
varchar, character varying, char varying	character varying	The same as VARCHAR2.
varchar2		Holds variable-length character data up to 4000 characters in length.

PostgreSQL Datatypes

As shown in Table 2-5, the PostgreSQL database supports most SQL99 datatypes, plus an extremely rich set of datatypes that store spacial and geometric data. As is evident, PostgreSQL supports additional versions of existing datatypes that are smaller and take up less disk space.

Table 2-5: PostgreSQL Datatypes

PostgresSQL Datatype	SQL92 or SQL99 Datatype	Description
bool	boolean	Contains a logical Boolean (true/false) value.
box		Contains a rectangular box in a 2D plane.
char(n)	character(n)	Contains fixed-length character string with spaces.
cidr		Describes an IP–version 4 network or host address.
circle		Describes a circle in a 2D plane.
date	date	Holds a calendar date without time of day.
datetime		Holds a calendar date and specific time of day.
decimal	decimal(precision, scale)	Stores exact numeric values.
float4	float(p)	Stores floating-point numbers with a precision of 8 or less and 6 decimal places.
float8	float(p), $7 <= p < 16$	Stores floating-point numbers with a precision of 16 or less and 15 decimal places.
inet		Stores an IP-Version 4 network or host address.
int2	smallint	Stores signed or unsigned 2-byte integers within a range of –32768 to 32767.
int4	int, integer	Stores signed or unsigned 4-byte integers within a range of –2147483648 to 2147483648.
int8		Stores signed or unsigned 8-byte integers with a range of 18 decimal places positive or negative.
interval	interval	Holds general-use time span values.
line		Holds infinite line in 2D plane values.
lseg		Holds values for line segments in a 2D plane.
macaddr		Holds a value for the MAC address of a computer's network interface card.
money	decimal(9,2)	Stores US-style currency values.
numeric(p,s)	numeric(p,s)	Stores exact numeric values for p = 9, s = 0.

Table 2-5: PostgreSQL Datatypes (continued)

PostgresSQL Datatype	SQL92 or SQL99 Datatype	Description
path		Describes an open and closed geometric path in a 2D plane.
point		Stores values for a geometric point in a 2D plane.
polygon		Stores values for a closed geometric path in a 2D plane.
serial		Stores a unique ID for indexing and cross-reference up to 2147483647.
time	time	Holds the time of day.
timespan		Holds a value that represents a specific span of time.
timestamp	timestamp with time zone	Stores the date and time. The optional *WITH TIME ZONE* keyword allows the declaration of a specially defined time zone value.
timetz	time with time zone	Holds the time of day, including time zone.
varchar(n)	character varying(n)	Stores variable-length character strings with spaces trimmed.

Processing NULLS

Most databases allow any of their supported datatypes to store NULL values. Inexperienced SQL programmers and developers tend to think of *NULL* as zero or blank. In fact, NULL is neither of these. In the relational database world, NULL literally means that the value is unknown or indeterminate. (This question alone—whether NULL should be considered unknown *or* indeterminate—is the subject of academic debate.) This differentiation enables a database designer to distinguish between those entries that represent a deliberately placed zero and those where either the data is not recorded in the system or where a NULL has been explicitly entered. For an example of this semantic difference, consider a system that tracks payments. A payment with a NULL amount does not mean that the product is free; instead, a NULL payment indicates that the amount is not known or perhaps not yet determined.

One side effect of the indeterminate nature of a NULL value is it cannot be used in a calculation or a comparison. Here are a few brief, but very important rules to remember about the behavior of NULL values:

- A NULL value cannot be inserted into a column defined as NOT NULL.

- NULL values are not equal to each other. It is a frequent mistake to compare two columns that contain NULL and expect the NULL values to match. (A NULL value can be identified in a *WHERE* clause or in a Boolean expression using phrases such as 'value IS NULL' and 'value IS NOT NULL'.)

- A column containing a NULL value is ignored in the calculation of aggregate values such as *AVG, SUM,* or *MAX.*

- When columns that contain NULL values in a *GROUP BY* clause of a query are listed, the query output contains rows for those NULL values.

- *Joins* between tables, in which one join condition contains values and the other contains NULL, are governed by the rules for "outer joins." Joins are described completely later in this chapter.

Categories of Syntax

SQL commands contains three main categories of syntax: identifiers, literals, and reserved and key words. *Identifiers* name objects that a user or a system process has created, such as a database, a table, the columns in a table, or a view. *Literals* are non-NULL values supplied to the system. *Reserved* and *key words* are words that have special meaning to the database SQL parser, such as *SELECT, GRANT, DELETE,* or *CREATE.*

Identifiers

Keep in mind that RDBMSs are built upon set theory: clusters contain sets of catalogs, catalogs contain sets of schemas, schemas contain sets of objects, and so on. At each level of this structure, each item requires a unique name or identifier.

This means that each object (whether a database, table, view, column, index, key, trigger, stored procedure, or constraint) in a RDBMS must be named. When issuing the command that creates a server object, a name for that new object must be specified.

There are two important sets of rules that experienced programmers keep in mind when choosing an identifier for a given item:

- The first set of rules include logical rules of thumb or conventions that ultimately create better database structures and data tracking. These are not so much required by SQL as they are the distilled experience of practiced programmers.

- The second set of rules are those set by the SQL standard and implemented by the vendors. The conventions for each vendor are covered later in this chapter.

Naming conventions

The naming conventions suggested for identifiers in the following list are based on long years of experience by many in the industry, although they aren't necessarily required by SQL:

Select a name that is meaningful, relevant, and descriptive
Do not name a database **XP03**; instead, name it **Expenses_2003**, showing that it stores expenses for the year 2003. Remember that other people will likely be using the database too, and the names should make sense at a glance. Each database vendor has limits on object name size, but names generally may be long enough to make sense to anyone reading them.

Choose and apply the same case throughout
Use either all uppercase or all lowercase for all objects throughout the database. Remember, too, that some database servers are case-sensitive, so using mixed-case identifiers might cause problems later.

Use abbreviations consistently

Once an abbreviation has been chosen, it should be used consistently throughout the database. For example, if EMP is used as an abbreviation for EMPLOYEE, then EMP should be used throughout the database. Do not use EMP in some places and EMPLOYEE in others.

Use complete, descriptive, meaningful names with underscores for reading clarity

A column name **UPPERCASEWITHUNDERSCORES** is not as easy to read as **UPPERCASE_WITH_UNDERSCORES**.

Do not put company or product names in database object names

Companies get acquired and products change names. These elements are too transitory to be included in database object names.

Do not use overly obvious prefixes or suffixes

For example, don't use "DB_" as a prefix for a database or prefix every view with "V_". However, some prefixes and suffixes are very useful when applied consistently.

Do not fill up all available space for the object name

If the database platform allows a 32-character table name, try to leave at least a few free bytes at the end. Different database vendors sometimes append prefixes or suffixes to the table name when manipulating temporary copies of the tables.

Do not use quoted identifiers

This is discussed in the following section, "Identity rules."

There are several benefits to following these guidelines. First, the SQL code becomes, in a sense, self-documenting, because the chosen names are meaningful and understandable to the reader. Second, the SQL code and database objects are easier to maintain—especially for users other than the original programmer—because they are consistently named. And finally, maintaining consistency increases database functionality. If the database ever has to be transferred or migrated to another application, consistent and descriptive naming saves both time and energy. Giving a few minutes of thought to naming SQL objects in the beginning can prevent problems later on.

Identity rules

Identity rules are rules for naming objects within the database, which are enforced by the database product. Note that the SQL99 standard specifies identity rules that may differ from those of a specific database vendor. Here are the SQL99 rules for naming server objects:

- The identifier can be no longer than 128 characters. (Many databases limit the identifier to 32 or fewer characters.)

- The identifier may contain numbers, characters, and symbols.

- The identifier must begin with a letter (or certain other allowable symbols).

- The identifier may not contain spaces or other special characters.

- The identifier may not be a reserved word or keyword (discussed shortly).

- In many circumstances, identifiers must be unique for each owner within its scope. For example, although Oracle allows two separate schemas to have an object with the same name, databases generally should be uniquely labeled and the tables of a database should all have unique names.

- Quoted identifiers (object names within double quotes) may be used to break some of the rules specified above. For example, a table could be named **"expense##ratios"**, but not named **expense##ratios** because the first table is a quoted identifier. These are sometimes known as *delimited identifiers*.

Literals

SQL judges literal values as any explicit numeric, character, string, date, or Boolean value that is not an identifier. SQL databases allow a variety of literal values in a SQL program. Literal values are allowed for most of the numeric, character, and date datatypes. For example, SQL Server numeric datatypes include (among others) *integer, real,* and *money.* Thus, *numeric literals* could look like:

```
30
-117
+883.3338
-6.66
$70000
2E5
7E-3
```

As the example illustrates, SQL Server allows signed or unsigned numerals, in scientific or normal notation. And since SQL has a money datatype, even a dollar sign can be included. SQL does not allow other symbols in numeric literals (besides 0 1 2 3 4 5 6 7 8 9 + - $. E e), so do not include commas. Most databases interpret a comma in a numeric literal as a *list item separator.* Thus, the literal value 3,000 would be interpreted by the database as 3 and, separately, 000.

 Oracle provides support for an interesting literal type called a *interval literal,* which is used to specify an interval of time. Refer to Oracle's documentation discussing *INTERVAL* for more information.

Character and *string literals* should always be enclosed by single quotation marks ("). As long as the literal is opened and closed with the same delimiter, SQL allows both kinds. The only difference between character and string literals is that a character literal contains only a single character, whereas a string literal contains lots of them. Additionally, character and string literals are not restricted just to the alphabet. In fact, any printable character in the server character set can be represented as a literal. All of the following are string literals:

```
'1998'
'$70,000 + 14000'
'There once was a man from Nantucket,'
'Oct 28, 1966'
```

All of these examples are, in fact, compatible with the *CHARACTER* datatype. Remember not to confuse the string literal '1998' with the numeric literal 1998. On one hand, string literals are associated with *CHAR* datatypes and cannot be used in arithmetic operations. On the other hand, many database products do perform automatic conversion of string literals when compared against *DATE* datatypes.

Doubling the delimiter can effectively represent a single quotation mark in a literal string, if necessary. These can be nested within the string. That is, use double quotation marks (even double double quotation marks) each time a single quotation mark (or double quotation mark) should appear. This example taken from Microsoft SQL Server illustrates the idea:

```
SELECT 'So he said "Who''s Le Petomaine?"!'
```

This gives the result:

```
------------------
So he said "Who's Le Petomaine?"!
```

In this example, single quotation marks serve as the outer delimiters of the string literal, while double quotation marks serve only as a string value, and the double apostrophe is used to show an apostrophe in the string. Except for Oracle, double quotation marks could have been used just as easily as delimiters and apostrophes within the string literal.

System Delimiters and Operators

String delimiters mark the boundaries of a string of alphanumeric characters. *System delimiters* are those symbols within the character set that have special significance to your database server. *Delimiters* are symbols that are used to judge the order or hierarchy of processes and list items. *Operators* are those delimiters used to judge values in comparison operations, including symbols commonly used for arithmetic or mathematic operations. Table 2-6 lists the system delimiters and operators allowed by SQL Server.

Table 2-6: SQL Delimiters and Operators

Symbol	Usage
+	Addition operator; also concatenation operator
-	Subtraction operator; also a range indicator in *CHECK* constraints
*	Multiplication operator
/	Division operator
=	Equality operator
<> !=	Inequality operators
<	Less-than operator
>	Greater-than operator
<=	Less-than or equal-to operator
>=	Greater-than or equal-to operator
(	Expression or hierarchy delimiter
)	Expression or hierarchy delimiter
%	Wildcard attribute indicator

Table 2-6: SQL Delimiters and Operators (continued)

Symbol	Usage
,	List item separator
@	Local variable indicator
@@	Global variable indicator
.	Identifier qualifier separator
' ' " "	Character string indicators
" "	Quoted identifier indicators
--	Single-line comment delimiter
/*	Beginning multiline comment delimiter
*/	Ending multiline comment indicator

Keywords and Reserved Words

Just as certain symbols have special meaning and functionality within SQL, certain words and phrases have special significance. SQL *keywords* are words whose meanings are so closely tied to the operation of the RDBMS that they cannot be used for any other purpose; generally, they are words used in a SQL command. For example, the word *SELECT* cannot be used as a table name.

 It is generally a good idea to avoid naming columns or tables after a keyword that occurs in a major database, because database applications are often converted from one implementation to another.

Reserved words, on the other hand, do not have special significance now, but they probably will in a future release. Thus, they are reserved for future use and should not be used as an object name. Unlike keywords, a reserved word is not always a word used in a SQL command. Most reserved words are words commonly associated with database technology, but they may or may not have an explicit link to commands in SQL. For example, the database term *CASCADE* is used to describe data manipulations that allow their action, such as a delete or update, to "flow down," or cascade, to any sub tables. Database vendors specify reserved words in current releases so that programmers will not encounter them as keywords at some later revision.

Although SQL99 specifies its own list of reserved words and keywords, so do vendors because they have their own extensions of the SQL command set. SQL keywords, as well as the keywords in the different vendor implementations, are shown in the Appendix, *SQL99 and Vendor-Specific Keywords*. Check the vendor documentation for reserved words information.

Using SQL

Up to this point, the chapter has been about the individual aspects of a SQL statement. Following is a high-level overview of the most important SQL command, *SELECT*, and some of its most salient points—namely, the relational operations known as *projections, selections,* and *joins.*

Although at first glance it might appear that the *SELECT* statement deals only with the selection operation; in actuality, *SELECT* embodies all three operations. (The *SELECT* statement is treated in detail in Chapter 3, *SQL Statements Command Reference.*) Projection operations retrieve specific columns of data. Selection operations retrieve specific rows of data. And join operations bring together the data from two or more different tables.

This overly simplified example of a *SELECT* statement focuses more on the underlying concepts than on difficult syntax:

```
SELECT select_list
FROM   table_list
WHERE  search_criteria
```

The following statement actually embodies two of the three relational operations, selection and projection:

```
SELECT expense_date, expense_amount, expense_description
FROM   expenses
WHERE  employee_last_name  = 'Fudd'
   AND employee_first_name = 'Elmer'
```

Projections

Projection is the relational operation of retrieving specific columns of data. As illustrated in the prior generic example, and the more realistic example that follows, the select_list is the component of a *SELECT* statement that allows the programmer to perform a projection. Here, we select the first and last names of an author, plus his home state, in the **authors** table:

```
SELECT au_fname, au_lname, state
FROM   authors
```

The results from any such *SELECT* statement are presented as another table of data:

au_fname	au_lname	state
Johnson	White	CA
Marjorie	Green	CA
Cheryl	Carson	CA
Michael	O'Leary	CA

The resulting data is sometimes called a *work table*, or a *derived table*, differentiating it from base tables in the database.

Selections

Selection is the relational operation of retrieving specific rows of data. This functionality is enabled through the use of the *WHERE* clause in a *SELECT* statement. *WHERE* acts to filter out unnecessary rows of data and retrieves only the requested rows. Building off the previous example, the following example selects authors from states other than California:

```
SELECT au_fname, au_lname, state
FROM   authors
WHERE  state <> 'CA'
```

The previous query retrieved all authors; the result of this query is a much smaller subset of records:

```
au_fname              au_lname                                    state
-------------------   ---------------------------------------     -----
Meander               Smith                                       KS
Morningstar           Greene                                      TN
Reginald              Blotchet-Halls                              OR
Innes                 del Castillo                                MI
```

Combining the capabilities of a projection and a selection together in a single query allows SQL to retrieve only the desired columns and records.

Joins

Joins are one of the most important operations in a relational database. Joins retrieve data from one or more tables in the result set of a single query. Different vendors allow varying numbers of tables to join in a single join operation. For example, Oracle is unlimited in the number of allowable joins, while Microsoft SQL Server allows up to 256 tables in a join operation.

The ANSI standard method of performing joins is to use the *JOIN* clause in a *SELECT* statement. An older method, know as a *theta join*, performs the join analysis in the *WHERE* clause. Here is an example of both approaches:

```
-- ANSI style
SELECT e.emp_id,
       e.fname,
       e.lname,
       j.job_desc
FROM   employee e
JOIN jobs j ON e.job_id = j.job_id

-- Theta style
SELECT e.emp_id,
       e.fname,
       e.lname,
       j.job_desc
FROM   employee e,
       jobs j
WHERE  e.job_id = j.job_id
```

For vendors that do not support ANSI *JOIN* syntax, outer joins are handled by placing special characters in the *WHERE* clause. For example, Oracle requires that the outer join operator, a plus sign (+), be placed next to the foreign key column in the join. In older versions, Microsoft SQL Server accomplished the same functionality using an asterisk (*). For example:

```
-- ANSI style
SELECT e.emp_id,
       e.fname,
       e.lname,
       j.job_desc
FROM   employee e
LEFT JOIN jobs j ON e.job_id = j.job_id
```

In the ANSI style example just shown, all employee records (the table on the left) will be returned along with job descriptions where available:

```
-- Theta-join on Microsoft SQL Server
SELECT  e.emp_id,
        e.fname,
        e.lname,
        j.job_desc
FROM    employee e,
        jobs     j
WHERE   e.job_id *= j.job_id
```

Although Microsoft SQL Server supports ANSI joins, the older theta-style outer join is still supported. The query shown before is functionally equivalent to the ASNI style query that precedes it:

```
-- Oracle Style
SELECT  e.emp_id,
        e.fname,
        e.lname,
        j.job_desc
FROM    employee e,
        jobs j
WHERE   e.job_id = j.job_id(+)
```

This query in Oracle is essentially the same as the other two. Here, all records from the **employee** table are required in the result set, while the values in the **job** table are optional and are returned only when there is a match between the two tables.

Conclusion

This chapter discussed the concepts that serve as the foundation for learning the Structured Query Language. The differences between row processing applications and set processing applications (such as relational databases) were discussed. The basic structure of the relational model, both in terms of the ANSI standard and typical database implementations, was illustrated. A quick overview of the datatypes provided by the SQL99 standard, as well as those provided by each database vendor, was also provided. The categories of SQL syntax, including identifiers, literals, system delimiters and operators, and keywords were described. Examples of SQL and an explanation of SQL projections, selections, and joins were included.

CHAPTER 3

SQL Statements Command Reference

This chapter is the heart of *SQL in a Nutshell*: it is an alphabetical listing of SQL commands with detailed explanations and examples. Each command and function is identified in a master table as being "supported," "supported with variations," "supported with limitations," or "not supported," for each of the four SQL dialects covered in this book: SQL Server, MySQL, Oracle, and PostgreSQL. After a brief description of the SQL99 standard, each vendor application is discussed briefly but thoroughly, with supporting examples and sample coding.

Recommended Reading Approach

When researching a command in this chapter, first read the introductory paragraph, vendor support table, and the section on SQL99 syntax and description. The reason for this is that any common features between all the implementations of the command are discussed once under the SQL99 topic. Thus, reading directly about a vendor's implementation of a particular command may not describe every aspect of that command, since some of its details may be covered in the opening comments.

Quick SQL Command Reference

The following list offers useful tips for reading Table 3-1, as well as what each abbreviation stands for. The sections that follow describe the table's commands in detail:

1. The first column contains the alphabetized SQL commands.

2. The SQL statement class for each command is indicated in the second left-hand column.

3. The command's implementation in SQL99 is indicated in the next column.

4. The subsequent columns list the vendor's level of support:

Supported (S)

The vendor supports the SQL99 standard for the particular command.

Supported, with variations (SWV)

The vendor supports the SQL99 standard for the particular command, using vendor-specific code or syntax.

Supported, with limitations (SWL)

The vendor supports some but not all of the functions specified by the SQL99 standard for the particular command.

Not supported (NS)

The vendor does not support the particular command according to the SQL99 standard.

5. Remember that even if a specific SQL99 command is listed as "Not Supported," the vendor usually has alternative coding or syntax to enact the same command or function. Therefore, be sure read the discussion and examples for each command later in this chapter.

Table 3-1: Alphabetical Quick SQL Command Reference

Command	SQL Statement Class	SQL99	Microsoft SQL Server	MySQL	Oracle	Postgre SQL
ALTER PROCEDURE	SQL-schema	Yes	SWV	NS	SWV	NS
ALTER TABLE	SQL-schema	Yes	SWV	SWL	SWV	SWV
ALTER TRIGGER	SQL-schema	No	SWV	NS	SWV	NS
ALTER VIEW	SQL-schema	No	SWV	NS	SWV	NS
CALL	SQL-control	Yes	NS	NS	S	S
CASE	SQL-data	Yes	S	S	NS	S
CAST	SQL-data	Yes	S	NS	NS	S
CLOSE CURSOR	SQL-data	Yes	S	NS	S	S
COMMIT TRANSACTION	SQL-transaction	Yes	SWV	NS	S	S
CONCAT-ENATION OPERATORS	SQL-data	Yes	SWV	SWV	S	S
CONNECT	SQL-connection	Yes	SWL	NS	S	NS
CREATE DATABASE	SQL-schema	No	SWV	S	S	SWV
CREATE FUNCTION	SQL-schema	Yes	SWV	SWV	SWV	SWV
CREATE INDEX	SQL-schema	Yes	SWV	SWV	SWV	SWV
CREATE PROCEDURE	SQL-schema	Yes	S	NS	S	NS

Table 3-1: Alphabetical Quick SQL Command Reference (continued)

Command	SQL Statement Class	SQL99	Microsoft SQL Server	MySQL	Oracle	Postgre SQL
CREATE ROLE	SQL-schema	Yes	NS	NS	SWV	NS
CREATE SCHEMA	SQL-schema	Yes	S	NS	S	NS
CREATE TABLE	SQL-schema	Yes	SWV	SWV	SWV	SWV
CREATE TRIGGER	SQL-schema	Yes	SWV	NS	SWV	SWV
CREATE VIEW	SQL-schema	Yes	SWV	NS	SWV	SWV
DECLARE CURSOR	SQL-data	Yes	S	NS	S	S
DELETE	SQL-data	Yes	SWV	SWV	S	S
DISCONNECT	SQL-connection	Yes	SWL	NS	SWV	NS
DROP DATABASE	SQL-schema	Yes	SWV	SWV	NS	SWV
DROP FUNCTION	SQL-schema	Yes	SWV	SWV	SWV	SWV
DROP INDEX	SQL-schema	Yes	SWV	SWV	SWV	SWV
DROP PROCEDURE	SQL-schema	Yes	S	NS	S	NS
DROP ROLE	SQL-schema	Yes	NS	NS	SWV	NS
DROP TABLE	SQL-schema	Yes	SWV	SWV	SWV	SWV
DROP TRIGGER	SQL-schema	Yes	SWV	NS	SWV	SWV
DROP VIEW	SQL-schema	Yes	S	NS	S	S
FETCH	SQL-data	Yes	S	NS	S	SWV
GRANT	SQL-schema	Yes	SWV	SWV	SWV	SWV
INSERT	SQL-schema	Yes	SWV	SWV	S	S
JOIN clause	SQL-data	Yes	S	SWL	NS (theta joins supp-orted)	SWV (theta joins supp-orted)
LIKE operator	SQL-schema	Yes	SWV	SWV	SWV	SWV
OPEN	SQL-schema	Yes	S	NS	S	S
OPERATORS	SQL-schema	Yes	SWV	SWV	SWV	SWV
RETURN	SQL-control	Yes	S	S	S	S

Statements

Table 3-1: Alphabetical Quick SQL Command Reference (continued)

Command	SQL Statement Class	SQL99	Microsoft SQL Server	MySQL	Oracle	Postgre SQL
REVOKE	SQL-schema	Yes	SWV	SWV	SWV	SWV
ROLLBACK	SQL-transaction	Yes	SWV	NS	S	S
SAVEPOINT	SQL-transaction	Yes	SWV	NS	S	NS
SELECT	SQL-data	Yes	SWV	SWV	SWV	SWV
SET CONNECTION	SQL-connection	Yes	SWL	NS	NS	NS
SET ROLE	SQL-session	Yes	NS	NS	SWV	NS
SET TIME ZONE	SQL-session	Yes	NS	NS	SWV	NS
SET TRANSACTION	SQL-session	Yes	SWV	NS	SWL	S
START TRANSACTION	SQL-transaction	Yes	NS (supports BEGIN TRAN)	NS	NS	NS (supports BEGIN TRAN)
TRUNCATE TABLE	SQL-data	Yes	S	NS	SWV	S
UPDATE	SQL-data	Yes	SWV	SWV	SWV	S

ALTER PROCEDURE

The *ALTER PROCEDURE* statement allows changes to be made to an existing stored procedure. Depending on the vendor, the kind and degree of change varies widely.

In SQL Server, this statement alters a previously created procedure (using the *CREATE PROCEDURE* statement) but doesn't change permissions or affect dependent stored procedures or triggers.

In Oracle, this command simply recompiles a PL/SQL stored procedure, but does not allow the code to be changed. Instead, use the Oracle command *CREATE OR REPLACE PROCEDURE* to achieve the same functionality.

Vendor	Command
SQL Server	Supported, with variations
MySQL	Not supported
Oracle	Supported, with variations
PostgreSQL	Not supported

SQL99 Syntax and Description

```
ALTER PROCEDURE procedure_name {CASCADE | RESTRICT}
[LANGUAGE | PARAMETER STYLE | <SQL data access> | <null clause behavior>
| DYNAMIC RESULT SETS | NAME]
[parameter datatype [,...n]
```

As discussed under *CREATE PROCEDURE*, the *LANGUAGE, PARAMETER STYLE*, SQL data access method (i.e., *NO SQL, CONTAINS SQL*, etc.), null clause behavior (e.g., *CALL ON NULL INPUT*), *DYNAMIC RESULT SET*, and the procedure *NAME* all may be altered.

The *ALTER PROCEDURE* command also may be used to alter the number or type of input parameters.

Microsoft SQL Server Syntax and Variations

```
ALTER PROC[EDURE] procedure_name [;number]
[ {@parameter datatype } [VARYING] [= default] [OUTPUT] ][,...n]
[WITH { RECOMPILE | ENCRYPTION | RECOMPILE , ENCRYPTION } ]
[FOR REPLICATION]
AS
T-SQL Block
```

In SQL Server, this command allows the change of any existing parameters for the previously created stored procedure. In effect, this command is just a shortcut around issuing a *DROP PROCEDURE* statement, followed by a modified *CREATE PROCEDURE* statement. Such grants or permissions to the stored procedure do not have to be reestablished. Review the command *CREATE PROCEDURE* for a full explanation of the syntax. This command may be executed on SQL Server by the owner of the stored procedure or a member of the **db_owner** and **ddl_admin** fixed database roles.

Oracle Syntax and Variations

```
ALTER PROCEDURE [user.]procedure_name COMPILE [DEBUG];
```

In Oracle, the procedure or package name that needs to be compiled must be provided. The *COMPILE* keyword is required. The *COMPILE [DEBUG]* option regenerates PL/SQL information. This command may be executed only by the owner of the stored procedure or by those who have specific privileges to *ALTER ANY PROCEDURE*.

Example

This example using Microsoft SQL Server creates a procedure called **get_next_br** that generates a unique CHAR(22) output string. Then, when the procedure must be changed to retrieve unique INT output value, *ALTER PROCEDURE* is used to redefine the stored procedure:

```
-- A Microsoft SQL Server stored procedure
CREATE PROCEDURE get_next_nbr
   @next_nbr CHAR(22) OUTPUT
AS
BEGIN
  DECLARE @random_nbr INT
  SELECT @random_nbr = RAND() * 1000000
```

```
SELECT @next_nbr =
  RIGHT('000000' + CAST(ROUND(RAND(@random_nbr)*1000000,0))AS CHAR(6), 6) +
  RIGHT('0000' + CAST(DATEPART (yy, GETDATE() ) AS CHAR(4)), 2) +
  RIGHT('000' + CAST(DATEPART (dy, GETDATE() ) AS CHAR(3)), 3) +
  RIGHT('00' + CAST(DATEPART (hh, GETDATE() ) AS CHAR(2)), 2) +
  RIGHT('00' + CAST(DATEPART (mi, GETDATE() ) AS CHAR(2)), 2) +
  RIGHT('00' + CAST(DATEPART (ss, GETDATE() ) AS CHAR(2)), 2) +
  RIGHT('000' + CAST(DATEPART (ms, GETDATE() ) AS CHAR(3)), 3)
END
GO


ALTER PROCEDURE get_next_nbr
   @next_nbr INT OUTPUT
AS
BEGIN
  DECLARE @convert_to_nbr CHAR(22)
  DECLARE @random_nbr INT
  SELECT  @random_nbr = RAND() * 1000000

SELECT @convert_to_nbr =
  RIGHT('000000' + CAST(ROUND(RAND(@random_nbr)*1000000,0))AS CHAR(6), 6) +
  RIGHT('0000' + CAST(DATEPART (yy, GETDATE() ) AS CHAR(4)), 2) +
  RIGHT('000' + CAST(DATEPART (dy, GETDATE() ) AS CHAR(3)), 3) +
  RIGHT('00' + CAST(DATEPART (hh, GETDATE() ) AS CHAR(2)), 2) +
  RIGHT('00' + CAST(DATEPART (mi, GETDATE() ) AS CHAR(2)), 2) +
  RIGHT('00' + CAST(DATEPART (ss, GETDATE() ) AS CHAR(2)), 2) +
  RIGHT('000' + CAST(DATEPART (ms, GETDATE() ) AS CHAR(3)), 3)

SELECT @next_nbr = CAST(@convert_to_nbr AS INT)

END
GO
```

ALTER TABLE

The *ALTER TABLE* statement allows an existing table to be modified without dropping the table or altering existing permissions on the table. In this way, certain incremental changes are performed easily on an existing table.

Both Oracle and Microsoft SQL Server support this command with a number of variations to service their differing physical file-allocation methods.

Vendor	Command
SQL Server	Supported, with variations
MySQL	Supported, with limitations
Oracle	Supported, with variations
PostgreSQL	Supported, with variations

SQL99 Syntax and Description

```
ALTER TABLE table_name
[ADD [COLUMN] column_name datatype attributes]
 | [ALTER [COLUMN] column_name SET DEFAULT default_value]
 | [ALTER [COLUMN] column_name DROP DEFAULT]
 | [ALTER [COLUMN] column_name ADD SCOPE table_name
 | [ALTER [COLUMN] column_name DROP SCOPE {RESTRICT | CASCADE}]
 | [DROP [COLUMN] column_name {RESTRICT | CASCADE}]
 | [ADD table_constraint_name]
 | [DROP CONSTRAINT table_constraint_name {RESTRICT | CASCADE}]
```

The SQL99 *ALTER TABLE* statement allows many useful modifications to be made to an existing table. This versatile command allows users to *ADD COLUMN* or table constraint; add or drop a *DEFAULT*; add or drop *SCOPE* on columns that are set up to reference a user-defined type; and *DROP* both a column and a table constraint. *DROP RESTRICT* tells the host DBMS to abort the command if it sees that other objects in the database depend on the column or table constraint. *DROP CASCADE* tells the host DBMS to drop any database object that depends on the column or table constraint. Refer to the *CREATE TABLE* statement for additional explanations of these elements of the command.

Microsoft SQL Server Syntax and Variations

```
ALTER TABLE table_name
[ALTER COLUMN column_name new_data_type attributes {ADD | DROP}
   ROWGUIDCOL]
 | [ADD [COLUMN] column_name datatype attributes][,...n]
 | [WITH CHECK | WITH NOCHECK] ADD table_constraint][,...n]
 | [DROP { [ CONSTRAINT ] constraint_name | COLUMN column_name }] [,...n]
 | [{ CHECK | NOCHECK } CONSTRAINT { ALL | constraint_name [,...n] }]
 | [{ ENABLE | DISABLE } TRIGGER { ALL | trigger_name [,...n] }]
```

Microsoft SQL Server offers many features in its implementation of *ALTER TABLE*. *ALTER COLUMN* allows the change of an existing column, such as datatype, nullability, identity functions, and so on. *ADD* puts a new column, computed column, or constraint in the table in the very last column position. (There is, at present, no way to insert a column in the middle or in some other position of the table.) The optional word *COLUMN* is provided for clarity, but is not necessary. The new column must be defined in the same way as using the *CREATE TABLE* statement, including any constraints, defaults, and collations.

The *WITH CHECK* and *WITH NOCHECK* clauses tell SQL Server whether the data in the table should be validated against any newly added constraints or keys. When constraints are added with *WITH NOCHECK*, the query optimizer ignores them until they are enabled via *ALTER TABLE table_name CHECK CONSTRAINT ALL*. Constraints may be dropped with *DROP CONSTRAINT* (though the *CONSTRAINT* keyword is not necessary) and enabled/disabled with *CHECK CONSTRAINT* and *NOCHECK CONSTRAINT*, respectively.

Similarly, a named trigger on a table may be enabled or disabled using the *ENABLE TRIGGER* and *DISABLE TRIGGER* clauses. All triggers on a table may be enabled or disabled by substituting the keyword *ALL* for the table name, as in *ALTER TABLE employee DISABLE TRIGGER ALL*.

MySQL Syntax and Variations

```
ALTER [IGNORE] TABLE table_name
[ADD [COLUMN] column_name datatype attributes ]
     [FIRST | AFTER column_name]] [,...n]
 | [ADD INDEX [index_name] (index_col_name,...)] [,...n]
 | [ADD PRIMARY KEY (index_col_name,...)] [,...n]
 | [ADD UNIQUE [index_name] (index_col_name,...)] [,...n]
 | [ALTER [COLUMN] column_name {SET DEFAULT literal | DROP DEFAULT}] [,...n]
 | [CHANGE [COLUMN] old_col_name create_definition] [,...n]
 | [MODIFY [COLUMN] column_name datatype attributes] [,...n]
 | [DROP [COLUMN] column_name] [,...n]
 | [DROP PRIMARY KEY] [,...n]
 | [DROP INDEX index_name] [,...n]
 | [RENAME [AS] new_tbl_name] [,...n]
 | [table_options]
```

Refer to the *CREATE TABLE* statement for more details on allowable column attributes and table constraints.

The *IGNORE* option tells MySQL to delete duplicate rows when defining a new unique key. If *IGNORE* is not specified, the operation aborts when duplicate records exist on the unique key.

The *FIRST* option is used when adding a new column as the first column of the table. The *AFTER column_name* may be to add a new column into a table after the specified **column_name**.

In addition, MySQL allows some additional flexibility in the *ALTER TABLE* statement by allowing users to issue multiple *ADD*, *ALTER*, *DROP*, and *CHANGE* clauses in a single *ALTER TABLE* statement. However, be aware that the *CHANGE column_name* and *DROP INDEX* clauses are MySQL extensions not found in SQL99. MySQL also supports the Oracle extension *MODIFY column_name*. The *ALTER COLUMN* clause allows a new default value for a column to be set or dropped.

A table may be renamed by using *RENAME AS,* and a column may be renamed using *CHANGE.* For example, this code renames both a table and a column:

```
ALTER TABLE employee RENAME AS emp;
ALTER TABLE employee CHANGE employee_ssn emp_ssn INTEGER;
```

Since MySQL allows the creation of indexes on a portion of a column (for example, on the first ten characters of a column), the *CHANGE* or *MODIFY* commands may not be used to create a column of less length than its indexes. When *DROP COLUMN* is used, the column is removed from both the table and any indexes built with that column.

DROP PRIMARY KEY does not automatically fail if there is no primary key on the table. Instead, MySQL will drop the first unique index on the table.

MySQL allows a datatype on an existing column to be redefined without losing any data. The values contained in the column must be compatible with the new datatype. For example, a date column could be redefined to a character datatype, but not a character datatype to an integer. Here's an example:

```
ALTER TABLE mytable MODIFY mycolumn LONGTEXT
```

MySQL allows the *FOREIGN KEY, CHECK,* and *REFERENCES* clauses, but they are empty. Commands containing these clauses may be issued, but they do nothing. They are provided primarily for porting compatibility.

Oracle Syntax and Variations

```
ALTER TABLE [owner_name.]table_name
[ADD column_name datatype attributes]
| [MODIFY {column_name datatype
    | column_constraint
    | physical_storage_attributes [LOGGING | NOLOGGING]
    | nested_table_attributes}]
| [MODIFY CONSTRAINT {constraint_name {constraint_state}
    | drop_constraint_clause
    | drop_column_clause
    | [ALLOCATE | DEALLOCATE extent_clause]
    | [CACHE | NOCACHE]
    | [LOGGING | NOLOGGING]
    | [MONITORING | NOMONITORING] ]
| [DROP {[COLUMN] column_name | constraint_name}]
| [ALLOCATE EXTENT details]
| [DEALLOCATE UNUSED details]
| [RENAME TO new_table_name]
| [OVERFLOW physical_storage_attributes]
| [ADD OVERFLOW physical_storage_attributes]
| [{ADD | DROP | MODIFY | MOVE | TRUNCATE | SPLIT | EXCHANGE | MODIFY}
    PARTITION partition_details]
```

The *ALTER TABLE* statement details Oracle's multitude of powerful features for controlling the physical storage and manipulation of a table, such as handling data extents, handling overflow extents, and partitioning tables to better handle extreme usage loads. Check Oracle's implementation of *CREATE TABLE* to see the specific syntax allowed for some of the previous lines, such as *column_constraint, physical_storage_attributes,* and *nested_table_attributes.*

This command may be used to *ADD* a new column or constraint or *MODIFY* and *DROP* existing columns and constraints. When a new column is added, it should be defined as *NULL,* unless the table has no rows. The *MODIFY* keyword allows you to alter characteristics of a previously created table. The *MODIFY CONSTRAINT* allows you to drop or alter constraints on a table, including whether *LOGGING, CACHE,* or *MONITOR* is activated, as well as whether to *ALLOCATE* or *DEALLOCATE* storage extents. It also utilizes the keywords *ENABLE* and *DISABLE* to activate or deactivate constraints on a table.

 Oracle's implementation of *ALTER TABLE* is very sophisticated and complex. Refer to the *CREATE TABLE* statement for complete discussions on subclauses to the commands that are held in common.

For example, the following code adds a new column to a table in Oracle and adds a new, unique constraint to that table:

```
ALTER TABLE titles
ADD subtitle VARCHAR2(32) NULL
CONSTRAINT unq_subtitle UNIQUE;
```

When a foreign key constraint is added to a table, the DBMS verifies that all existing data in the table meets that constraint. If they do not, the *ALTER TABLE* fails.

 Any applications that use **SELECT** * return the new columns, even if this was not planned. On the other hand, precompiled objects, such as stored procedures, may not return any new columns.

Oracle also allows multiple actions, such as *ADD* or *MODIFY,* to multiple columns to be performed by enclosing the action within parentheses. For example, the following command adds several columns to a table with this single statement:

```
ALTER TABLE titles
ADD (subtitles VARCHAR2(32) NULL,
    year_of_copyright INT,
    date_of_origin DATE);
```

PostgreSQL Syntax and Variations

```
ALTER TABLE table [*]
[ADD [COLUMN] column_name datatype attributes]
 | [ALTER [COLUMN] column_name {SET DEFAULT value | DROP DEFAULT}]
 | [RENAME [COLUMN] column_name TO new_column_name]
 | [RENAME TO new_table_name]
```

PostgreSQL's implementation of *ALTER TABLE* allows the addition of extra columns using the *ADD* keyword. Existing columns may have new default values assigned to them using *ALTER COLUMN . . . SET DEFAULT,* while *ALTER COLUMN . . . DROP DEFAULT* allows the complete erasure of a column-based default. In addition, new defaults may be added to columns using the *ALTER* clause, but only newly inserted rows will be affected by the default value. *RENAME* allows new names for existing columns and tables.

ALTER TRIGGER

The *ALTER TRIGGER* statement modifies a preexisting trigger definition without altering permissions or dependencies.

Vendor	Command
SQL Server	Supported, with variations
MySQL	Not supported
Oracle	Supported, with variations
PostgreSQL	Not supported

SQL99 Syntax and Description

Currently, there is no SQL99 standard for this command.

Microsoft SQL Server Syntax and Variations

```
ALTER TRIGGER trigger_name
ON {table_name | view_name}
[WITH ENCRYPTION]
{FOR | AFTER | INSTEAD OF} {[DELETE] [,] [INSERT] [,] [UPDATE]}
[WITH APPEND]
[NOT FOR REPLICATION]
AS
  T-SQL_block
| [FOR { [INSERT] [,] [UPDATE] }
[NOT FOR REPLICATION]
AS

  { IF UPDATE(column) [{AND | OR} UPDATE(column)] [...n]
    |
    IF (COLUMNS_UPDATED() {bitwise_operator} updated_bitmask)
    { comparison_operator} column_bitmask [...n] }
    T-SQL_block ] } ]
```

Microsoft SQL Server allows the specification of *FOR | AFTER | INSTEAD OF { [DELETE] [,] [UPDATE] [,][INSERT] } | { [INSERT] [,] [UPDATE] }* to describe which data-modification statement trigger is affected by the command. At least one of these is required, but any combination is allowed with extra options separated by commas. The options *FOR* and *AFTER* are essentially the same, causing the trigger code to fire after the data-manipulation operation has completed. Alternately, the *INSTEAD OF* key phrase tells SQL Server to substitute the data-manipulation operation completely with the code of the trigger.

The *WITH APPEND* key phrase tells SQL Server to append an additional trigger of the specified type to the base table. This option is allowed only on *FOR* triggers. The *NOT FOR REPLICATION* key phrase tells SQL Server not to execute the trigger when the action is caused by a replication login, such as *sqlrepl*. The *IF UPDATE (column)* clause tests for an *INSERT* or *UPDATE* action (but not *DELETE*) on a specific column and is very useful when doing row-based operations using a cursor. The *{AND | OR}* operators allow additional columns in the same phrase to be tested. The *IF (COLUMNS_UPDATED())* test an *INSERT* or *UPDATE* trigger to see if the mentioned column(s) were affected. The results are returned as bitwise operators.

Oracle Syntax and Variations

```
ALTER TRIGGER [user.]trigger_name [ENABLE | DISABLE | COMPILE [DEBUG] ];
```

Oracle does not allow the underlying code of the trigger to be completely altered using this command (although the same functionality can be attained using Oracle's implementation of *CREATE OR REPLACE TRIGGER*). Oracle's *ALTER TRIGGER* allows a trigger to be enabled, disabled, or recompiled. The *COMPILE [DEBUG]* option regenerates PL/SQL information.

Oracle allows triggers *only* on tables (though *INSTEAD OF* triggers are allowed on views). Microsoft SQL Server allows triggers on tables and updateable views.

ALTER VIEW

While there is currently no SQL99 standard for the *ALTER VIEW*, it is important to note that this command behaves differently in each major vendor application that supports it. Oracle uses this command to recompile a view; Microsoft SQL Server uses this command to allow modifications to a view without also updating any dependent stored procedures, triggers, or permissions.

Vendor	Command
SQL Server	Supported, with variations
MySQL	Not supported
Oracle	Supported, with variations
PostgreSQL	Not supported

SQL99 Syntax and Description

Currently, there is no SQL99 standard for this command.

Microsoft SQL Server Syntax and Variations

```
ALTER VIEW view_name [(column [,...n])]
[WITH {ENCRYPTION | SCHEMABINDING | VIEW_METADATA]
AS
select_statement
[WITH CHECK OPTION]
```

As with the *CREATE VIEW* statement, *ALTER VIEW* allows a programmer to specify the column aliases that the view uses to name the columns, as well as the entire *SELECT* statement that is the core component of the view.

The other clauses of the *ALTER VIEW* statement are described under the *CREATE VIEW* statement.

Microsoft SQL Server can maintain the column permissions only if the column names remain the same after the command has been executed. The *ENCRYPTION* keyword allows the encryption of the views code within the syscomments system table in SQL Server. The keywords *CHECK OPTION* force all data modifications executed against the view to pass the criteria of its defining *select_statement*. If the view previously contained either of these options, they must be enabled with the *ALTER VIEW* statement to stay active.

Oracle Syntax and Variations

```
ALTER VIEW [user.]view_name COMPILE
```

The *ALTER VIEW* statement recompiles a view in Oracle. It is useful to validate a view after making changes to a base table. A view becomes invalid if its base tables have changed and it is not recompiled.

Example

This example from SQL Server creates a view called **california_authors** that contains authors from California. Then, *ALTER VIEW* is used to expand and replace the view:

```
CREATE VIEW california_authors
AS
SELECT au_lname, au_fname, city, state
FROM authors
WHERE state = 'CA'
WITH CHECK OPTION
GO

ALTER VIEW california_authors
AS
SELECT au_fname, au_lname, address, city, state, zip
FROM pubs..authors
WHERE state = "CA"
GO
```

CALL

The *CALL* statement invokes a stored procedure.

Vendor	Command
SQL Server	Not supported
MySQL	Not supported
Oracle	Supported
PostgreSQL	Supported

SQL99 Syntax and Description

```
CALL procedure_name [ (parameter [, ...n] ) ]
```

The *CALL* statement makes it easy to invoke a stored procedure. Simply provide the name of the stored procedure and include any parameters used by the stored procedure, enclosing them within parentheses. If the stored procedure has only *OUT* parameters, or has no parameters, empty parentheses may be included.

 Microsoft SQL Server does not support the *CALL* statement. However, nearly identical functionality can be achieved using the *EXECUTE* statement. Refer to the vendor documentation for a full explanation of this SQL Server extension.

Oracle Syntax and Variations

```
CALL [schema.][{type_name | package_name}.]procedure_name@dblink
[(parameter [, ...n] )]
[INTO :variable_name [INDICATOR :indicator_name] ]
```

Oracle allows the *CALL* statement to invoke standalone stored procedures, functions, methods, as well as stored procedures and functions contained within a type or package. If the procedure or function resides in another database, simply declare the database via a dblink statement, stating where the object resides, as part of the *CALL* statement. dblink must refer to a previously created database link.

If the called routine is a function, Oracle requires the *INTO* clause. Conversely, INTO can be used only when invoking functions. The variable that will store the value returned by the function must be provided. Finally, an indicator also may be specified to retain the condition of the host variable, if the function is a precompiled Pro*C/C++ routine.

Example

This example creates a simple stored procedure, then calls it independently:

```
CREATE PROCEDURE update_employee_salary
(emp_id NUMBER, updated_salary NUMBER)
IS
BEGIN
   UPDATE employee SET salary = updated_salary WHERE employee_id =emp_id ;
END;

CALL update_employee_salary(1517, 95000);
```

CASE

The *CASE* function provides *IF-THEN-ELSE* functionality within a *SELECT* or *UPDATE* statement. It evaluates a list of conditions and returns one value out of several possible values.

Vendor	Command
SQL Server	Supported
MySQL	Supported
Oracle	Not Supported (refer to the *DECODE* function in vendor documentation for similar functionality)
PostgreSQL	Supported

CASE has two usages: simple and searched. Simple *CASE* expressions compare one value, the *input_value*, with a list of other values, and return a result associated with the first matching value. Searched *CASE* expressions allow the analysis of several logical conditions and return a result associated with the first one that is true.

SQL99 Syntax and Description

```
-- Simple comparison operation
CASE input_value
WHEN when_condition THEN resulting_value
[...n]
[ELSE else_result_value]
END
```

```
-- Boolean searched operation
CASE
WHEN Boolean_condition THEN resulting_value
[...n]
[ELSE else_result_expression]
END
```

In the simple *CASE* function, the *input_value* is evaluated against each *WHEN* clause. The *resulting_value* is returned for the first TRUE instance of *input_value = when_condition*. If no *when_condition* evaluates as TRUE, the *else_result_value* is returned. If no *else_result_value* is specified, then NULL is returned.

In the more elaborate Boolean searched operation, the structure is essentially the same as the simple comparison operation, except that each *WHEN* clause has its own Boolean comparison operation.

In either usage, multiple *WHEN* clauses are used, although only one *ELSE* clause is necessary.

Examples

Here is a simple comparison operation where the *CASE* function alters the display of the contract column to make it more understandable:

```
SELECT  au_fname,
        au_lname,
        CASE contract
            WHEN 1 THEN 'Yes'
            ELSE 'No'
        END 'contract'
FROM    authors
WHERE   state = 'CA'
```

Here is an elaborate searched *CASE* function in a *SELECT* statement that reports how many titles have been sold in different year-to-date sales ranges:

```
SELECT CASE
            WHEN ytd_sales IS NULL  THEN 'Unknown'
            WHEN ytd_sales <=   200 THEN 'Not more than 200'
            WHEN ytd_sales <=  1000 THEN 'Between  201 and  1000'
            WHEN ytd_sales <=  5000 THEN 'Between 1001 and  5000'
            WHEN ytd_sales <= 10000 THEN 'Between 5001 and 10000'
            ELSE 'Over 10000'
        END 'YTD Sales',
        COUNT(*) 'Number of Titles'
FROM   titles
GROUP BY CASE
            WHEN ytd_sales IS NULL  THEN 'Unknown'
            WHEN ytd_sales <=   200 THEN 'Not more than 200'
            WHEN ytd_sales <=  1000 THEN 'Between  201 and  1000'
            WHEN ytd_sales <=  5000 THEN 'Between 1001 and  5000'
            WHEN ytd_sales <= 10000 THEN 'Between 5001 and 10000'
            ELSE 'Over 10000'
        END
ORDER BY MIN( ytd_sales )
```

This results in the following:

```
YTD Sales                 Number of Titles
---------------------     ----------------
Unknown                   2
Not more than 200         1
Between  201 and  1000    2
Between 1001 and  5000    9
Between 5001 and 10000    1
Over 10000                3
```

Here is an *UPDATE* statement that applies discounts to all the titles. The more complicated command that follows discounts all personal computer-related titles by 25%, all other titles by 10%, and applies only a 5% discount to titles with year-to-date sales exceeding 10,000 units.

The following *UPDATE* query uses a searched *CASE* expression to perform price adjustment:

```
UPDATE  titles
SET     price = price *
        CASE
            WHEN ytd_sales > 10000      THEN 0.95  -- 5% discount
            WHEN type = 'popular_comp'  THEN 0.75  -- 25% discount
            ELSE 0.9                               -- 10% discount
        END
WHERE   pub_date IS NOT NULL
```

The update has now completed three separate update operations in a single statement.

CAST

The *CAST* command explicitly converts an expression of one datatype to another.

Vendor	Command
SQL Server	Supported
MySQL	Not supported
Oracle	Not supported
PostgreSQL	Supported

SQL99 Syntax and Description

```
CAST(expression AS data_type[(length)])
```

The *CAST* function converts any expression, such as a column value or variable, into another defined datatype. The length of the datatype may be supplied optionally for those datatypes (such as *CHAR* or *VARCHAR*) that support lengths.

Be aware that some conversions, such as *DECIMAL* values to *INTEGER*, result in rounding operations. Also, some conversion operations may result in an error if the new datatype does not have sufficient space to display the converted value.

Example

This example retrieves the year-to-date sales as a *CHAR* and concatenates it with a literal string and a portion of the book title. It converts *ytd_sales* to *CHAR(5)*, plus it shortens the length of the *title* to make the results more readable:

```
SELECT CAST(ytd_sales AS CHAR(5)) + "Copies sold of " + CAST(title AS
VARCHAR(30))
FROM titles
WHERE ytd_sales IS NOT NULL
   AND ytd_sales > 10000
ORDER BY ytd_sales DESC
```

This results in the following:

```
--------------------------------------------------
22246 Copies sold of The Gourmet Microwave
18722 Copies sold of You Can Combat Computer Stress
15096 Copies sold of Fifty Years in Buckingham Pala
```

CLOSE CURSOR

The *CLOSE CURSOR* command closes a server-side cursor created with a *DECLARE CURSOR* statement. MySQL does not support server-side cursors, but does support extensive C programming extensions.

Vendor	Command
SQL Server	Supported
MySQL	Not supported
Oracle	Supported
PostgreSQL	Supported

SQL99 Syntax and Description

```
CLOSE { cursor_name }
```

The *cursor_name* is the name of the cursor created with the *DECLARE CURSOR* command.

Example

This example from Microsoft SQL Server opens a cursor and fetches all the rows:

```
DECLARE employee_cursor CURSOR FOR
   SELECT lname, fname
   FROM pubs.dbo.authors
   WHERE lname LIKE 'K%'

OPEN employee_cursor

FETCH NEXT FROM employee_cursor

WHILE @@FETCH_STATUS = 0
BEGIN
   FETCH NEXT FROM Employee_Cursor
END

CLOSE employee_cursor

DEALLOCATE employee_cursor
```

 The *DEALLOCATE* statement in Microsoft SQL Server releases the resources and data structures used by the cursor, but Oracle, PostgreSQL, and MySQL do not use it.

COMMIT TRANSACTION

The *COMMIT TRANSACTION* statement explicitly ends an open transaction, whether explicitly opened with *BEGIN,* or implicitly opened as part of an *INSERT, UPDATE,* or *DELETE* statement. This command allows the manual and permanent end to a data-manipulation operation.

Vendor	Command
SQL Server	Supported, with variations
MySQL	Not supported
Oracle	Supported
PostgreSQL	Supported

SQL99 Syntax and Description

```
COMMIT [WORK]
```

In addition to finalizing a single or group of data-manipulation operation(s), *COMMIT* has some interesting effects on other aspects of a transaction. First, it closes any associated open cursors. Second, any temporary table(s) specified with *ON COMMIT DELETE ROWS* are cleared of data. Third, all locks opened by the transaction are released. Finally, all deferred constraints are checked. If the deferred constraints are violated, the transaction is rolled back.

Please note that SQL99 dictates that transactions are *implicitly opened* when one of these statements is executed:

ALTER
CLOSE
COMMIT AND CHAIN (new for SQL99)
CREATE
DELETE
DROP
FETCH
FREE LOCATOR
GRANT
HOLD LOCATOR
INSERT
OPEN
RETURN
REVOKE
ROLLBACK AND CHAIN (new for SQL99)
SELECT
START TRANSACTION (new for SQL99)
UPDATE

SQL99 offers the new, optional keywords *AND CHAIN*. None of our vendors yet support this command. This new syntax is:

```
COMMIT [WORK] [AND [NO] CHAIN]
```

The *AND CHAIN* option tells the DBMS to treat the following transaction as if it were a part of the preceding. In effect, the two transactions are separate units of work, but they share a common transaction environment (such as transaction isolation level). The *AND NO CHAIN* option simply ends the single transaction. The *COMMIT* command is functionally equivalent to the command *COMMIT WORK AND NO CHAIN*.

Microsoft SQL Server Syntax and Variations

```
COMMIT [TRAN[SACTION] [transaction_name | @tran_name_variable] ]
|
COMMIT [WORK]
GO
```

Microsoft SQL Server allows a specific, named transaction to be made permanent. The *COMMIT* command must be paired with a *BEGIN TRAN* command. The *COMMIT TRANSACTION* syntax allows programmers to specify an explicit transaction to close or to store a transaction name in a variable. Curiously, SQL Server still commits only the last open transaction, despite the name of the transaction that is specified. When using *COMMIT WORK*, a transaction name or a variable containing a transaction name may not be specified.

However, this syntax is misleading in the event of nested named triggers, since it closes the outermost transaction. Transactions in SQL Server are identified numerically by the *@@TRANCOUNT* global variable. All transactions are committed only when *@@TRANCOUNT* equals 0.

Oracle Syntax and Variations

```
COMMIT [WORK];
```

Oracle does not allow specifically named transactions (but it does allow save-points); thus, the *COMMIT* command simply makes permanent all data-manipulation operations since the last implicit or explicit *COMMIT* statement was executed. Oracle allows the *WORK* keyword, but it is entirely optional.

PostgreSQL Syntax and Variations

```
COMMIT [WORK | TRANSACTION];
```

In PostgreSQL, both the *WORK* and *TRANSACTION* keywords are optional. The effect of the command is the same with or without either keyword. When completed, all committed transactions have been written to disk and are visible to other users.

Example

```
INSERT INTO sales VALUES('7896','JR3435','Oct 28 1997',25,'Net
60','BU7832');

COMMIT WORK;
```

Concatenation Operators

When it is necessary to combine the data of multiple columns into a single column in *SELECT* result set, the concatenation symbol supported by the DBMS may be used to achieve this result.

Vendor	Command
SQL Server	Supported, with variations
MySQL	Supported, with variations
Oracle	Supported
PostgreSQL	Supported

Example and Description

```
SELECT lname || ', ' || fname FROM customers WHERE cust_id = 41;
```

The ANSI standard is a double-pipe mark (||), as shown in the previous code example, and is supported by Oracle and PostgreSQL.

Microsoft SQL Server uses a plus sign (+) as its concatenation symbol.

MySQL uses the *CONCAT(string1, numeric1, string2, numeric2 [,...n])* function to accomplish concatenation.

CONNECT

The *CONNECT* statement establishes a connection to the DBMS and to a specific database within the DBMS.

Vendor	Command
SQL Server	Supported, with limitations
MySQL	Not supported
Oracle	Supported
PostgreSQL	Not supported

SQL99 Syntax and Description

```
CONNECT [TO] DEFAULT
  | {[server_specification] [AS connection_name] [USER user_name ] }
```

If the *CONNECT* statement is invoked without explicitly disconnecting, the old session becomes dormant and the new session becomes active. The period between issuing the *CONNECT* and *DISCONNECT* statements is commonly called a *session*. Typically, users complete all work on a DBMS during an explicitly invoked session.

 The Oracle tool SQL*Plus uses the *CONNECT* command somewhat differently: to connect a user to a specific schema.

The *CONNECT TO DEFAULT* statement has somewhat variable results, since different vendors implement it differently. But according to the standard, this command should initiate a default session with the server where the user authorization is the default and the current database is the default.

In contrast to *CONNECT TO DEFAULT, CONNECT TO server_name* allows you to specify the server. Here, the connection is made to the server that is explicitly named. In addition, the connection may be declared using *AS* and a specific user with *USER*.

Oracle Syntax and Variations

```
CONN[ECT] [[username/password] [AS [SYSOPER | SYSDBA] ] ]
```

The *CONNECT* clause allows a database connection as a specific username. Alternately, a connection can be established for special privileges with *AS SYSOPER* or *AS SYSDBA*. If another connection is already open, *CONNECT* commits any open transactions, closes the current session, and opens the new one.

 PostgreSQL does not explicitly support the *CONNECT* command. However, it does support the statement *SPI_CONNECT* under the Server Programming Interface and *PG_CONNECT* under the PG/tcl programming package.

Examples

To connect under a specific user ID, a user or automated program might issue the command:

```
CONNECT TO USER pubs_admin
```

If the DBMS requires named connections, then alternative syntax might be used:

```
CONNECT TO USER pubs_admin AS pubs_administrative_session;
```

Microsoft SQL Server supports *CONNECT TO* only within embedded SQL (ESQL):

```
EXEC SQL CONNECT TO new_york.pubs USER pubs_admin
```

CREATE DATABASE

SQL99 does not actually contain a *CREATE DATABASE* statement. The closest SQL99 gets to the *CREATE DATABASE* statement is the *CREATE SCHEMA* and *CREATE CATALOG* statements. (*CREATE SCHEMA* is detailed later.) However, it is nearly impossible to operate a SQL database without this command. Almost all database vendors support some version of this command.

Vendor	Command
SQL Server	Supported, with variations
MySQL	Supported
Oracle	Supported
PostgreSQL	Supported, with variations

SQL99 Syntax and Description

```
CREATE database_name
```

In this syntax, *database_name* is the identifier of the new database to be created. This command creates a new, blank database with a specific name. Most vendors require a user to be in the root, master, or system database to create a new database. Once the new database is created, it can then be filled with database objects (such as tables, views, triggers, and so on), and the tables populated with data.

Microsoft SQL Server Syntax and Variations

In SQL Server and Oracle, the database is instantiated in a pre-created file structure. These files act as go-betweens for the database system and the operating system. As a result, the SQL Server and Oracle variants of *CREATE DATABASE* are similarly more sophisticated.

The syntax for Microsoft SQL Server looks like this:

```
CREATE DATABASE database_name
[ ON [PRIMARY]
[ <file> [,...n] ]
[, <file_group> [,...n] ]
]
[ LOG ON { <file> [,...n]} ]
[ FOR LOAD | FOR ATTACH ]
GO
```

In this implementation, not only can the name of the database be supplied, but the location where the database is to be stored also can be specified. Both Oracle and SQL Server use *files* (a predefined space created on the disk structure) to act as a repository for databases. The databases may be stored on one or more files or filegroups. SQL Server also allows the transaction log to be placed in a separate location from the database using the *LOG ON* clause. These functions allow sophisticated file planning for optimal control of disk I/O.

The *FOR LOAD* clauses specify that the database will be immediately loaded from a backup after creation, thus speeding up the initial creation. The *FOR ATTACH* clause tells SQL Server that the database is attached from an existing operating-system file structure, such as a DVD-ROM, CD-ROM, or portable hard drive.

MySQL and PostgreSQL Syntax and Variations

In MySQL, *CREATE DATABASE* essentially creates a new directory that holds the database objects. So, with these vendors, creating a database is just a step above creating a filesystem directory. The database is created as a directory under the vendor's main directory, and any new objects created within the database are placed in that folder. PostgreSQL provides the same functionality, although PostgreSQL allows the database's location to be specified using the *WITH LOCATION* option:

```
CREATE DATABASE name [ WITH LOCATION = 'dbpath' ];
```

For example, to create the database **sales_revenue** in the */home/teddy/private_db* directory:

```
CREATE DATABASE sales_revenue WITH LOCATION = '/home/teddy/private_db';
```

Oracle Syntax and Variations

```
CREATE DATABASE [database_name]
[CONTROLFILE REUSE]
[LOGFILE [GROUP1 integer] file1 integer [K | M] [,...n] [REUSE]]
    [MAXLOGFILES integer]
    [[MAXLOGMEMBERS] integer]
    [[MAXLOGHISTORY] integer]
[DATAFILE file1 [AUTOEXTEND [,...n] [ON | OFF]]
      [NEXT integer [K | M]]
      [MAXSIZE [UNLIMITED | integer [K | M]]
    [MAXDATAFILES integer]
    [,...n]]
[MAXINSTANCES integer]
[MAXDATAFILES integer]
[ARCHIVELOG | NOARCHIVELOG]
{CHARACTER SET charset}
{NATIONAL CHARACTER SET charset};
```

CREATE DATABASE is a very powerful command in Oracle and should be utilized only by experienced DBAs. Novices should be aware that the existing database can be destroyed using this command.

As with Microsoft SQL Server, Oracle provides an extraordinary level of control over the database file structures beyond merely naming the database and specifying a path for the database files. Also unique to the Oracle environment is the *INIT.ORA* file, which specifies the database name and a variety of other options when creating and starting up the database. The *INIT.ORA* file always must be used and point to the control files, or the database does not start up.

When *the file1 [,…n]* option is available, the filename and file size may be specified in bytes, kilobytes, or megabytes in this format:

```
'file_path_and_name' SIZE bytes [K | M] REUSE
```

The *[K | M]* options multiply the file's byte size by 1024 and 1048576, respectively. While the *REUSE* option creates the file if it does not exist, and reuses it if it does, the *CONTROLFILE REUSE* option causes control files to be overwritten. Similarly, *LOGFILE . . . REUSE* causes logfiles to be overwritten.

When a group of logfiles are listed, they are usually shown in parentheses. The parentheses aren't needed when creating a group with only one member, but this is seldom done. Here's an example of a parenthetical list of logfiles:

```
CREATE DATABASE publications
LOGFILE ('/s01/oradata/loga01','/s01/oradata/loga02') SIZE 5M
DATAFILE
```

Additionally, the *LOGFILE* and *DATAFILE* options and suboptions allow precise control of the size and growth patterns of the database's redo logs and database files. The *MAXLOGFILES* and *MAXDATAFILES* define the absolute upper limit of files allowed for redo logs and database files, respectively. When *AUTOEXTEND* is enabled, the datafile grows in increments of *NEXT* until it reaches *MAXSIZE,* unless it is set to *UNLIMITED. MAXLOGMEMBERS* controls the maximum number of copies of a redo log group. *MAXLOGHISTORY,* used in Oracle Parallel Server, controls the maximum number of archived redo logs so that the right amount of space is recorded in the control file.

The *MAXINSTANCES* parameter sets the maximum number of instances that may mount the database being created. *ARCHIVELOG | NOARCHIVELOG* are mutually exclusive options that define how redo logs operate. *ARCHIVELOG* saves data to an additional archiving file, providing for media recoverability. Both options provide recoverability, although *NOARCHIVELOG* (the default) usually does not provide media recovery. *CHARACTER SET,* which is operating-system dependent, controls the language and character set in which the data is stored.

CREATE FUNCTION

The *CREATE FUNCTION* statement creates a *user-defined function* (UDF), which takes input arguments and returns a single value in the same way as *CAST()*. A UDF can be called in a query just like any other system function.

See Chapter 4, *SQL Functions,* for a full description of SQL functions and the individual vendor implementations.

Vendor	Command
SQL Server	Supported, with variations
MySQL	Supported, with variations
Oracle	Supported, with variations
PostgreSQL	Supported, with variations

The *CREATE FUNCTION* statement allows database programmers to create user-defined functions. These functions, once created, can be called in queries and data-manipulation operations, such as *INSERT, UPDATE,* and the *WHERE* clause of *DELETE* statements. Although the basic syntax for the statement was shown before, there is so much variety in how vendors have implemented the command that they are each described later in this section.

SQL99 Syntax and Description

```
CREATE FUNCTION function_name
[(parameter datatype attributes [,...n])]
RETURNS datatype

[LANGUAGE {ADA | C | FORTRAN | MUMPS | PASCAL | PLI | SQL}]
[PARAMETER STYLE {SQL | GENERAL}]
[SPECIFIC specific_name]
[DETERMINISTIC | NOT DETERMINISTIC]
[NO SQL | CONTAINS SQL | READS SQL DATA | MODIFIES SQL DATA]
[RETURNS NULL ON NULL INPUT | CALL ON NULL INPUT]
[STATIC DISPATCH]

code block
```

The SQL99 standard for the *CREATE FUNCTION* statement has a primary component and a more advanced component that is used less often. In most UDFs, users define the function name, any input parameters, and the value that the UDF returns. These form the basic uses of the command.

However, the SQL99 standard allows much more. The *LANGUAGE* clause allows the language in which the function is written (e.g., PostgreSQL) to be declared. The *PARAMETER STYLE* clause is used to declare a parameter style, other than the typical SQL style, via the *GENERAL* keyword. (SQL is the default.) The *SPECIFIC* declaration is used to further refine the function name in a user-defined type. The *DETERMINISTIC* versus *NOT DETERMINISTIC* clause tells the host DBMS whether the function will always return the same result when given the same input parameters (i.e., it is deterministic). Only deterministic functions may be used in constraints.

The SQL data access clause tells the host DBMS whether the function contains *NO SQL*, contains SQL code with *CONTAINS SQL*, uses the *SELECT* or *FETCH* statement with *READS SQL DATA*, or uses any of the data-modification statements with *MODIFIES SQL DATA*. The default is *CONTAINS SQL*.

For host languages that cannot handle nulls, *RETURNS NULL ON NULL INPUT* may be declared, telling the function to immediately return a null when handed a null.

In contrast, *CALL ON NULL INPUT* (the default) processes the null parameter normally with possible unknown results.

The *STATIC DISPATCH* clause is used for non-SQL functions that contain parameters that use user-defined types or *ARRAYS*.

Microsoft SQL Server Syntax and Variations

```
CREATE FUNCTION [owner_name.]function_name
( [ {@parameter1 datatype [=default]} [,...n] ] )
RETURNS {datatype | TABLE]
[WITH {ENCRYPTION | SCHEMABINDING}]
AS <Transact-SQL body>
GO
```

SQL Server functions can return multiple values via the *TABLE* datatype. The *TABLE* datatype is considered *inline* if it has no accompanying column list and is defined with a single *SELECT* statement. If the *RETURN* clause returns multiple values via the *TABLE* datatype, and if the *TABLE* has defined columns and their datatypes, this function is a *multistatement* table-valued function.

SQL Server requires that one or more user-supplied parameters be declared for a given user-defined function. All SQL Server datatypes are supported as parameters, except *timestamp*. Values returned by the function can be any datatype except *timestamp, text, ntext,* or *image*. If an inline table value is required, the *TABLE* option without an accompanying column list may be used.

Microsoft SQL Server user-defined functions, like many other database objects in SQL Server, may be created with the *ENCRYPTION* or *SCHEMABINDING* option. The *ENCRYPTION* option tells SQL Server to encrypt the system column table that stores the text of the function, thus preventing unwarranted review of the function code. The *SCHEMABINDING* option specifies that the function is bound to a specific database object, such as a table or view. That database object cannot be altered or dropped as long as the function exists (or maintains the *SCHEMABINDING* option).

The Transact-SQL body of code is either a single *SELECT* statement for an inline function, in the format *RETURN (SELECT . . .)*, or a series of Transact-SQL statements for a multistatement operation. The Transact-SQL body held within a *BEGIN . . . END* block cannot make any permanent changes to data or cause other lasting side effects. The last statement of the block must be an unconditional *RETURN* that returns a single datatype value or *TABLE* value.

The Transact-SQL block may not contain any global variables that return a perpetually changing value, such as *@@CONNECTIONS* or *GETDATE*. But it may contain those that return a single unchanging value, such as *@@SERVERNAME*. A number of other restrictions exist, since the code cannot make any permanent changes to data or cause other lasting side effects. For example, *INSERT, UPDATE,* and *DELETE* statements may modify only *TABLE* variables local to the function.

The following is an example of a scalar function that returns a single value:

```
CREATE FUNCTION metric_volume -- Input dimensions in centimeters.
    (@length decimal(4,1),
```

```
    @width decimal(4,1),
    @height decimal(4,1) )
RETURNS decimal(12,3) -- Cubic Centimeters.
AS BEGIN
     RETURN ( @length * @width * @height )
   END
GO
```

This user-defined function could then be utilized in a query or other operation just like any other function. For example, the project name and metric volume for all construction projects with more than 300,000 in metric volume can be found like this:

```
SELECT project_name,
   metric_volume(construction_height,
      construction_length,
      construction_width)
FROM housing_construction
WHERE metric_volume(construction_height,
      construction_length,
      construction_width) >= 300000
GO
```

User-defined functions that return a table value are often selected as a result set value or are used in the *FROM* clause of a *SELECT* statement, just as a regular table is used. In a *FROM* clause, a table alias function can be assigned just like a regular table. For example:

```
SELECT co.order_id, co.order_price
FROM   construction_orders AS co,
       fn_construction_projects('Cancelled') AS fcp
WHERE  co.construction_id = fcp.construction_id
ORDER BY co.order_id
GO
```

MySQL Syntax and Variations

```
CREATE [AGGREGATE] FUNCTION function_name
RETURNS {STRING | REAL | INTEGER}
SONAME shared_program_library_name ;
```

CREATE FUNCTION under MySQL aggregates user-defined functions, such as *SUM()* and *COUNT()*, using the *AGGREGATE* option. The type of value returned may be either *STRING* for character data, *REAL* for floating point numbers, or *INTEGER* for whole numbers.

The implementation of *CREATE FUNCTION* in MySQL differs dramatically from the other vendors, since the procedural code must be C/C++ under an operating system that supports dynamic loading. The C/C++ program is named in the *shared_program_library_name* option. The function may be compiled either directly into the MySQL server, making the function permanently available, or as a dynamically callable program. Since the user-defined function is written as a C/C++ program, a full description of this implementation is beyond the scope of this book.

Oracle Syntax and Variations

```
CREATE [OR REPLACE] FUNCTION [owner_name.]function_name
[(parameter1 [IN | OUT | IN OUT] [NOCOPY] datatype][,...n)]]
RETURN datatype [DETERMINISTIC | AUTHID {CURRENT_USER | DEFINER} ]
   {IS | AS} {PL/SQL block | external program};
```

In Oracle, user-defined functions and stored procedures are very similar in composition and structure. The primary difference is that stored procedures cannot return a value to the invoking process, while a function may return a single value to the invoking process.

In Oracle user-defined functions, the arguments and parameters specified include *IN, OUT,* and *IN OUT.* The *IN* qualifier is provided when invoking the function, and it passes a value to the function; *OUT* arguments pass a value back to the invoking process. In other words, the *IN* qualifier is supplied by the user or process that calls the function, while the *OUT* argument is returned by the function. *IN OUT* arguments perform both *IN* and *OUT* functionality. The NOCOPY keyword is used to speed up performance when an *OUT* or *IN OUT* argument is very large, as with a varray or record datatype.

The *RETURN* keyword specifies the datatype of the return value provided by the function. The *DETERMINISTIC* keyword is used to speed processing by functions that have been declared explicitly as deterministic. The stored returning value might come from a materialized view, another concurrent function call to the same function, or a function-based index. The function also may be forced to run in the permission context of either the current user or the person who owns the function, using the *AUTHID CURRENT_USER* or *AUTHID DEFINER* phrases, respectively.

For example, a construction project's profit can be determined by passing in the name of the project in this function:

```
CREATE FUNCTION project_revenue (project IN varchar2)
RETURN NUMBER
AS
   proj_rev NUMBER(10,2);
BEGIN
   SELECT SUM(DECODE(action,'COMPLETED',amount,0)) -
          SUM(DECODE(action,'STARTED',amount,0))   +
          SUM(DECODE(action,'PAYMENT',amount,0))
   INTO proj_rev
   FROM construction_actions
   WHERE project_name = project;
   RETURN (proj_rev);
END;
```

In this example, the user-defined function accepts the project name as an argument. Then, it processes the project revenue, behind the scenes, by subtracting the starting costs from the completion payment and adding any other payments into the amount. The RETURN(proj_rev); line returns the amount to the invoking process.

PostgreSQL Syntax and Variations

```
CREATE FUNCTION name ( [ parameter1 [,...n] ] )
RETURNS datatype
```

```
AS {definition | object_file, link_symbol}
LANGUAGE {'C' | 'SQL' | 'PLPGSQL' | 'PLTCL' | 'PLTCLU' | 'PLPERL'
    | 'internal'}
[WITH ISCACHABLE];
```

The PostgreSQL variation of *CREATE FUNCTION* is among the most flexible implementations of the command. As with the other implementations, *parameters* are
invoked and return a value of datatype. PostgreSQL also allows function *overloading* where the same function name is allowed for different functions, as long
as they accept distinct input parameters.

The *WITH ISCACHABLE* datatype attribute optimizes PostgreSQL performance by
indicating that the function always returns the same values when provided with
the same parameter values. This setting then allows the optimizer to preevaluate
the call of the function.

The *definition* can be a string defining the function (dependent on the language in
which the function is written), such as an internal function name, the path and
name of an object file, SQL query, or the text of a procedural language. The definition also can be an *object file* and *link symbol* to a C-language function.

Here's an example of a simple SQL function in PostgreSQL:

```
CREATE FUNCTION max_project_nbr
RETURNS int4
AS "SELECT MAX(project_ID) FROM housing_construction AS RESULT"
LANGUAGE 'sql';
```

 PostgreSQL uses *CREATE FUNCTION* as a substitute for *CREATE
PROCEDURE*, as well as to define actions for *CREATE TRIGGER*.

The *LANGUAGE* keyword allows the PostgreSQL function to call an external
program. Since these are programs compiled in other languages, they are beyond
the scope of this book. However, the *LANGUAGE 'sql'* clause should be used when
writing SQL user-defined functions.

CREATE INDEX

Indexes are special objects built on top of tables that speed many data-
manipulation operations, such as *SELECT, UPDATE,* and *DELETE* statements. When
an index is created, the location and spread of values (called statistics) are built for
the column that is indexed. The selectivity of a given *WHERE* clause is usually
based upon the quality of indexes that have been placed on the table.

Vendor	Command
SQL Server	Supported, with variations
MySQL	Supported, with variations
Oracle	Supported, with variations
PostgreSQL	Supported, with variations

The *CREATE INDEX* command varies greatly among vendors. One reason is that some DBMS vendors use the *CREATE INDEX* command to direct how the data in a given table is physically sorted and arranged on disk.

SQL99 Syntax and Description

```
CREATE INDEX index_name ON table_name (column_name [, ...n])
```

All major vendors support *composite indexes*, also known as *concatenated indexes*. These indexes are used when two or more columns are best searched as a unit—for example, last name and first name.

Microsoft SQL Server Syntax and Variations

```
CREATE [UNIQUE] [CLUSTERED | NONCLUSTERED] INDEX index_name
ON {table | view} (column [ASC | DESC] [,...n])
[WITH [PAD_INDEX]
    [[,] FILLFACTOR = fillfactor]
    [[,] IGNORE_DUP_KEY]
    [[,] DROP_EXISTING]
    [[,] STATISTICS_NORECOMPUTE] ]
[ON filegroup]
GO
```

Microsoft SQL Server has some important options. For example, ascending or descending indexes can be created on tables, as can indexes on views and calculated columns (such as *UPPER(book_name)* or *((qty * amt) / royalty)*). SQL Server also allows specification of several optional arguments: *UNIQUE, CLUSTERED*, or *NONCLUSTERED* (the default). *Unique indexes* require that no two values in the indexed column(s) are identical. Any attempt to insert or update a value so that there are duplicate values within the index will fail with an error. *Clustered indexes* specify the physical sort order of the data on the disk. *Nonclustered indexes* create a logical ordering of the table, which is used to speed data-manipulation operations.

SQL Server allows some additional syntax:

- *PAD_INDEX* specifies that space should be left open on each index data page, according to the value established by the *FILLFACTOR* setting.

- *FILLFACTOR* is a percentage value (from 1 to 100) and tells SQL Server how much of its 8K data page should be filled at the time the index is created. This is useful to reduce page splits when an 8K data page fills up, thus reducing I/O-intensive disk operations. Creating a clustered index with an explicitly defined fillfactor can increase the size of the index and speed up processing in certain circumstances.

- *IGNORE_DUP_KEY* controls what happens when a duplicate record is placed into a unique index through an insert or update operation. If this value is set for a column, only the duplicate row is excluded from the operation. If this value is not set, then all records in the operation (even nonduplicate records) are rolled back.

- *DROP_EXISTING* is a helpful feature that tells SQL Server to drop any preexisting indexes and rebuild the specified index.

- *STATISTICS_NORECOMPUTE* stops SQL Server from recomputing index statistics. This can speed the *CREATE INDEX* operation, but it may mean that the index is less valuable.

- ON *filegroup* creates the index on a given preexisting filegroup. This creates the capability of placing indexes on a specific hard disk or RAID device.

 Creating an index usually takes 1.2 to 1.5 times more space than the table currently occupies. Most of that space is released after the index has been created.

MySQL Syntax and Variations

```
CREATE [UNIQUE] INDEX index_name ON table_name (column_name(length) [,...n])
```

MySQL supports the basic ANSI standard for the *CREATE INDEX* statement, including the ability to build an index upon multiple columns. An index may be defined further as *UNIQUE*, forcing that index to accept only unique values. Any insertion of a non-unique value to the table with a *UNIQUE* index is rejected.

Interestingly, MySQL also lets you build an index on the first *(length)* characters of a *CHAR* or *VARCHAR* column. This can be useful when selectivity is sufficient in the first, say, 10 characters of a column, and in those situations where saving disk space is very important.

Oracle Syntax and Variations

```
CREATE [UNIQUE | BITMAP] INDEX [owner_name.]index_name
ON [schema.]{table ({column | expression} [ASC | DESC] [,...n])
    | CLUSTER cluster_name}
[physical_attributes_clause | {LOGGING | NOLOGGING} |
    | [ONLINE] | [COMPUTE [STATISTICS] ]
    | {TABLESPACE tablespace_name | DEFAULT}
    | {COMPRESS int | NOCOMPRESS}
    | {NOSORT |REVERSE} ],...
  [GLOBAL PARTITION BY RANGE (column_list)
    (PARTITION [partition_name] VALUES LESS THAN (value_list)
    [physical_attributes_clause | {LOGGING | NOLOGGING} ] ,...n )
  | LOCAL [ (PARTITION [partition_name]
    [physical_attributes_clause | {LOGGING | NOLOGGING} ] ,...n ) ] ]
  [PARALLEL [int] | NOPARALLEL]
```

Oracle allows the creation of indexes that are based not only on column values, but also on calculated expressions, such as *UPPER(book_name)* or *((qty * amt) / royalty)*. Indexes may be *UNIQUE* or non-unique. Oracle also allows the creation of a *BITMAP* index, which is useful for columns that have few distinct values. In addition, Oracle allows the construction of both ascending *(ASC)* and descending *(DESC)* indexes. However, be aware Oracle treats *DESC* indexes as function-based indexes. There is some difference in functionality between *ASC* indexes and *DESC* indexes. A cluster key also may be specified for the index using the *CLUSTER* option. (Clusters are created with the Oracle-specific command *CREATE CLUSTER*.)

Oracle and SQL Server differ significantly in their definition of a clustered index. In SQL Server, a *clustered index* designates the physical sort order of the data held in a table. In Oracle, a *cluster* is a special index between two or more tables that greatly speeds join operations.

The *physical_attributes_clause* refers to the settings that can be established for the following:

```
[ PCTFREE int
| PCTUSED int
| INITRANS int
| MAXTRANS int
| STORAGE storage...]
```

PCTFREE is similar to SQL Server's *FILLFACTOR*; that is, it designates the percentage of free space to leave in the index for new entries and updates. *PCTFREE* can be used only for indexes that are not *UNIQUE*. *PCTUSED* is the percentage of space available in a block that must exist before Oracle will allow insertions to that block. *PCTUSED* is allowable for tables, but may not be used for indexes. *STORAGE, INITRANS,* and *MAXTRANS* are discussed in the *CREATE TABLE* statement topic, in the section, "Oracle Syntax and Variations."

The *TABLESPACE* clause assigns the index to a specific tablespace. Leaving out the *TABLESPACE* clause places the index on the default tablespace, or the *DEFAULT* keyword achieves the same results.

LOGGING tells Oracle to log the creation of the index on the redo log file, while *NOLOGGING* prevents such logging. This keyword also sets the default behavior for subsequent bulk loads using Oracle Direct Loader. When building index partitions, there are some special behaviors for these keywords, so refer to the vendor documentation when attempting such activities.

ONLINE tells Oracle to allow data manipulations on the table while the index is being created. The *COMPUTE STATISTICS* command collects statistics while the index is created. The statistics are collected at relatively little cost. *COMPRESS* activates key compression on nonpartitioned indexes, which frees space by eliminating repeated key values. The integer value that accompanies *COMPRESS* gives the number of prefix columns to compress. *NOCOMPRESS*, the default, disables compression.

Oracle allows the creation of partitioned indexes and tables with the *PARTITION* clause. Consequently, Oracle's indexes also support partitioned tables. The *LOCAL* clause tells Oracle to create separate indexes for each partition of a table. The *GLOBAL* clause tells Oracle to create a common index for all the partitions, though specific index value ranges may differ from the ranges stored by the partitions.

The *NOSORT* option allows an index to be created quickly for a column that is already sorted in ascending order. If the values of the column are not in perfect ascending order, the operation aborts, allowing a retry without the *NOSORT* option. *REVERSE*, by contrast, places the index blocks in storage by reverse order (excluding rowed). *REVERSE* is mutually exclusive of *NOSORT* and cannot be used on a bitmap index or an index-organized table.

The *PARALLEL* clause allows for the parallel creation of the index by distinct CPUs to speed the operation. An optional integer value may be supplied to define the exact number of parallel threads used in the operation. *NOPARALLEL*, the default, causes the index to be created serially.

PostgreSQL Syntax and Variations

```
CREATE [UNIQUE] INDEX index_name ON table
[USING [BTREE | RTREE | HASH] ]
(function_name (column [operator_class] [, ...] ))
```

PostgreSQL allows the creation of standard ascending-order indexes, as well as *UNIQUE* indexes. Its implementation also includes a performance enhancement under the *WITH access_method* clause. This clause allows one of three dynamic access methods to optimize performance:

BTREE
>   This is the default method when no other is specified. This method utilizes Lehman-Yao high-concurrency btrees.

RTREE
>   This method utilizes standard rtrees using Guttman's quadratic-split algorithm.

HASH
>   This method is an implementation of Litwin's linear hashing.

In PostgreSQL, columns also may have an associated *operator class* based on the datatype of the column. An operator class specifies the operators for a particular index. Although users are free to define any valid operator class for a given column, the default operator class is the appropriate operator class for that field type.

PostgreSQL also allows users to define an index using a function, a user-defined function, or an expression. For example, an index could be defined on *UPPER(book_name)* to speed a transformation operation that is regularly applied to the base data of the index.

Examples

This example in MySQL creates a simple ascending index on the **au_id** column of the **authors** table:

```
CREATE INDEX au_id_ind
ON authors (au_id);
```

This example creates a **housing_construction** table (as used in the *CREATE FUNCTION* topic) and places a clustered index on it. This index physically orders the data on disk because the *CLUSTERED* clause is specified:

```
CREATE TABLE housing_construction
    (project_number      INT NOT NULL,
    project_date         DATETIME NULL,
    project_name         VARCHAR(50)
        COLLATE SQL_Latin1_General_CP1_CI_AS NULL ,
    construction_color   NCHAR(20)
        COLLATE SQL_Latin1_General_CP1_CI_AS NULL ,
    construction_height  DECIMAL(4, 1) NULL ,
```

```
      construction_length  DECIMAL(4, 1) NULL ,
      construction_width   DECIMAL(4, 1) NULL ,
      construction_volume  INT NULL
GO


CREATE UNIQUE CLUSTERED INDEX project_id_ind
ON housing_construction(project_id)
GO
```

It is often necessary to build indexes that span several columns—i.e., a *concatenated key*. Here is an example:

```
CREATE UNIQUE INDEX project2_ind
ON housing_construction(project_name, project_date)
WITH PAD_INDEX, FILLFACTOR = 80
GO
```

Adding the *PAD_INDEX* clause and setting the *FILLFACTOR* to 80 tells SQL Server to leave the index and data pages 80% full, rather than 100% full.

The following example constructs the same index in Oracle on a specific tablespace with specific instructions for how the data is to be stored:

```
CREATE UNIQUE INDEX project2_ind
ON housing_construction(project_name, project_date)
STORAGE (INITIAL 10M NEXT 5M PCTINCREASE 0)
TABLESPACE construction;
```

If the **housing_construction** table is created as a partitioned table on an Oracle server, a partitioned index should also be created:

```
CREATE UNIQUE CLUSTERED INDEX project_id_ind
ON housing_construction(project_id)
GLOBAL PARTITION BY RANGE (project_id)
   (PARTITION part1 VALUES LESS THAN ('K')
      TABLESPACE construction_part1_ndx_ts,
   PARTITION part2 VALUES LESS THAN (MAXVALUE)
      TABLESPACE construction_part2_ndx_ts);
```

CREATE PROCEDURE

Stored procedures provide conditional processing and programmatic capabilities in the database-server environment. Stored procedures are capsules of programming code that may accept passed parameters and accomplish complicated tasks. Stored procedures also are very valuable because they are precompiled: they execute their tasks quickly and efficiently because the database optimizer has already built an execution plan for the code.

Vendor	Command
SQL Server	Supported
MySQL	Not supported (see the "CREATE FUNCTION" command)
Oracle	Supported
PostgreSQL	Not supported

Like many of the other *CREATE* statements, the vendors have built a great deal of variety into this command.

SQL99 Syntax and Description

```
CREATE PROCEDURE procedure_name
[parameter data_type attributes ][,...n]
AS
code block
```

For a more complete listing of the SQL99 syntax, refer to *CREATE FUNCTION*. The advanced features of *CREATE FUNCTION* also apply to *CREATE PROCEDURE*.

Because each vendor has implemented his own procedural extensions to the SQL language, a broad discussion about coding stored procedures is not appropriate for this book. However, the basics of stored-procedure programming is discussed. Other O'Reilly books, such as *Transact-SQL Programming,* by Kevin Kline, Lee Gould & Andrew Zanevsky (1999), and *Oracle PL/SQL Programming, Second Edition,* by Steven Feuerstein with Bill Pribyl (1997), provide excellent discussions about their respective programming languages.

Microsoft SQL Server Syntax and Variations

```
CREATE PROC[EDURE] procedure_name [;number]
[{@parameter_name datatype} [VARYING] [= default] [OUTPUT]][,...n]
[WITH {RECOMPILE | ENCRYPTION | RECOMPILE, ENCRYPTION}]
[FOR REPLICATION]
AS
Transact-SQL_block
GO
```

In addition to a procedure name, Microsoft SQL Server also lets you specify a version number in the format *procedure_name;1,* where 1 is an integer indicating the version number. This allows multiple versions of a single stored procedure to be accessed.

Like tables (see *CREATE TABLE*), local and global temporary procedures may be declared by prefixing a pound symbol (#) and double-pound symbol (##) to the name of the procedure, respectively. Temporary procedures exist only for the duration of the user or process session that created them. When that session ends, the temporary procedure automatically deletes itself.

A SQL Server stored procedure may have as many as 1024 input parameters, specified by the "at" symbol (@) and any acceptable SQL Server datatype. (Parameters of cursor datatype must be both *VARYING* and *OUTPUT.*) The *VARYING* keyword is used only with parameters of the cursor datatype to indicate that the result set is constructed dynamically by the procedure.

The values for input parameters must be supplied by the user or calling process. However, a default value can be supplied to allow the procedure to execute without a user- or process-supplied value. The default must be a constant or NULL, but it may contain wildcard characters, as discussed under the topic *LIKE.*

Similarly, a parameter may be declared a return parameter by using the *OUTPUT* keyword. The value stored in the return parameter is passed back to any calling procedure through the return variables of the SQL Server *EXEC[UTE]* command. Output parameters can be any datatype except *TEXT* and *IMAGE*.

The options *WITH RECOMPILE*, *WITH ENCRYPTION*, and *WITH RECOMPILE, ENCRYPTION* are as follows:

WITH RECOMPILE
> Tells SQL Server not to store a cache plan for the stored procedure, but instead to recompile the cache plan each time it is executed. This is useful when using atypical or temporary values in the procedure.

WITH ENCRYPTION
> Encrypts the code of the stored procedure in the SQL Server **syscomments** table.

WITH RECOMPILE, ENCRYPTION
> Allows both options at one time.

The *FOR REPLICATION* clause, which is mutually exclusive of *WITH RECOMPILE*, disables execution of the stored procedure on a subscribing server. It is used primarily to create a filtering stored procedure that is executed only by SQL Server's built-in replication engine.

The *AS Transact-SQL_block* clause contains one or more Transact-SQL commands, up to a maximum size of 128 MB. Microsoft SQL Server allows most valid Transact-SQL statements, but *SET SHOWPLAN_TEXT* and *SET SHOWPLAN_ALL* are prohibited. Some other commands have restricted usages within stored procedures, including *ALTER TABLE*, *CREATE INDEX*, *CREATE TABLE*, all *DBCC* statements, *DROP TABLE*, *DROP INDEX*, *TRUNCATE TABLE*, and *UPDATE STATISTICS*.

SQL Server allows deferred name resolution, meaning that the stored procedure compiles without an error even though it references an object that has not yet been created. It creates an execution plan and fails only at execution time, if the object still doesn't exist.

Stored procedures can be nested easily in SQL Server. Whenever a stored procedure invokes another stored procedure, the system variable *@@NESTLEVEL* is incremented by 1. It is decreased by 1 when the called procedure completes. *SELECT @@NESTLEVEL* is specified to find how many layers of nesting occur in the current session.

Oracle Syntax and Variations

```
CREATE [OR REPLACE] PROCEDURE [owner_name.]procedure_name
[(parameter1 [IN | OUT | IN OUT] [NOCOPY] datatype][,...n)]]
[AUTHID {CURRENT_USER | DEFINER} ]
{IS | AS} {PL/SQL block | LANGUAGE {java_spec | C_spec}};
```

In Oracle, user-defined functions and stored procedures are very similar in composition and structure. The primary difference is that stored procedures cannot return a value to the invoking process, while a function may return a single value to the invoking process.

In an Oracle stored procedure, the specified arguments and parameters include *IN*, *OUT*, or *IN OUT*. The *IN* qualifier is provided when invoking the function and passes a value in to the function, while *OUT* arguments pass a value back to the invoking process. In other words, the *IN* qualifier is supplied by the user or process that calls the function, while the *OUT* argument is returned by the function. *IN OUT* arguments perform both *IN* and *OUT* functionality. The *NOCOPY* keyword is used to speed performance when an *OUT* or *IN OUT* argument is very large, like a varray or record datatype.

The function also may be forced to run in the permission context of either the current user or the person who owns the function, using the *AUTHID CURRENT_USER* or *AUTHID DEFINER* phrases, respectively.

Oracle also allows the procedure to call external programs through the *LANGUAGE* keyword. The external programs must be C or Java programs; the specific syntax for calling external programs is beyond the scope of this book. Refer to the vendor documentation for more information on this capability.

 Microsoft SQL Server stored procedures *can* be used to return result sets, while Oracle stored procedures *cannot* return a result set to the calling process.

Example

This Microsoft SQL Server stored procedure generates a unique 22-digit value (based on elements of the system date and time) and returns it to the calling process:

```
-- A Microsoft SQL Server stored procedure
CREATE PROCEDURE get_next_nbr
   @next_nbr CHAR(22) OUTPUT
AS
BEGIN
  DECLARE @random_nbr INT
  SELECT @random_nbr = RAND() * 1000000

SELECT @next_nbr =
  RIGHT('000000' + CAST(ROUND(RAND(@random_nbr)*1000000,0))AS CHAR(6), 6) +
  RIGHT('0000' + CAST(DATEPART (yy, GETDATE() ) AS CHAR(4)), 2) +
  RIGHT('000'  + CAST(DATEPART (dy, GETDATE() ) AS CHAR(3)), 3) +
  RIGHT('00'   + CAST(DATEPART (hh, GETDATE() ) AS CHAR(2)), 2) +
  RIGHT('00'   + CAST(DATEPART (mi, GETDATE() ) AS CHAR(2)), 2) +
  RIGHT('00'   + CAST(DATEPART (ss, GETDATE() ) AS CHAR(2)), 2) +
  RIGHT('000'  + CAST(DATEPART (ms, GETDATE() ) AS CHAR(3)), 3)
END
GO
```

CREATE ROLE

CREATE ROLE allows the creation of a named set of privileges that may be assigned to users of a database. When a user is granted a role, that user also gets all the privileges and permissions of that role.

Vendor	Command
SQL Server	Not supported
MySQL	Not supported
Oracle	Supported, with variations
PostgreSQL	Not supported

Microsoft SQL Server does not support the *CREATE ROLE* command, but has the equivalent capability via the system stored procedure *sp_add_role*.

SQL99 Syntax and Description

```
CREATE ROLE role_name [WITH ADMIN {CURRENT_USER | CURRENT_ROLE}]
```

This statement creates a new role, and differentiates that role from a host-DBMS user. The *WITH ADMIN* clause allows assigns a role immediately to the currently active user or currently active role. By default, the statement defaults to *WITH ADMIN CURRENT_USER*.

Oracle Syntax and Variations

```
CREATE ROLE role_name [NOT IDENTIFIED | IDENTIFIED
    {BY password | EXTERNALLY | GLOBALLY}]
```

In Oracle, the role is created first, then granted privileges and permissions as if it is a user via the *GRANT* command. When users want to get access to the permissions of a role protected by a password, they use the *SET ROLE* command. If a password is placed on the role, any user wishing to access it must provide the password with the *SET ROLE* command.

Oracle ships with several preconfigured roles. *CONNECT, DBA,* and *RESOURCE* are available in all versions of Oracle. *EXP_FULL_DATABASE* and *IMP_FULL_DATABASE* are newer roles used for import and export operations.

Example

The following example uses *CREATE* to specify a new role in Oracle, *GRANT* it privileges, assign it a password with *ALTER ROLE*, and *GRANT* that role to a couple of users:

```
CREATE ROLE boss;

GRANT ALL ON employee TO boss;
GRANT CREATE SESSION, CREATE DATABASE LINK TO boss;

ALTER ROLE boss IDENTIFIED BY le_grande_fromage;

GRANT boss TO nancy, dale;
```

CREATE SCHEMA

This statement creates a *schema*—i.e., a named group of related objects. A schema is a collection of tables, views, and their associated permissions. The schema is associated with an existing, valid user ID (called the *owner*).

Vendor	Command
SQL Server	Supported
MySQL	Not supported
Oracle	Supported, with variations
PostgreSQL	Not supported

SQL99 Syntax and Description

```
CREATE SCHEMA [schema_name] [AUTHORIZATION owner_name]
[DEFAULT CHARACTER SET char_set_name]
[PATH schema_name [,...n] ]

    [ <create_table_statement1> [...n] ]
    [ <create_view_statement1>  [...n] ]
    [ <grant statement1> [...n] ]
```

The *CREATE SCHEMA* statement is a container that can hold many other *CREATE* and *GRANT* statements. As an option, a *DEFAULT CHARACTER SET* names the schema's default character set. The *PATH* also may be declared for any objects in the schema that reside on the filesystem.

Microsoft SQL Server and Oracle Syntax

```
CREATE SCHEMA AUTHORIZATION owner_name
    [ <create_table_statement1> [...n] ]
    [ <create_view_statement1>  [...n] ]
    [ <grant statement1> [...n] ]
```

If any statement fails within the *CREATE SCHEMA* statement, then the entire statement fails. One good thing about *CREATE SCHEMA* is that the objects within do not need to be organized according to any dependency. For example, a *GRANT* statement normally could not be issued for a table that does not exist yet. However, all the *GRANT* statements first could be placed in the *CREATE SCHEMA* statement, followed by the *CREATE* statements where the grants are being given.

Many implementations do not explicitly support the *CREATE SCHEMA* command. However, they implicitly create a schema when a user creates database objects. On the other hand, Oracle creates a schema whenever a user is created. The *CREATE SCHEMA* command is simply a single-step method of creating all the tables, views, and other database objects along with their permissions.

Example

In Oracle, the *CREATE SCHEMA* does not create a schema—only *CREATE USER* does that. *CREATE SCHEMA* allows a user to perform multiple steps in one SQL statement. The following Oracle example places the permissions before the objects within the *CREATE SCHEMA* statement:

```
CREATE SCHEMA AUTHORIZATION emily
    GRANT SELECT, INSERT ON view_1 TO sarah
    GRANT ALL ON table_1 TO sarah

    CREATE VIEW view_1 AS
        SELECT column_1, column_2
```

```
FROM table_1
ORDER BY column_2

CREATE TABLE table_1(column_1 INT, column_2 CHAR(20));
```

CREATE TABLE

The *CREATE TABLE* statement does what it says: create a table. However, most vendors also allow a wide variety of other functions to be exercised through the *CREATE TABLE* statement, such as the assignment of keys, cascading referential integrity, constraints, and default values.

Vendor	Command
SQL Server	Supported, with variations
MySQL	Supported, with variations
Oracle	Supported, with variations
PostgreSQL	Supported, with variations

This command defines a table name, its constituent columns, and any properties to the columns and/or table. Typically, a great deal of consideration goes into the design and creation of a table. This discipline is known as *database design*. The discipline of analyzing the relationship of a table to its own data and to other tables within the database is known as *normalization*.

 It is strongly recommended that programmers and developers study both database design and normalization principles thoroughly before issuing *CREATE TABLE* commands.

In general, the table name always starts with an alphabetic character. The allowable length of the name varies by vendor; Oracle allows only 30 characters, but it can be much bigger than 30 characters when necessary. Numbers may be used in the name of the table, but do not use any symbol other than the underscore (_). Some vendors allow many other symbols in the name of a table, but it's good practice not to use them since they can create confusing identifiers.

When defining column characteristics, all vendors support the *NULL* and *NOT NULL* options. (A bare *NULL* is not a requirement of SQL99.) When a column is defined as *NULL*, regardless of its datatype, that column may contain null values. Typically, nullable columns consume an extra bit of space per record. If *NOT NULL* is specified, the column can never contain null values. Any *INSERT* operation that attempts to insert a null value or any *UPDATE* operation that attempts to modify a value to null on a *NOT NULL* column fails and is rolled back.

All vendors also support the *PRIMARY KEY* declaration, at both the column- and table-level. A *primary key* is a special designation that describes how each row of a table is uniquely identified. The primary key is composed of one or more columns in the table that provide each row with a unique identity. A table may have only one primary key. All values in the primary key must be unique and may not be null. Foreign keys then can be declared on a table that establishes a direct relationship to the primary key of another table. In this way, parent/child or master/detail relationships among tables may be created. A cascading action may further augment this action. For example, a user may wish to prevent the deletion of a customer record from the **customer** table, if sales records exist for that customer in the **sales** table. The syntax for a foreign key varies among the vendors.

Most vendors also support a *DEFAULT* value for a given column. Any time a record is inserted in a table and no value is provided for the column, its default value is inserted.

The basic syntax for *CREATE TABLE* is shown here; this is enough to get started building tables and populating them with data:

```
CREATE TABLE table_name
    (
    column_name datatype[(length)] [NULL | NOT NULL],...n
    )
```

Here's a simple example:

```
CREATE TABLE housing_construction
      (project_number      INT NOT NULL,
      project_date         DATETIME NOT NULL,
      project_name         VARCHAR(50) NOT NULL,
      construction_color   NCHAR(20) NULL,
      construction_height  DECIMAL(4,1) NULL,
      construction_length  DECIMAL(4,1) NULL,
      construction_width   DECIMAL(4,1) NULL,
      construction_volume  INT NULL)
GO
```

In Microsoft SQL Server, this statement defines a table called **housing_construction** that contains eight columns. Each column is defined as *NULL* or *NOT NULL*, with a datatype appropriate for the type of information it contains. Notice that the list of column definitions is always encapsulated in parentheses and that a comma closes each column definition when another definition follows it.

SQL99 Syntax and Description

```
CREATE [GLOBAL TEMPORARY | LOCAL TEMPORARY] TABLE table_name
[ON COMMIT {PRESERVE ROWS | DELETE ROWS}
(column_name datatype attributes [,...n]
  | [LIKE  table_name]
  | [table_constraint][,...n] ]
```

The SQL99 *CREATE TABLE* statement creates *TEMPORARY* tables that are instantiated when the table is created and are automatically dropped when the current user session ends. Temporary tables may be *GLOBAL* and available to all active user sessions, or *LOCAL* and available only to the user session that created it. An *ON COMMIT* value for the temporary table also may be specified. *ON COMMIT PRESERVE ROWS* preserves any data modifications to the temporary table on a *COMMIT*, while *ON COMMIT DELETE ROWS* flushes the table after a *COMMIT*.

The *LIKE table_name* option creates a new table with the same column definitions and table constraints as a preexisting table. When using *LIKE*, column or table constraints do not need to be defined.

Because the implementation of *CREATE TABLE* varies so widely and the command is such an important one, each vendor implementation is dealt with separately and in detail.

Microsoft SQL Server Syntax and Variations

```
CREATE TABLE [database_name.[owner]. | owner.] table_name
({column_name datatype [ [DEFAULT default_value]
    | {IDENTITY [(seed,increment) [NOT FOR REPLICATION]]]
    [ROWGIDCOL] ]
    [NULL | NOT NULL]
    | [{PRIMARY KEY | UNIQUE}
        [CLUSTERED | NONCLUSTERED]
        [WITH FILLFACTOR = int] [ON {filegroup | DEFAULT}] ]
    | [[FOREIGN KEY]
        REFERENCES reference_table[(reference_column[,...n])]
        [ON DELETE {CASCADE | NO ACTION}]
        [ON UPDATE {CASCADE | NO ACTION}]
        [NOT FOR REPLICATION]
    | [CHECK [NOT FOR REPLICATION] (expression)]
    | [COLLATE collation_name]
|column_name AS computed_column_expression
[,...n]
|[table_constraint][,...n] )
[ON {filegroup | DEFAULT} ]
[TEXTIMAGE_ON {filegroup | DEFAULT} ]
```

SQL Server offers a plethora of options when defining a table, its columns, and its table-level constraints. SQL Server allows any column-level constraint to be named by specifying *CONSTRAINT constraint_name. . .*, and then the text of the constraint. Several constraints may be applied to a single column, as long as they are not mutually exclusive (for example, *PRIMARY KEY* and *NULL*).

SQL Server also allows a local temporary table to be created, which is stored in the **tempdb** database, by prefixing a single pound sign (#) to the name of the table. The local temporary table is usable by the person or process that created it, and is deleted when the person logs out or the process terminates. A global temporary table, which is usable to all people and processes that are currently logged in, can be established by prefixing two pound signs (##) to the name of the table. The global temporary table is deleted when its process terminates or its creator logs out.

Since SQL Server supports built-in replication, many of the properties of a column can be set to *NOT FOR REPLICATION*, meaning that the values of an *IDENTITY* or *FOREIGN KEY* is not replicated to subscribing servers. This helps in situations in which different servers require the same table structures, but not the exact same data.

Also useful for replication is *ROWGUIDCOL*. This identifies a column as a global unique identifier, which ensures no two values are ever repeated across any number of servers. Only one such column may be identified per table. It does not, however, create the unique values itself. They must be inserted using the *NEWID* function.

The *IDENTITY* property, when applied to an integer column, is similar to MySQL's *AUTO_INCREMENT*, automatically creating and populating the column with a monotonically increasing number. However, it is more versatile and flexible. Where *AUTO_INCREMENT* always starts at 1, the *IDENTITY* starts counting at the value of *seed*. Where *AUTO_INCREMENT* increases by 1 each time a new row is inserted, *IDENTITY* increases by the value of *increment*.

In SQL Server, *DEFAULT* can be applied to any column except those with a timestamp datatype or an *IDENTITY* property. The *DEFAULT* must be a constant value such as a character string or a number, and a system function such as *GETDATE()* or *NULL*.

One *PRIMARY KEY* called *name per table* also may be specified, and multiple *UNIQUE* or *FOREIGN KEY* columns may be specified per table. They may be clustered or nonclustered, and may be defined with a starting fillfactor. Refer to the topic *CREATE INDEX* for more information.

When specifying a *FOREIGN KEY*, the table and columns that maintain referential integrity may be specified using the *REFERENCES* clause. It can only reference columns that are defined as a *PRIMARY KEY* or *UNIQUE* index on the referencing table. A referential action may be specified to take place on the **reference_table** when the record is deleted or updated. If *NO ACTION* is specified, then nothing happens on the referring table when a record is deleted or updated. If *CASCADE* is specified, then the delete or update also takes place on the referring table to any records dependent on the value of the *FOREIGN KEY*.

The *CHECK* constraint ensures that a value inserted into the specified column of the table is a valid value based on the *CHECK* expression. For example, the following shows a table with several column-level constraints:

```
CREATE TABLE people
    (people_id    CHAR(4)
        CONSTRAINT pk_dist_id PRIMARY KEY CLUSTERED
        CONSTRAINT ck_dist_id CHECK (dist_id LIKE '[A-Z][A-Z][A-Z][A-Z]'),
    people_name   VARCHAR(40) NULL,
    people_addr1  VARCHAR(40) NULL,
    people_addr2  VARCHAR(40) NULL,
    city          VARCHAR(20) NULL,
    state         CHAR(2)     NULL
        CONSTRAINT def_st DEFAULT ("CA")
        CONSTRAINT chk_st REFERENCES states(state_ID),
    zip           CHAR(5)     NULL
        CONSTRAINT ck_dist_zip
        CHECK(zip LIKE '[0-9][0-9][0-9][0-9][0-9]'),
    phone         CHAR(12)    NULL,
    sales_rep     empid       NOT NULL DEFAULT USER)
GO
```

The *CHECK* constraint on the *people_id* ensures an all-alphabetic ID, while the one on *zip* ensures an all-numeric value. The *REFERENCES* constraint on *state* performs a look-up on the **states** table. The *REFERENCES* constraint is essentially the same as a *CHECK* constraint, except that it derives its list of acceptable values from the values stored in another column. This example illustrates how column-level constraints are named using the *CONSTRAINT constraint_name. . .* syntax.

Also new to SQL Server 2000 is the *COLLATE* column-level property. This feature allows programmers to change, on a column-by-column basis, the sort order and character set that is used by the column. Since this is an advanced technique, refer to the vendor documentation if the default sort order or character set of a given column needs to be changed. The *CREATE FUNCTION* topic shows an example of this syntax.

SQL Server also allows the creation of tables with columns that contain a computed value. The column does not actually contain data. Instead, it is a virtual column containing an expression using other columns already in the table. For example, a computed column could have an expression, such as *order_cost AS (price * qty)*. Computed columns also can be a constant, function, variable, noncomputed column, or any of these combined with each other with operators.

Any of the column-level constraints shown earlier also may be declared at the table level. That is, *PRIMARY KEY* constraints, *FOREIGN KEY* constraints, *CHECK* constraints, and others may be declared after all the columns have been defined in the *CREATE TABLE* statement. This is very useful for constraints that cover more than one column. For example, when declaring a column-level *UNIQUE* constraint, it can be applied only to that column. However, declaring the constraint at the table level allows it to span several columns. Here is an example of both column-level and table-level constraints:

```
-- Creating a column-level constraint
CREATE TABLE favorite_books
    (isbn           CHAR(100)     PRIMARY KEY NONCLUSTERED,
    book_name       VARCHAR(40)   UNIQUE,
    category        VARCHAR(40)   NULL,
    subcategory     VARCHAR(40)   NULL,
    pub_date        DATETIME      NOT NULL,
    purchase_date   DATETIME      NOT NULL)
GO


-- Creating a table-level constraint
CREATE TABLE favorite_books
    (isbn           CHAR(100)     NOT NULL,
    book_name       VARCHAR(40)   NOT NULL,
    category        VARCHAR(40)   NULL,
    subcategory     VARCHAR(40)   NULL,
    pub_date        DATETIME      NOT NULL,
    purchase_date   DATETIME      NOT NULL,
        CONSTRAINT pk_book_id   PRIMARY KEY NONCLUSTERED (isbn)
            WITH FILLFACTOR=70,
        CONSTRAINT unq_book     UNIQUE CLUSTERED (book_name,pub_date))
GO
```

These two commands provide nearly the same results, except that the table-level *UNIQUE* constraint has two columns, whereas only one column is included in the column-level *UNIQUE* constraint.

Finally, Microsoft SQL Server has two separate clauses controlling how the table (or primary key or unique indexes) are to be physically placed: *[ON {filegroup | DEFAULT}]* and *[TEXTIMAGE_ON {filegroup | DEFAULT}]*. The *ON filegroup* clause stores the table or index within the named file group, as long as it exists within the database. If *ON DEFAULT* is specified or the *ON* clause is not used at all, the table or index is stored in the default filegroup for the database. The *TEXTIMAGE* clause works in very much the same way, except that it controls the placement of **text**, **ntext**, and **image** columns. These columns are normally stored in the default filegroup with all other tables and database objects.

MySQL Syntax and Variations

```
CREATE [TEMPORARY] TABLE [IF NOT EXISTS] table_name
(column_name datatype [NULL | NOT NULL] [DEFAULT default_value]
   [AUTO_INCREMENT]
   [PRIMARY KEY] [reference_definition] |
   [CHECK (expression) |
   [INDEX [index_name] index_col_name1[(length)],...n)] |
   [UNIQUE [INDEX] [index_name] (index_col_name1,...n)] |
   [CONSTRAINT symbol] FOREIGN KEY index_name (index_col_name1,...n)
      [REFERENCES table_name [(index_col_name,...)]
      [MATCH FULL | MATCH PARTIAL]
      [ON DELETE {RESTRICT | CASCADE | SET NULL | NO ACTION | SET
DEFAULT}]
      [ON UPDATE {RESTRICT | CASCADE | SET NULL | NO ACTION | SET
DEFAULT}])
{[TYPE = {ISAM | MYISAM | HEAP} |
   AUTO_INCREMENT = int |
   AVG_ROW_LENGTH = int |
   CHECKSUM = {0 | 1} |
   COMMENT = "string" |
   DELAY_KEY_WRITE = {0 | 1} |
   MAX_ROWS = int |
   MIN_ROWS = int |
   PACK_KEYS = {0 | 1} |
   PASSWORD = "string" |
   ROW_FORMAT= { default | dynamic | static | compressed }] }
   [[IGNORE | REPLACE] SELECT_statement]
```

MySQL allows a great many options when creating a table. The *TEMPORARY* option creates a table that persists for the duration of the connection under which it was created. Once that connection closes, the temporary table is automatically deleted. The *IF NOT EXISTS* option prevents an error if the table already exists.

When a table is created in MySQL, three operating-system files are typically created: a table definition file with the extension *.frm*, a datafile with the extension *.myd*, and an index file with the extension *.myi*.

The *AUTO_INCREMENT* clause sets up an integer column so that it automatically increases its value by 1 (starting with a value of 1). MySQL only allows one *AUTO_INCREMENT* column per table. When the max value is deleted, the value is reused. When all records are deleted, the values start over.

A *PRIMARY KEY* column or columns may be defined, as long as they also are defined as *NOT NULL*. When an *INDEX* characteristic is assigned to a column, a name for the index also can be included. (A MySQL synonym for *INDEX* is *KEY*.) If a name is not assigned, MySQL assigns a name of **index_column_name** plus a numeric suffix (_2, _3,. . .) to make it unique. Only the MyISAM table type supports indexes on *NULL* columns or on *BLOB* or *TEXT* datatype columns.

The *FOREIGN KEY*, *CHECK*, and *REFERENCES* clauses do nothing. They add no functionality to the table and are supported only to improve compatibility with other SQL databases.

The table *TYPE* options describe how the data should be physically stored. *ISAM* is the original table definition. *MyISAM* is a newer, binary, more portable storage structure. *HEAP* stores the table in memory. Other options exist to optimize performance for the table:

AUTO_INCREMENT
Sets the *auto_increment* value for the table (MyISAM only).

AVG_ROW_LENGTH
Sets an approximate average row length for tables with variable-size records. MySQL uses *avg_row_length* * *max_rows* to decide how big a table may be.

CHECKSUM
When set to 1, maintains a checksum for all rows in the table (MyISAM only). Makes processing slower, but less prone to corruption.

COMMENT
Allows a comment of up to 60 characters.

DELAY_KEY_WRITE
When set to 1, delays key table updates until the table is closed (MyISAM only).

MAX_ROWS
Sets a maximum number of rows to store in the table. The default max is 4 GB of space.

MIN_ROWS
Sets a minimum number of rows to store in the table.

PACK_KEYS
When set to 1, compacts the indexes of the table, making reads faster but updates slower (MyISAM and ISAM only). By default, only strings are packed. When set to 1, both strings and numeric values are packed.

PASSWORD
Encrypts the *.frm* file with a password, but not the table.

ROW_FORMAT
Determines how future rows should be stored in the table.

The *SELECT_statement* clause creates a table whose fields are based upon the elements in the *SELECT* statement. If it does not, as some implementations do, then the table can be populated with the results of the *SELECT* statement. For example:

```
CREATE TABLE test_example
  (column_a INT NOT NULL AUTO_INCREMENT,
  PRIMARY KEY(column_a),
```

```
    INDEX(column_b))
    TYPE=HEAP
    SELECT column_b,column_c FROM samples;
```

This creates a heap table with three columns: **column_a**, **column_b**, and **column_c**.

Oracle Syntax and Variations

```
CREATE [GLOBAL TEMPORARY] TABLE [schema.]table_name
( column_name datatype [DEFAULT] {column_constraint [...]} [,...n]
| table_constraint [,...n] } )
[ON COMMIT {DELETE | PRESERVE} ROWS]
( physical_characteristics )
( table_characteristics )
```

This simple and small block of code is deceptive! Oracle's extremely sophisticated implementation of the *CREATE TABLE* statement has the potential to become one of the most complex single commands in just about any programming language under the sun.

 The code for Oracle's *CREATE TABLE* clause contains many sub-clauses. Rather than show them all in one command, the command is broken out into subclauses that in turn contain other subclauses. The average SQL programmer might never use some of these subclauses.

To explain the most immediate differences between the SQL99 version of *CREATE TABLE* and Oracle's version, note that tables created as *GLOBAL TEMPORARY* must be basic tables. Global temporary tables cannot possess most of the special features that Oracle allows for regular tables, such as partitioning, index organizing, or clustering tables. A global temporary table is available to all sessions, but the data stored within a global temporary table is visible only to the session that inserted it. The *ON COMMIT* clause, which is allowed only when creating temporary tables, tells Oracle either to truncate the table after each commit against the table (*DELETE ROWS*) or to truncate the table when the session terminates (*PRESERVE ROWS*). For example:

```
CREATE GLOBAL TEMPORARY TABLE shipping_schedule
    (ship_date DATE,
     receipt_date DATE,
     received_by VARCHAR2(30),
     amt NUMBER)
ON COMMIT PRESERVE ROWS;
```

The *CREATE TABLE* statement shown earlier creates a global temporary table, **shipping_schedule**, that retains inserted rows across multiple sessions.

The physical characteristics of an Oracle table are defined using the next several blocks of code and their subblocks of code:

```
-- physical_characteristics
{[{[physical_attributes]
| TABLESPACE tablespace_name
```

```
|  {LOGGING | NOLOGGING} }]
|  {ORGANIZATION {HEAP [{[physical_attributes]
    | TABLESPACE tablespace_name
    | {LOGGING | NOLOGGING} }]
|  INDEX indexed_table_clause)}
|  CLUSTER cluster_name (column [,...n]) }
[special_storage_clause]
```

The *physical_characteristics* clause controls how data is stored physically on the disk subsystem.

The *TABLESPACE* clause assigns the table to a specific, preexisting tablespace. The *TABLESPACE* clause can be left out, which places the index on the default tablespace, or *DEFAULT* keyword can be used to achieve the same results.

The *LOGGING* and *NOLOGGING* clauses define whether the table, large object (LOB), or partition is logged in the redo log.

The *ORGANIZATION HEAP* clause tells Oracle to physically place the rows of the table in any order. It may optionally be associated with a *segment_characteristic* clause. Alternately, the rows of the table may be physically ordered according to a named index using *ORGANIZATION INDEX index_name*.

The *physical_attributes* clause (as shown in the following code block) defines storage characteristics for the entire table, or if the table is partitioned, for a specific partition (discussed later):

```
-- physical_attributes
[{PCTFREE int | PCTUSED int | INITRANS int | MAXTRANS int | storage_
    clause}]
```

PCTFREE defines the percentage of free space reserved for each data block in the table. For example, a value of 10 reserves 10% of the data space for new rows to be inserted. *PCTUSED* defines the minimum percentage of space allowed in a block before it can receive new rows. For example, a value of 90 means new rows are inserted in the data block when the space used falls below 90%. The sum of *PCTFREE* and *PCTUSED* cannot exceed 100. *INITRANS* is rarely tinkered with; it defines the allocation of from 1 to 255 initial transactions to a data block. *MAXTRANS* defines the maximum number of concurrent transactions on a data block.

The *storage_clause* controls a number of attributes governing the physical storage of data:

```
-- storage_clause
STORAGE ( [ {INITIAL int [K | M]
            | NEXT int [K | M]
            | MINEXTENTS int
            | MAXEXTENTS {int | UNLIMITED}
            | PCTINCREASE int
            | FREELISTS int
            | FREELIST GROUPS int
            | OPTIMAL [{int [K | M] | NULL}]
            | BUFFER_POOL {KEEP | RECYCLE | DEFAULT} ] [...] )
```

When delineating the storage clause attributes, enclose them in parentheses and separate them with spaces—for example, *(INITIAL 32M NEXT8M)*. *INITIAL int [K | M]* sets the initial extent size of the table in bytes, kilobytes *(K)*, or megabytes *(M)*. *NEXT int [K | M]* tells how much additional space to allocate after *INITIAL* is filled. *PCTINCREASE int* controls the growth rate of the object after the first growth. The initial extent gets allocated as specified. The second extent is the size specified by *NEXT.* The third extent is *NEXT + (NEXT * PCTINCREASE).* When *PCTINCREASE* is set to 0, *NEXT* is always used. Otherwise, each added extent of storage space is *PCTINCREASE* larger than the previous extent.

MINEXTENTS int tells Oracle to create a minimum number of extents. By default, only 1 is created, but more can be created when the object is initialized. *MAXEXTENTS int* tells Oracle the maximum extents allowed. It may be set to *UNLIMITED.* (Note that UNLIMITED should be used with caution. There are situations in which it can cause database damage.) *FREELISTS int* establishes the number of freelists for each group, defaulting to 1. *FREELIST GROUPS int* sets the number of groups of freelists, defaulting to 1. For example:

```
CREATE TABLE book_sales
  (qty NUMBER,
   period_end_date DATE,
   period_nbr NUMBER)
TABLESPACE sales
STORAGE (INITIAL 8M NEXT 8M MINEXTENTS 1 MAXEXTENTS 8);
```

The table **books_sales** is defined on the **sales** tablespace as consuming an initial 8 MB of space, to grow by no less than 8 MB when the first extent is full. The table has no less than 1 and no more than 8 extents, limiting its maximum size to 64 MB.

The *ORGANIZATION HEAP* clause tells Oracle to physically place the rows of the table in any order. It may be optionally associated with a *segment_characteristic_ clause.* Alternately, the rows of the table may be physically ordered according to a named *INDEX.*

The *CLUSTER* clause includes the table in an existing cluster based upon a clustered key. (Refer to Oracle's *CREATE CLUSTER* command.) All tables in the cluster must possess columns that correspond to the columns of the clustered key.

The *special_storage_clause* details three special types of data storage possible within an Oracle table: LOB (large object, such as image files), varrays, and nested tables:

```
{LOB { (LOB_item [,n]) STORE AS {ENABLE | DISABLE} STORAGE IN ROW
      | (LOB_item) STORE AS
            {LOB_segment_name ({ENABLE | DISABLE} STORAGE IN ROW)
            | LOB_segment_name
            | ({ENABLE | DISABLE} STORAGE IN ROW)}
    | VARRAY varray_item STORE AS
    | NESTED TABLE nested_item STORE AS storage_table
      [(physical_characteristics)]
      [RETURN AS {LOCATOR | VALUE}] }
```

The *LOB* clause defines the storage attributes of LOB data segment. The LOB item is the name of the LOB column or columns declared in the table. The LOB objects may be stored within the row if they are less than 4000 bytes in length, using the *ENABLE STORAGE IN ROW* clause, or they may be stored outside the row regardless of size, using the *DISABLE STORAGE IN ROW* clause. Refer to the Oracle documentation for more information about the LOB storage using the *LOB_storage_clause*. For example:

```
CREATE TABLE large_objects
    (pretty_picture BLOB,
     interesting_text CLOB)
STORAGE (INITIAL 256M NEXT 256M)
LOG (pretty_picture, interesting_text)
    STORE AS (TABLESPACE large_object_segment
        STORAGE (INITIAL 512M NEXT 512M)
        NOCACHE LOGGING);
```

The **large_objects** table is used to store pictures and text. The storage characteristics, as well as logging and caching characteristics, are also detailed.

A varray is a special Oracle object. Oracle allows distinct storage parameters for LOBs stored in a varray, using essentially the same syntax as the LOB clause. Refer to the vendor documentation for more information for varrays.

Oracle allows declaration of a *NESTED TABLE* clause in which a table is virtually stored within a column of another table. The *STORE AS* clause enables a proxy name for the table within a table, but the nested table must be created initially as a user-defined datatype. This capability is valuable for sparse arrays of values, but it is not a generally recommended approach for day-to-day tasks. For example:

```
CREATE TYPE prop_nested_tbl AS TABLE OF props_nt;

CREATE TABLE proposal_types
    (proposal_category VARCHAR2(50),
     proposals         PROPS_NT)
NESTED TABLE props_nt STORE AS props_nt_table;
```

Oracle allows a wide variety of table characteristics to be defined for a given table. Some of those characteristics are shown in the following list:

```
-- table_characteristics
{ PARTITION characteristics }
[CACHE | NOCACHE] [MONITORING | NOMONITORING]
[{NOPARALLEL | PARALLEL [int] }]
[{ENABLE | DISABLE} [VALIDATE | NOVALIDATE]
  {UNIQUE (column [,...n] )
  | PRIMARY KEY
  | CONSTRAINT constraint_name}
[index_clause]
[EXCEPTION INTO [schema.]table_name]
[CASCADE] ]
[AS select_statement]
```

Oracle uses the *PARTITION* clause as a performance enhancement by spreading the table across multiple partitions. However, the full syntax describing all permutations of a table partition would be prohibitively long. Furthermore, it is not used by most beginning SQL programmers. Refer to the Oracle vendor documentation for more information on table partitioning.

CACHE buffers a table for rapid reads, while *NOCACHE* turns off this behavior. Index-organized tables offer *CACHE* behavior. *MONITORING* collects statistics on a table for added performance, while *NOMONITORING* turns this function off.

For the *CREATE TABLE* statement, the *INDEX* clause is just for primary key and unique indexes that are created along with the table. Refer to the Oracle documentation for a full discussion on the available means of manipulating an index using the *CREATE TABLE* command. For most purposes, the *CREATE INDEX* command is the recommended approach. (Note that Oracle automatically creates an index when creating a table with a primary key constraint. There is no need for the user to create an index in that situation.)

The *PARALLEL* clause allows for the parallel creation of the table by distinct CPUs to speed the operation. It also enables parallelism for queries and other data-manipulation operations against the table after its creation. An optional integer value may be supplied to define the exact number of parallel threads used in the operation, as well as the parallel threads allowed to service the table in the future. (Oracle calculates the best number of threads to use in a given parallel operation, so this is an optional feature.) *NOPARALLEL*, the default, creates the table serially and disallows future parallel queries and data-manipulation operations.

The *DISABLE* and *ENABLE* clauses deactivate or activate constraints on a table, respectively. Basically, the *DISABLE* clause can deactivate any active integrity constraint or trigger. Conversely, *ENABLE* can activate any disabled integrity constraint or trigger. The syntax for this clause is:

```
DISABLE | ENABLE {{UNIQUE(column[,...n] |
    PRIMARY KEY |
    CONSTRAINT constraint_name}
        [CASCADE]}
        [EXCEPTIONS INTO [owner.]table_name]
        [USING INDEX [INITRANS int][MAXTRANS int]
            [TABLESPACE tablespace_name][storage_characteristics]
            [PCTFREE int] |
```

The *CASCADE* keyword, usable only with *DISABLE*, does not disable a cascading constraint or trigger. Instead, it cascades the disablement/enablement to any integrity constraints that depend on the constraint named in the clause. The *EXCEPTIONS INTO* clause, usable only with *ENABLE*, tells Oracle to store the information of any integrity-constraint violation in an existing exceptions table. The *USING INDEX* clause, also usable only with *ENABLE*, provides a mechanism to specify different storage characteristics for the named index, particularly primary and unique keys. The default is for all constraints to be enabled.

The *AS SELECT_statement* clause populates the new table with records from a valid *SELECT* statement. Unlike PostgreSQL's implementation of *CREATE . . . AS SELECT*, the columns of the *CREATE TABLE* statement must match those in the *SELECT* statement. Logging of *CREATE . . . AS SELECT* may be turned off by using the *NOLOGGING* keyword. Logging to the redo log is the default behavior.

Oracle supports a number of object-oriented features that are beyond the scope of this book.

PostgreSQL Syntax and Variations

```
CREATE [TEMPORARY | TEMP] TABLE table
(column_name datatype [NULL | NOT NULL] [DEFAULT value]
    | [UNIQUE]
    | [PRIMARY KEY (column[,...n])]
    | [CHECK (expression) ]
    | REFERENCES reference_table (reference_column)
        [MATCH {FULL | PARTIAL | default}]
        [ON DELETE {CASCADE | NO ACTION | RESTRICT | SET NULL | SET
            DEFAULT}]
        [ON UPDATE {CASCADE | NO ACTION | RESTRICT | SET NULL | SET
            DEFAULT}]
        [[NOT] DEFERRABLE] [INITIALLY {DEFERRED | IMMEDIATE}] } [,...n]
 |[table_constraint][,...n]
 [INHERITS (inherited_table [,...n])]


 | [ON COMMIT {DELETE | PRESERVE} ROWS]


 | AS SELECT_statement
```

Using a syntax similar to MySQL, PostgreSQL allows the creation of a *TEMPORARY* table. Temporary tables exist only for the session in which they were created and automatically drop themselves when the session ends.

Constraints such as *UNIQUE*, *PRIMARY KEY*, and *CHECK* are essentially the same as in Microsoft SQL Server. However, unique to PostgreSQL is the ability to create column-level constraints with multiple columns. Since PostgreSQL also supports standard table-level constraints, the ANSI-standard approach is still the recommended approach.

The *REFERENCES* constraint is similar to a *CHECK* constraint, except that it checks a value against the values of another column in another table. It also can be used as part of a *FOREIGN KEY* declaration. The *MATCH* options are *FULL*, *PARTIAL*, and default (where *MATCH* has no other keyword). Full match forces all columns of a multicolumn foreign key either to be null or to contain a valid value. The default allows mixed nulls and values. Partial matching is a valid syntax, but is not supported.

The *REFERENCES* clause also allows several different behaviors to be declared for *ON DELETE* and/or *ON UPDATE* referential integrity:

NO ACTION
> Produces an error when the foreign key is violated (the default)

RESTRICT
> A synonym for *NO ACTION*

CASCADE
> Sets the value of the referencing column to the value of the referenced column

SET NULL
> Sets the referencing column value to NULL

SET DEFAULT
> Sets the referencing column to its declared default value or null, if no default value exists

---

The *DEFERRABLE* option of the *REFERENCES* clause tells PostgreSQL to defer all constraints to the end of a transaction. *NOT DEFERRABLE* is the default behavior for the *REFERENCES* clause. Similar to the *DEFERRABLE* clause is the *INITIALLY* clause. Specifying *INITIALLY DEFERRED* checks constraints at the end of a transaction; *INITIALLY IMMEDIATE* checks constraints after each statement (the default).

Note that, like Microsoft SQL Server, all column-level constraints may be declared as table-level constraints. Importantly, the *FOREIGN KEY* constraint can be declared only as a table-level constraint and not as a column-level constraint. All options for the *REFERENCES* clause are supported as part of the *FOREIGN KEYS* clause. The syntax follows:

```
[FOREIGN KEY (column[,...n]) REFERENCES...]
```

The *INHERITS inherited_table* clause specifies a table or tables from which this table inherits all columns. The newly created table also inherits functions attached to tables higher in the hierarchy. If any inherited column appears more than once, the statement fails.

If a temporary or global temporary table is created in PostgreSQL, the *ON COMMIT* clause also may be appended to the command. This clause controls the behavior of the temporary table after records are committed to the table. *ON COMMIT DELETE ROWS* clears the temporary table of all rows after each commit. This is the default. *ON COMMIT PRESERVE ROWS* saves the rows in the temporary table after the transaction has committed.

The *AS SELECT_statement* clause enables a programmer to create and populate a table with data from a valid *SELECT* statement. The columns, datatypes, or constraints do not need to be defined, since they are inherited from the query. It is similar in functionality to *SELECT . . . INTO*, but its syntax seems more readable.

Examples

This example adds a foreign key to the example table:

```
-- Creating a column-level constraint
CREATE TABLE favorite_books
    (isbn         CHAR(100)    PRIMARY KEY NONCLUSTERED,
    book_name     VARCHAR(40)  UNIQUE,
    category      VARCHAR(40)  NULL,
    subcategory   VARCHAR(40)  NULL,
    pub_date      DATETIME     NOT NULL,
    purchase_date DATETIME     NOT NULL,
        CONSTRAINT fk_categories FOREIGN KEY (category)
            REFERENCES category(cat_name));
```

The foreign key on the **categories** column relates it to the **cat_name** table in the **category** table. This syntax is supported by all the vendors mentioned in this book. Similarly, the foreign key could have been declared as a multicolumn key including both the **category** and **subcategory** columns:

```
...
CONSTRAINT fk_categories FOREIGN KEY (category, subcategory)
        REFERENCES category(cat_name, subcat_name));
```

Listed here are two more full examples from the **pubs** database (**jobs** and **employee**):

```
-- For a Microsoft SQL Server database
CREATE TABLE jobs
   (job_id  SMALLINT IDENTITY(1,1) PRIMARY KEY CLUSTERED,
   job_desc VARCHAR(50) NOT NULL DEFAULT 'New Position',
   min_lvl  TINYINT NOT NULL CHECK (min_lvl >= 10),
   max_lvl  TINYINT NOT NULL CHECK (max_lvl <= 250))

-- For a MySQL  database
CREATE TABLE employee
   (emp_id INT AUTO_INCREMENT CONSTRAINT PK_emp_id PRIMARY KEY,
   fname VARCHAR(20) NOT NULL,
   minit CHAR(1) NULL,
   lname VARCHAR(30) NOT NULL,
   job_id SMALLINT NOT NULL DEFAULT 1
      REFERENCES jobs(job_id),
   job_lvl TINYINT DEFAULT 10,
   pub_id CHAR(4) NOT NULL DEFAULT ('9952')
      REFERENCES publishers(pub_id),
   hire_date DATETIME NOT NULL DEFAULT (CURRENT_DATE());

CREATE TABLE publishers
   (pub_id char(4) NOT NULL
      CONSTRAINT UPKCL_pubind PRIMARY KEY CLUSTERED
      CHECK (pub_id IN ('1389', '0736', '0877', '1622', '1756')
      OR pub_id LIKE '99[0-9][0-9]'),
   pub_name varchar(40) NULL,
   city varchar(20) NULL,
   state char(2) NULL,
   country varchar(30) NULL DEFAULT('USA'))
```

The following is an example of an Oracle *CREATE TABLE* statement with many storage properties:

```
CREATE TABLE classical_music_cds
   (music_id        INT,
   composition     VARCHAR2(50),
   composer        VARCHAR2(50),
   performer       VARCHAR2(50),
   performance_date DATE DEFAULT SYSDATE,
   duration        INT,
   cd_name         VARCHAR2(100),
CONSTRAINT pk_class_cds PRIMARY KEY (music_id)
   USING INDEX TABLESPACE index_ts
   STORAGE (INITIAL 100K NEXT 20K),
CONSTRAINT uq_class_cds UNIQUE (composition, performer, performance_date)
   USING INDEX TABLESPACE index_ts
   STORAGE (INITIAL 100K NEXT 20K))
TABLESPACE tabledata_ts;
```

CREATE TRIGGER

A trigger is a special kind of stored procedure that fires automatically (hence, the term trigger) when a data-modification statement is executed. Triggers are associated with a specific data-modification statement (*INSERT, UPDATE,* or *DELETE*) on a specific table.

Vendor	Command
SQL Server	Supported, with variations
MySQL	Not supported
Oracle	Supported, with variations
PostgreSQL	Supported, with variations

SQL99 Syntax and Description

```
CREATE TRIGGER trigger_name
{BEFORE | AFTER} {[DELETE] | [INSERT] | [UPDATE] [OF column [,...n]}
ON table_name
[REFERENCING {OLD [ROW] [AS] old_name | NEW [ROW] [AS] new_name
  OLD TABLE [AS] old_name | NEW TABLE [AS] new_name}]
[FOR EACH { ROW | STATEMENT }]
[WHEN (conditions)]
code block
```

Triggers, by default, fire once at the *statement level.* That is, a single *INSERT* statement might insert 500 rows into a table, but an insert trigger on that table fires only one time. Some vendors allow a trigger to fire for each row of the data-modification operation. So, a statement that inserts 500 rows into a table that has a row-level insert trigger fires 500 times, once for each inserted row.

In addition to being associated with a specific data-modification statement (*INSERT, UPDATE,* or *DELETE*) on a given table, triggers are associated with a specific *time* of firing. In general, triggers can fire *BEFORE* the data-modification statement is processed, *AFTER* it is processed, or (when supported by the vendor) *INSTEAD OF* processing the statement. Triggers that fire before or instead of the data-modification statement do not see the changes that the statement renders, while those that fire afterwards can see and act upon the changes that the data-modification statement renders.

Microsoft SQL Server Syntax and Variations

```
CREATE TRIGGER trigger_name
ON {table_name | view_name}
[WITH ENCRYPTION]
{FOR | AFTER | INSTEAD OF} {[DELETE] [,] [INSERT] [,] [UPDATE]}
[WITH APPEND]
[NOT FOR REPLICATION]
AS
  {
  T-SQL_block
  |
```

```
{ IF UPDATE(column) [{AND | OR} UPDATE(column)] [...n]
  |
  IF (COLUMNS_UPDATED() {bitwise_operator} updated_bitmask)
  { comparison_operator} column_bitmask [...n] }
  T-SQL_block [...n]
}
```

Microsoft SQL Server supports a number of interesting features in its *CREATE TRIGGER* statement. First, SQL Server allows multiple triggers for a given data-manipulation operation on a table or *view*. Thus, three *UPDATE* triggers are possible on a single table.

The *WITH ENCRYPTION* clause encrypts the text of the trigger where it is stored in the **syscomments** system table. The *WITH APPEND* clause adds an additional trigger of an existing type to a table or view. This clause is added for backward compatibility with earlier versions of the product and can be used only with *FOR* triggers. The *NOT FOR REPLICATION* clause disables the trigger on data-manipulation operations invoked through SQL Server's built-in replication capabilities.

The *FOR*, *AFTER*, and *INSTEAD OF* clauses tell SQL Server when the trigger should fire. The *FOR* and *AFTER* keywords are synonymous and serve the same function. In effect, they specify that the trigger fire only after the triggering data-modification statement (and any cascading actions and constraint checks) have completed successfully. Many *AFTER* triggers are possible on a given table. Their order is undefined, though the first and last triggers can be specified using the *sp_settriggerorder* system stored procedure.

 AFTER triggers cannot be defined on views.

The *INSTEAD OF* clause is functionally equivalent to Oracle's *BEFORE* trigger. It specifies that the trigger fire before (and thus, instead of) the triggering data-modification statement, but only one *INSTEAD OF* trigger is possible per *INSERT*, *UPDATE*, or *DELETE* statement on a given table (though multiple *AFTER* triggers are possible). This kind of trigger is usable on views, but only if they do not use the *WITH CHECK OPTION* clause. *INSTEAD OF DELETE* triggers cannot be used when there is a cascading action on the delete.

The *DELETE*, *INSERT*, and *UPDATE* specifications identify the data-modification statement that fires the trigger. In SQL Server, any combination of these are made possible in a trigger definition by separating each option with a comma. (When doing so, the same code fires for each statement in the combination definition.)

The *AS T-SQL_block* clause contains the procedural code that the trigger fires whenever the data-manipulation operation is performed. This section should be enclosed within the Transact-SQL *BEGIN* and *END* clauses. Traditionally, this section contains control-of-flow commands and checks against the type and amount of data changed.

SQL Server instantiates two important pseudo-tables when a trigger is fired: **deleted** and **inserted**. These tables are identical in structure to the table on which the triggers are defined, except that they contain the old data before the data-modification statement fired (**deleted**) and the new values of the table after the data-modification statement fired (**inserted**).

Only *INSTEAD OF* triggers can access **text**, **ntext**, or **image** columns.

The *AS IF UPDATE(column)* clause tests specifically for *INSERT* or *UPDATE* actions on a given column or columns. Multiple columns may be specified by adding separate *UPDATE(column)* clauses after the first; follow the clause with a Transact-SQL *BEGIN . . . END* block to allow multiple Transact-SQL operations to fire when the condition is met. This clause is functionally equivalent to the *IF . . . THEN . . . ELSE* operation.

The *AS IF (COLUMNS_UPDATE( ))* clause is similar to the *AS IF UPDATE()* clause in that it fires only on an *INSERT* or *UPDATE* operation against the column specified. It returns a *varbinary* bit pattern that tells which columns were inserted or updated and allows bitwise operations that compare the column values in various ways. The comparison operators are the equal sign (=), used to check if all columns specified in the updated bitmask were changed, and the greater-than sign (>), used to check whether one or some of the columns were changed.

Triggers are used often to control declarative referential integrity. However, primary and foreign key declarations via a *CREATE TABLE* or *ALTER TABLE* statement are preferable.

SQL Server *does not* allow the following statements within the Transact-SQL block of a trigger: *ALTER, CREATE, DROP, DENY, GRANT, REVOKE, LOAD, RESTORE, RECONFIGURE,* or *TRUNCATE.* In addition, it does not allow any *DISK* statements or the *UPDATE STATISTICS* command.

SQL Server also allows triggers to fire recursively using the *recursive triggers* setting of the *sp_dboption* system stored procedure. Recursive triggers, by their own action, cause themselves to fire again. For example, if an *INSERT* trigger on table **T1** performs an *INSERT* operation on table **T1**, it might perform a recursive operation. Since recursive triggers can be dangerous, this functionality is disabled by default.

Similarly, SQL Server allows *nested triggers* up to 32 levels deep. If any one of the nested triggers performs a *ROLLBACK* operation, no further triggers execute. An example of nested triggers is a trigger on table **T1** firing an operation against table **T2**, which also has a trigger that fires an operation against table **T3**. The triggers cancel if an infinite loop is encountered. Nested triggers are enabled with the nested triggers setting of the system stored procedure *sp_configure*. If nested triggers are disabled, recursive triggers are disabled as well, despite the recursive triggers' setting of *sp_dboption*.

SQL Server *CREATE* statements allow *deferred name resolution*, meaning that the command is processed even if it refers to a database object that does not yet exist in the database.

Oracle Syntax and Variations

```
CREATE [OR REPLACE] TRIGGER [owner.]trigger_name
{BEFORE | AFTER | INSTEAD OF}
{[DELETE] [OR] [INSERT] [OR] [UPDATE [OF column [,...n] ]] [...n]}
ON {table_name | view_name}
[REFERENCING {OLD [AS] old_name | NEW [AS] new_name}]
[FOR EACH { ROW | STATEMENT }]
[WHEN (conditions)]
PL/SQL block
```

As is typical of the *CREATE TRIGGER* statement, the command specifies the data-modification operation (*INSERT, UPDATE,* or *DELETE*) that fires the PL/SQL block of code and when it is fired (*BEFORE, AFTER,* or *INSTEAD OF* the data-modification operation). On *UPDATE* operations, an *UPDATE OF* a column or columns may be specified to indicate that the update trigger should fire only when those specific column(s) are changed.

Oracle allows *INSTEAD OF* triggers to process only against views, not tables.

Oracle also allows triggers to fire on certain database events, such as *DROP TABLE* or *SHUTDOWN*.

The *REFERENCING* clause specifies a name for the pseudo-tables that hold the *OLD* and *NEW* versions of the table. (SQL Server automatically names these pseudo-tables **inserted** and **deleted**.) In Oracle, the default name for these pseudo-tables is **OLD** and **NEW**, respectively. These pseudo-tables compare record values before they are altered by the data-manipulation operation (via the **OLD** pseudo-table) and compared to the values after the data-manipulation operation (via the **NEW** pseudo-table). Pseudo-tables also perform conditional operations on the *PL/SQL_block*.

 When referencing values in the OLD and NEW pseudo-tables, the value must be prefaced with a colon (:), except in the trigger's WHEN clause, where no colons are used.

The *FOR EACH ROW* clause tells the trigger to operate on each individual row (firing once for each row affected by the operation), rather than operate as an implicit statement trigger (firing once for the entire transaction). The *WHEN* clause specifies a SQL condition that restricts the execution of the trigger to happen only when the condition is met. The *WHEN* clause also allows comparisons of the **OLD** and **NEW** tables without having to build a PL/SQL block to compare them.

Multiple trigger types may be combined into a single trigger command if they are of the same level (row or statement) and they are on the same table. When triggers are combined in a single statement, the clauses *IF INSERTING THEN, IF*

UPDATING THEN, and *IF DELETING THEN* may be used in the PL/SQL block to break the code logic into distinct segments. An *ELSE* clause also can be used in this structure.

PostgreSQL Syntax and Variations

```
CREATE TRIGGER trigger_name
{ BEFORE | AFTER }
{ {[DELETE] [OR | ,] [INSERT] [OR | ,] [UPDATE]} [OR ...] }
ON table_name
FOR EACH { ROW | STATEMENT }
EXECUTE PROCEDURE function_name (parameters)
```

The PostgreSQL implementation of *CREATE TRIGGER* functions in a similar manner to that of the other vendors. It may fire *BEFORE* the data-modification operation is attempted on the record and before any constraints are fired. Or it may fire *AFTER* the data-manipulation operation has processed (and after constraints have been checked), making all operations involved in the transaction visible to the trigger.

Rather than process a block of procedural code (as Oracle and SQL Server do), PostgreSQL executes a function via the *EXECUTE PROCEDURE* clause created using the *CREATE FUNCTION*. Also, other vendors implicitly process upon all rows in the transaction. PostgreSQL executes the trigger on each row or once for the entire transaction, using the *FOR EACH ROW* and *FOR EACH STATEMENT* clauses, respectively.

Examples

Following is an example of a PostgreSQL *BEFORE* trigger that checks at a row level to ensure that the specified distributor code exists in the **distributors** table before inserting or updating a row in the **sales** table:

```
CREATE TRIGGER if_dist_exists
BEFORE INSERT OR UPDATE ON sales
FOR EACH ROW
EXECUTE PROCEDURE check_primary_key ('did', 'distributors', 'did');
```

BEFORE triggers alter the values committed to a table by a data-modification operation, since the processing on the affected records happens before they are changed in the table. *AFTER* triggers are used often for auditing processes, since they cannot fire until after the row has been changed in the table. *INSTEAD OF* completely skips the data-modification operation in favor of code that the user provides for the transaction.

Here is an Oracle *BEFORE* trigger that uses the **OLD** and **NEW** pseudo-tables to compare values. (By way of comparison, SQL Server uses the **DELETED** and **INSERTED** pseudo-tables in the same way.) This trigger creates an audit record before changing an employee's pay record:

```
CREATE TRIGGER if_emp_changes
BEFORE DELETE OR UPDATE ON employee
FOR EACH ROW
WHEN (new.emp_salary <> old.emp_salary)
BEGIN
```

```
    INSERT INTO employee_audit
    VALUES ('old', :old.emp_id, :old.emp_salary, :old.emp_ssn);
END;
```

The following example builds an Oracle insert and update trigger that uses the *IF INSERTED THEN* clauses:

```
CREATE TRIGGER if_emp_changes
BEFORE DELETE OR UPDATE ON employee
FOR EACH ROW
BEGIN
  IF DELETING THEN
    INSERT INTO employee_audit
    VALUES ('DELETED', :old.emp_id, :old.emp_salary, :old.emp_ssn);
  ELSE
    INSERT INTO employee_audit
    VALUES ('UPDATED', :old.emp_id, :new.emp_salary, :old.emp_ssn);
  END IF;
END;
```

This SQL Server example adds a new table called **contractor** to the database. All records in the **employee** table that indicate that the employee is a contractor were moved into the **contractor** table. Now all new employees inserted into the **employee** table will go into the **contractor** table instead through an *INSTEAD OF* trigger:

```
CREATE TRIGGER if_emp_is_contractor
INSTEAD OF INSERT ON employee
BEGIN
  INSERT INTO contractor
  SELECT * FROM inserted WHERE status = 'CON'

  INSERT INTO employee
  SELECT * FROM inserted WHERE status = 'FTE'
END
GO
```

CREATE VIEW

This statement creates a *view*, also known as a *virtual table*. A view acts just like a table but is actually defined as a query. Almost any valid *SELECT* statement can define the contents of a view, though an *ORDER BY* clause is usually prohibited.

When a view is referenced in a statement, the result set of the query becomes the content of the view for the duration of that statement. In some cases, views can be updated, causing the view changes to be translated to the underlying data in the base tables.

Vendor	Command
SQL Server	Supported, with variations
MySQL	Not supported
Oracle	Supported, with variations
PostgreSQL	Supported, with variations

Views even can be built upon other views, but this is inadvisable and usually considered bad practice.

SQL99 Syntax and Description

```
CREATE VIEW view_name [(column list)]
AS
(SELECT_statement
[WITH [CASCADED | LOCAL] CHECK OPTION] )
```

Views are usually as effective as the query upon which they are based. That is why it is important to be sure that the defining *SELECT* statement is speedy and well-written.

A *column list* also may be specified after the view name. The optional column list contains aliases serving as names for each element in the result set of the *SELECT* statement.

The *WITH CHECK OPTION* clause is used *only* on views that allow updates to the base table. It ensures that only data that may be read by the view may be inserted, updated, or deleted by the view. For example, if a view of **employees** showed only salaried employees, but not hourly employees, it would be impossible to insert, update, or delete hourly employees through that view. The *CASCADE* and *LOCAL* options of the *CHECK OPTION* clause are used for nested views. The *CASCADE* option performs the check option for the current view and all views it is built on top of. The *LOCAL* option performs the check option only for the current view, even when it is built upon other views.

ANSI SQL99 views can update the base table(s) they are based upon if they meet the following conditions:

- The defining *SELECT* statement is based upon one table.

- The view does not have *UNION, MINUS,* or *INTERSECT* operators.

- The defining *SELECT* statement does not contain *GROUP BY* or *HAVING* clauses.

- The defining *SELECT* statement does not contain any reference to pseudo-columns such as **ROWNUM** or **ROWGUIDCOL.**

- The defining *SELECT* statement does not contain any group functions.

- The defining *SELECT* statement does not contain the *DISTINCT* clause.

Microsoft SQL Server Syntax and Variations

```
CREATE [owner_name.]VIEW view_name [(column [,...n])]
[WITH {ENCRYPTION | SCHEMABINDING | VIEW_METADATA} [,...n]]
AS
select_statement
[WITH CHECK OPTION]
```

Microsoft SQL Server allows two new options not in SQL99: *ENCRYPTION* and *SCHEMABINDING*. The *ENCRYPTION* option encrypts the text of the view in the **syscomments** table. The *SCHEMABINDING* option binds the view to a specific schema, meaning that all objects in the view must be referenced by their full name (both owner and object name). Views created with *SCHEMABINDING* (and tables referenced by these views) must have the schema binding dropped (via *ALTER VIEW*) before they may be dropped or altered. *VIEW_METADATA* specifies that SQL Server returns metadata about the view (rather than the base table) to calls made from DBLIB and OLEDB APIs. Views created or altered with *VIEW_METADATA* enable their columns to be updated by *INSERT* and *UPDATE INSTEAD OF* triggers.

SQL Server allows indexes to be created on views (see *CREATE INDEX*). By creating a unique, clustered index on a view, a SQL Server essentially stores a physical copy of the view on the database. Changes to the base table are automatically updated in the indexed view.

 Indexed views should be built on base tables using only the *SCHEMABINDING* clause. This is an advanced technique and should be used only by experts. Refer to the vendor documentation for more information on this technique.

Oracle Syntax and Variations

```
CREATE [OR REPLACE] [FORCE | NO FORCE] VIEW [owner_name.]view_name
   [(column [,...n])]
AS
SELECT_statement
[WITH [READ ONLY | CHECK OPTION [CONSTRAINT constraint_name] ] ]
```

The *OR REPLACE* clause tells Oracle that any existing view with the same name should be replaced by the new view. The *FORCE* clause creates the view regardless of whether the base tables exist or the user creating the view has privileges to the base tables. The *NO FORCE* clause creates the view only if the base tables and proper privileges are in place.

Oracle allows the use of the *CHECK OPTION*, including the ability to name the constraint using the *CONSTRAINT* clause. The *CHECK OPTION* clause may be used on nested views, but only if the top level view's *CHECK OPTION* is enforced. If the constraint is not named, Oracle names the constraint *SYS_Cn*, where **n** is an integer.

Oracle allows data-manipulation operations through views, as long as they meet the SQL99 requirements, and the added requirement does not contain any expressions. The *WITH READ ONLY* clause ensures the view is used only to retrieve data.

PostgreSQL Syntax and Variations

```
CREATE VIEW view_name AS SELECT_statement
```

PostgreSQL's *CREATE VIEW* does not support some of the more complex options that other vendors do. However, it does allow views to be built on tables and other defined class objects. PostgreSQL views are typically built only upon other tables, not upon other views, and are not used to perform data modifications on the underlying base tables.

Examples

The simplest view is based on the entire contents of a single table:

```
CREATE VIEW employees
AS
SELECT *
FROM employee_tbl;
```

This example shows a view named **california_authors** that allows data modifications to apply only to authors within the state of California:

```
CREATE VIEW california_authors
AS
SELECT au_lname, au_fname, city, state
FROM authors
WHERE state = 'CA'
WITH CHECK OPTION
GO
```

DECLARE CURSOR

The *DECLARE CURSOR* command enables the retrieval and manipulation of records from a table one row at a time. This provides row-by-row processing, rather than the traditional set processing offered by SQL. To use this procedure properly, you should:

1. *DECLARE* the cursor

2. *OPEN* the cursor

3. *FETCH* rows from the cursor

4. When finished, *CLOSE* the cursor

MySQL does not support server-side cursors in the ANSI SQL style, but does support extensive C-programming extensions that provide the same functionality.

Vendor	Command
SQL Server	Supported
MySQL	Not supported
Oracle	Supported
PostgreSQL	Supported

SQL99 Syntax and Description

The *DECLARE CURSOR* command works by specifying a *SELECT* statement. Each row returned by the *SELECT* statement may be individually retrieved and manipulated. The *DECLARE CURSOR* command also defines the characteristics of a server-side cursor. The characteristics might include how the cursor scrolls and the *SELECT* statement used to retrieve a result set.

Microsoft SQL Server allows the *INSENSITIVE* and *SCROLL* options to be identified. The *INSENSITIVE* keyword specifies that the cursor build a temporary copy of the result set used by the cursor. All requests to the cursor are answered from the temporary table, not the base table. The cursor does not allow modifications. Subsequent fetches by the cursor do not reflect any changes made by the cursor. The *SCROLL* keyword enables all *FETCH* options for the cursor (*FIRST, LAST, PRIOR, NEXT, RELATIVE,* and *ABSOLUTE*). Refer to the *FETCH* command for more details. If *SCROLL* is not declared, only *NEXT* is available as a *FETCH* option. A read-only cursor also can be declared using the *FOR READ ONLY* clause.

In Oracle, variables are not allowed in the *WHERE* clause of the *SELECT* statement unless they are first declared as variables. The parameters are not assigned at the *DECLARE*; instead, they are assigned values at the *OPEN* command.

PostgreSQL has an implementation that is very similar to Microsoft SQL Server, except that it allows a *BINARY* option. *BINARY* forces the cursor to retrieve binary-formatted data rather than text-formatted data.

Microsoft SQL Server Syntax

```
DECLARE cursor_name [INSENSITIVE] [SCROLL] CURSOR
FOR select_statement
[FOR {READ ONLY | UPDATE [OF column_name [,...n]]}]
```

Oracle Syntax

```
DECLARE CURSOR cursor_name [parameter1 datatype1 [,...parameterN
datatypeN]
IS select_statement
[FOR UPDATE [OF column_name [,...n]]}]
```

PostgreSQL Syntax

```
DECLARE cursor_name [BINARY] [INSENSITIVE] [SCROLL] CURSOR
FOR select_statement
[FOR {READ ONLY | UPDATE [OF column_name [,...n]]}]
```

Microsoft SQL Server Syntax and Variations

Microsoft SQL Server supports the standard format described previously in this chapter, but also has a more elaborate extension. The syntax for this is:

```
DECLARE cursor_name CURSOR
[LOCAL | GLOBAL] [FORWARD_ONLY | SCROLL]
[STATIC | KEYSET | DYNAMIC | FAST_FORWARD]
[READ_ONLY | SCROLL_LOCKS | OPTIMISTIC]
[TYPE_WARNING]
FOR select_statement
[FOR UPDATE [OF column_name [,...n]]]
```

This syntax works in the same way as the ANSI-standard cursor declaration, but it offers many new functionalities. First, the scope of the cursor may be declared as *LOCAL* or *GLOBAL*. If *LOCAL*, the cursor is available only within the current Transact-SQL batch, stored procedure, or trigger in which it was declared. If *GLOBAL*, the cursor is available as the *OPEN* and *FETCH* commands throughout the connection.

Transact-SQL notation should not be mixed with the ANSI-standard cursor declaration in Microsoft SQL Server.

The next several options determine how the cursor searches through the record set. *FORWARD_ONLY*, as opposed to *SCROLL*, specifies that the cursor can scroll only from the first record to the last. It cannot be used in conjunction with *STATIC*, *KEYSET*, or *DYNAMIC*. It acts as a *DYNAMIC* cursor.

STATIC functions similarly to the keyword *INSENSITIVE*. *KEYSET* is similar to *STATIC* and *INSENSITIVE*, except that it allows modifications to the result set. The keyset is unaware of records inserted by other users once the cursor has been opened, though records deleted by other users produce an *@@FETCH_STATUS* of -2. New values are made visible when updates are done by specifying *WHERE CURRENT OF*. *DYNAMIC* reflects all data changes made to the result set during work with the cursor. The result set can change during any *FETCH*. *FETCH ABSOLUTE* is not supported by *DYNAMIC* cursors. *FAST_FORWARD* is shorthand for *FORWARD_ONLY*, *READ_ONLY*, but it also enables extra functionality. *FAST_FORWARD* is mutually exclusive of *SCROLL*, *FOR_UPDATE*, *SCROLL_LOCKS*, *OPTIMISTIC*, and *FORWARD_ONLY*.

Two other options also are allowed for *READ_ONLY*: *SCROLL_LOCKS* and *OPTIMISTIC*. *SCROLL_LOCKS* forces a record-level lock whenever a new record is fetched, ensuring that updates and deletes made through the cursor succeed. *OPTIMISTIC* specifies that positioned updates and deletes made through the cursor fail if the row is changed by another user.

Finally, the *TYPE_WARNING* option tells SQL Server that a warning message should be sent to the client if it is transformed from one type to another (for example, *KEYSET* to *DYNAMIC*).

Examples

In this simple example from Microsoft SQL Server, a cursor from the **publishers** table is declared and opened. The cursor takes the first record from **publisher** that matches the *SELECT* statement and inserts it into another table; it then moves to the next record and the next, until all records are processed. Finally, the cursor is closed and deallocated (*deallocate* is only used in Microsoft SQL Server):

```
DECLARE @publisher_name VARCHAR(20)

DECLARE pub_cursor CURSOR
FOR SELECT pub_name FROM publishers
    WHERE country <> 'USA'
```

```
OPEN pub_cursor
FETCH NEXT FROM pub_cursor INTO @publisher_name
WHILE @@FETCH_STATUS = 0
BEGIN
    INSERT INTO foreign_publishers VALUES(@publisher_name)
END

CLOSE pub_cursor
DEALLOCATE pub_cursor
```

In this Oracle example, the cursor is declared in the declaration block along with some other variables, and the rest of the cursor is then processed:

```
DECLARE
    new_price NUMBER(10,2);
    CURSOR title_price_cursor IS
        SELECT title, price
        FROM titles
        WHERE price IS NOT NULL;
    title_price_val title_price_cursor%ROWTYPE;
BEGIN
    OPEN title_price_cursor;
    FETCH title_price_cursor INTO title_price_val;
    new_price := "title_price_val.price" * 1.25
    INSERT INTO new_title_price VALUES (title_price_val.title, new_price)
    CLOSE title_price_cursor;
END;
```

Because this example uses a lot of PL/SQL, much of the code is beyond the scope of this book. However, the *DECLARE* block clearly shows that the cursor is declared. In the PL/SQL execution block, the cursor is initialized with the *OPEN* command, values are retrieved with the *FETCH* command, and the cursor finally is terminated with the *CLOSE* command.

DELETE

The *DELETE* statement erases records from a specified table or tables. It is a logged operation, meaning that it can be undone with a *ROLLBACK* command.

Vendor	Command
SQL Server	Supported, with variations
MySQL	Supported, with variations
Oracle	Supported
PostgreSQL	Supported

 It is rare to issue a *DELETE* statement without a *WHERE* clause, because this results in deleting *all* rows from the affected table.

SQL99 Syntax and Description

```
DELETE [FROM] [owner.]table_name [WHERE clause]
```

If it becomes necessary to remove all the rows in a table, it is preferable to use the *TRUNCATE TABLE* statement. In those databases that support the command, this is usually a faster method to physically remove all rows. *TRUNCATE TABLE* is faster than *DELETE* because *TRUNCATE* is not logged, making rollback impossible. The reduction of logging overhead saves considerable time when erasing a large number of records.

Microsoft SQL Server Syntax and Variations

```
DELETE [FROM] [owner.] {table_name | view_name}
[WITH (query_hint[,...n]]
[FROM table_source[,...n]]
[WHERE clause | [CURRENT OF [GLOBAL] cursor_name]]
[OPTION (query_hint[,...n])]
```

Microsoft SQL Server allows records to be deleted both from tables and from views that describe a single table. (There are some other special rules that allow deletion from a multitable view, but they are quite complex and beyond the scope of this book.) At two points in the command, after the first *FROM* and at the end of the statement, SQL Server's default optimizer behavior can be overridden, but this should be done only by experts. These hints are not a part of the ANSI standard, but they are part of most vendor documentation.

Additionally, SQL Server allows a second *FROM* clause. The second *FROM* allows the use of the *JOIN* statement and makes it quite easy to delete rows from the table in the first *FROM* (based on corresponding rows of a table declared in the second *FROM*).

The *WHERE CURRENT OF* clause is used for positioned deletes through a cursor. In conjunction with a cursor, this form of *DELETE* erases only the row that currently is opened by the cursor.

MySQL Syntax and Variations

```
DELETE [LOW_PRIORITY] FROM table_name [WHERE clause] [LIMIT rows]
```

MySQL is optimized for speed. With that in mind, it allows the option of specifying *LOW PRIORITY*, which delays the execution of *DELETE* until no other clients are reading from the table. MySQL also can place an arbitrary cap on the number of records deleted before control is passed back to the client using the *LIMIT nbr_of_rows* clause.

Oracle Syntax and Variations

```
DELETE FROM [schema.]{table_name | view_name | snapshot_name}
    {PARTITION (partition_name) | SUBPARTITION (subpartition_name)} |
[WHERE clause]
[subquery WITH {READ ONLY | CHECK OPTION [CONSTRAINT constraint_name]} ]
[RETURNING expression[,...] INTO variable[,...]
```

Oracle allows you to delete rows from tables, views, and partitioned views and tables.

PARTITION and *SUBPARTITION* specify the name of the partition or subpartition within the table that should be deleted.

The *WITH* clause is used in conjunction with a subquery. It restricts the actions of the *DELETE* statement. The *WITH READ ONLY* option specifies that any subquery used in the command cannot be updated. *WITH CHECK OPTION* tells Oracle to *DELETE* any rows that are not in the subquery.

RETURNING retrieves the rows affected by the command. When used for a single-row delete, the values of the row are stored in PL/SQL variables and bind variables. When used for a multirow delete, the values of the rows are stored in bind arrays. The *INTO* keyword specifies that the deleted values should be stored in the variables list.

PostgreSQL Syntax and Variations

```
DELETE FROM [ONLY] table
[WHERE {clause | CURRENT OF cursor_name}]
```

PostgreSQL uses the *DELETE* command to remove rows from the table and any defined subclasses from the table. When deleting rows from only the table specified, use the *ONLY* clause. The *WHERE CURRENT OF* clause tells PostgreSQL to delete only the currently open row of the named, open cursor.

Examples

To delete all records from the **titles** table:

```
DELETE titles
```

To delete all records in the **authors** table where the last name starts with 'Mc':

```
DELETE FROM authors
WHERE au_lname LIKE 'Mc%'
```

To delete all titles with an old ID number:

```
DELETE titles WHERE title_id >= 40
```

To delete all titles that have no sales:

```
DELETE titles WHERE ytd_sales IS NULL
```

To delete all records in one table based on the results of a subquery against another table (in this case, the records are erased in the **titleauthor** table that have a match concerning 'computers' in the **titles** table):

```
DELETE FROM titleauthor
WHERE title_id IN
  (SELECT title_id
  FROM titles
  WHERE title LIKE '%computers%')
```

DISCONNECT

The *DISCONNECT* statement terminates a connection to the DBMS.

Vendor	Command
SQL Server	Supported, with limitations
MySQL	Not supported
Oracle	Supported, with variations
PostgreSQL	Not supported

SQL99 Syntax and Description

```
DISCONNECT {CURRENT | ALL | connection_name}
```

This command ends one or more connections created between the current SQL process and the database server. The *CURRENT* clause closes the currently active user connection. The *ALL* clause closes all open connections for the current user. Alternately, it's possible to close only a specific connection.

Microsoft SQL Server Syntax and Variations

Microsoft SQL Server supports *DISCONNECT* in Embedded-SQL (ESQL) only, not within its ad hoc querying tool, SQL Query Analyzer. It supports the full SQL99 syntax. When disconnecting from Microsoft SQL Server in an ESQL program, the *DISCONNECT ALL* command should be used to disconnect cleanly from the database server.

Oracle Syntax and Variations

```
DISC[ONNECT]
```

In contrast to SQL Server, Oracle allows *DISCONNECT only* in its ad hoc query tool, SQL*Plus. In this usage, the command ends the current session with the database server but otherwise allows work in SQL*Plus to continue. For example, a programmer can continue to edit the buffer, save run files, and so on. However, a reconnection must be established to issue any SQL commands. Exiting SQL*Plus and returning to the filesystem requires the *EXIT* or *QUIT* commands.

Oracle also supports this functionality with the command *ALTER SYSTEM DISCONNECT SESSION*. However, this is a privileged command available only to the DBA for forcibly disconnecting a session (usually a rogue session) from the database.

PostgreSQL

PostgreSQL does not explicitly support the DISCONNECT command. However, every programming interface does support a disconnect operation; for example, SPI_FINISH is available under the Server Programming Interface, and PG_CONNECT is available under the PL/tcl programming package.

Examples

End the current connection with an Oracle server:

```
DISCONNECT;
```

Microsoft SQL Server supports *DISCONNECT* within ESQL programs only:

```
EXEC SQL DISCONNECT new_york;
```

DROP Statements

All of the database objects created with *CREATE* commands may be destroyed using complementary *DROP* statements. The *DROP* command is irreversible and permanent, so it must be used with care. The syntax follows this format:

```
DROP object_type [owner_name.]object_name
```

With most vendors, the *DROP* command fails if the database object is in use by another user. With some vendors, the *DROP* command fails if the database object has other characteristics. For example, Microsoft SQL Server does not drop a table that is replicated. The table must be removed from replication before it can be dropped.

 It is important to be aware that most vendors do not notify a user if the *DROP* command creates a dependency problem. Thus, if a table is dropped that is used by a few views and stored procedures else- where in the database, no warning is issued. Those other objects simply return failures when they are accessed.

DROP DATABASE

DROP DATABASE undoes all the work done by the *CREATE DATABASE* command. It drops all existing database objects and releases the space used by them. With most vendors this command cannot be executed while users (including the owner) are active in the database.

Vendor	Command
SQL Server	Supported
MySQL	Supported
Oracle	Not supported
PostgreSQL	Supported

SQL99 Syntax and Description

```
DROP DATABASE database_name
```

Like *CREATE DATABASE*, *DROP DATABASE* is supported by ANSI SQL only as an extension and not as a core command. SQL99 prefers commands relating to *SCHEMA* and *DOMAIN* to cover areas that roughly correspond to what most imple- mentations would consider "database" issues.

The system databases created by the database vendor should never be dropped. Dropping a database requires explicit permissions, unless performed by the database owner or the system administrator.

Microsoft SQL Server Syntax and Variations

```
DROP DATABASE database_name [,...n]
```

In SQL Server, multiple databases may be dropped in the same command by adding a comma between each database name. A database may be dropped only by a user in the master database, a user who has sys admin privileges, or the database owner. The database must be *ONLINE* to be dropped.

MySQL and PostgreSQL Syntax and Variations

In MySQL and PostgreSQL, this command removes an entire database and all associated files. The DB sends a message indicating how many files were deleted. A database that is open and in use under the PostgreSQL implementation may not be dropped.

Oracle Syntax and Variations

Oracle does not support *DROP DATABASE*. A database may be destroyed by issuing the command *CREATE DATABASE database_name* (without parameters), using the same name as the database to be destroyed.

DROP FUNCTION

This command removes a user-defined function from the current database.

Vendor	Command
SQL Server	Supported, with variations
MySQL	Supported, with variations
Oracle	Supported, with variations
PostgreSQL	Supported, with variations

SQL99 Syntax and Description

```
DROP FUNCTION function_name {RESTRICT | CASCADE}
```

This command permanently destroys a function. The *RESTRICT* clause ensures that the command fails if other database objects, such as a view, depend upon the function. On the other hand, the *CASCADE* option drops the function, any grants based on the function, and any dependent database objects!

Microsoft SQL Server Syntax and Variations

```
DROP FUNCTION [owner_name.]function_name [,...n]
```

As with other SQL Server *DROP* commands, more than one database object of the same type may be dropped by placing a comma between the names of each database object.

MySQL Syntax and Variations

This command does not actually delete the file containing the function. Instead, it deletes the function reference from the system table, which can be added back by using the *CREATE FUNCTION* statement.

Oracle Syntax and Variations

```
DROP FUNCTION [owner_name.]function_name
```

As with other Oracle *DROP* commands, the name of the function owner may be specified. Otherwise, Oracle assumes the current-user context, and only functions owned by the current user to be dropped. Alternately, those users with *DROP ANY FUNCTION* system privilege are allowed to drop any function anywhere.

PostgreSQL Syntax and Variations

```
DROP FUNCTION name ( [ type [,...n] ] )
```

PostgreSQL allows functions declared in any programming language to be dropped. *Type* is the input argument of the function to be dropped. Type must be specified, since only the function with the given name and parameter types is destroyed.

DROP INDEX

The *DROP INDEX* command destroys one or more indexes within the current database. When an index is dropped, all the space it previously consumed is immediately regained. *DROP INDEX* does not, however, destroy *PRIMARY KEY* or *UNIQUE* constraints, which must be done with the *ALTER TABLE . . . DROP* command. Refer to the *CREATE TABLE* command for more information about primary key and unique constraints.

Vendor	Command
SQL Server	Supported, with variations
MySQL	Supported, with variations
Oracle	Supported, with variations
PostgreSQL	Supported, with variations

SQL99 Syntax and Description

```
DROP INDEX table_name.index_name
```

PostgreSQL follows the SQL99 standard, with variations.

Microsoft SQL Server Syntax and Variations

```
DROP INDEX {table_name | view_name}.index_name [,...n]
```

Microsoft SQL Server allows indexes created on both tables and views to be dropped. If a clustered index on a table that contains nonclustered indexes is dropped, all nonclustered indexes are rebuilt and assigned new pointers.

MySQL Syntax and Variations

```
DROP INDEX table_name.index_name [,...n]
```

Older versions of MySQL include this command only for compatibility reasons; however, newer versions actually destroy the specified index. The statement is functionally equivalent to the MySQL statement *ALTER TABLE . . . DROP INDEX*.

MySQL allows multiple indexes to be dropped by separating each table and index name with a comma.

Oracle Syntax and Variations

```
DROP INDEX [owner_name.]index_name
```

Oracle allows indexes to be dropped directly by name without providing the table name. Oracle also allows the index to be dropped based on the owner name.

DROP PROCEDURE

This command destroys an existing stored procedure in the current user database.

Vendor	Command
SQL Server	Supported
MySQL	Not supported
Oracle	Supported
PostgreSQL	Not supported

SQL99 Syntax and Description

```
DROP PROCEDURE procedure_name {RESTRICT | CASCADE}
```

This command is essentially the same as *DROP FUNCTION*, except that it acts upon stored procedures rather than functions.

Microsoft SQL Server Syntax and Variations

```
DROP PROCEDURE [owner_name.]procedure_name [,...n]
```

Microsoft SQL Server allows the removal of multiple stored procedures by placing a comma between the name of each one. Individual versions of stored procedures cannot be dropped. The entire group of stored-procedure versions must be dropped.

Oracle Syntax and Variations

```
DROP PROCEDURE [owner_name.]procedure_name
```

Oracle also allows any procedure to be dropped based on the owner name. Users with the system privilege, *DROP ANY PROCEDURE*, may drop procedures owned by other users.

DROP ROLE

This command destroys a named set of user privileges in the current user database.

Vendor	Command
SQL Server	Not supported
MySQL	Not supported
Oracle	Supported, with variations
PostgreSQL	Not supported

SQL99 Syntax and Description

```
DROP ROLE role_name
```

The *DROP ROLE* command destroys the specified role. Only users who have *WITH ADMIN OPTION* may drop roles.

Oracle Syntax

```
DROP ROLE [owner_name.]role_name;
```

Executing the *DROP ROLE* command destroys the role in the current user database. It is no longer usable by any users or roles who previously had the role assigned to them.

DROP TABLE

This command removes a table definition and all data, indexes, triggers, constraints, and permission specifications for that table. Any view or stored procedure that references the dropped table encounters problems, unless they are explicitly altered or dropped as well.

Some vendors do not allow a table to be dropped unless certain other characteristics of the table are dropped first. For example, Microsoft SQL Server requires that the table be dropped from any replication scheme and *FOREIGN KEY* references be dropped before the table itself is dropped.

Vendor	Command
SQL Server	Supported, with variations
MySQL	Supported, with variations
Oracle	Supported, with variations
PostgreSQL	Supported, with variations

SQL99 Syntax and Description

```
DROP TABLE table_name RESTRICT | CASCADE
```

In the SQL99 syntax, *RESTRICT* prohibits the DBMS from executing the command if views or constraints currently reference the table to be dropped. The *CASCADE* clause causes any referencing objects to be dropped along with the table.

Microsoft SQL Server Syntax and Variations

```
DROP TABLE [database_name.][owner_name.]table_name [,...n]
GO
```

Microsoft SQL Server allows more than one table to be dropped at a time by including a comma between each table name. Tables also may be dropped in databases outside of the current context by specifying the database name (assuming the user has the right permissions). Any constraints or triggers on the table are dropped with the table. Explicitly declared rules and defaults lose their bindings when their underlying table is dropped. Views and stored procedures that reference a dropped table produce an error when they are executed and the table is found to be missing.

MySQL Syntax and Variations

```
DROP TABLE [IF EXISTS] table_name;
```

MySQL permanently and completely deletes the table and all associated files when this command is executed. The *IF EXISTS* syntax can be added to avert a returned error when attempting to drop a table that might not exist.

Oracle Syntax and Variations

```
DROP TABLE [owner_name.]table_name [CASCADE CONSTRAINTS];
```

Dropping a table in Oracle frees the space used by the table and commits any pending changes to the database. When a table is dropped, all the space it previously consumed is immediately regained. All indexes and grants associated with the table are lost. Objects, such as views, stored procedures, and synonyms built upon the table, are marked invalid and cease to function.

Take into account that in Oracle, executing any *ALTER*, *CREATE*, or *DROP* command causes any other pending transactions to commit.

The *CASCADE CONSTRAINTS* clause drops all integrity constraints referring to keys in the dropped table.

PostgreSQL Syntax and Variations

```
DROP TABLE table_name;
```

PostgreSQL supports only the basic *DROP TABLE* command.

DROP TRIGGER

The *DROP TRIGGER* command removes a trigger for a table within the current database.

Vendor	Command
SQL Server	Supported, with variations
MySQL	Not supported
Oracle	Supported, with variations
PostgreSQL	Supported, with variations

SQL99 Syntax and Description

```
DROP TRIGGER trigger_name
```

DROP TRIGGER removes a trigger from the current database. MySQL does not support this command.

Microsoft SQL Server Syntax and Variations

```
DROP TRIGGER [owner_name.]trigger_name [,...n]
GO
```

Microsoft SQL Server allows multiple triggers to be dropped by placing a comma between each trigger name.

Oracle Syntax and Variations

```
DROP TRIGGER [owner_name.]trigger_name;
```

Oracle drops the indicated trigger and commits pending changes to the database when this command is executed.

PostgreSQL Syntax and Variations

```
DROP TRIGGER trigger_name ON table_name;
```

PostgreSQL requires that the table where the trigger resides is named. It then drops all references to an existing trigger when this command is executed.

DROP VIEW

This command permanently removes a view from the current database.

Vendor	Command
SQL Server	Supported
MySQL	Not supported
Oracle	Supported
PostgreSQL	Supported

SQL99 Syntax and Description

```
DROP VIEW view_name RESTRICT | CASCADE
```

In the SQL99 syntax, *RESTRICT* tells the DBMS to prohibit the drop if views or assertions that currently reference the table are to be dropped. The *CASCADE* clause causes any referencing objects to be dropped along with the view.

This command is not currently supported by MySQL.

Microsoft SQL Server Syntax and Variations

```
DROP VIEW [owner_name.]view_name [,...n]
GO
```

Microsoft SQL Server allows multiple views to be dropped in a single command by placing a comma between each view name. The views must reside in the same database. Information about the view is removed from all system tables.

Oracle Syntax and Variations

```
DROP VIEW [owner_name.]view_name;
```

As with other Oracle *DROP* commands, the owner name may be specified along with the view name. Users with the system privilege, *DROP ANY VIEW,* may drop views owned by other users.

PostgreSQL Syntax and Variations

```
DROP VIEW view_name;
```

In PostgreSQL, the *DROP VIEW* command drops an existing view from the current database. Only the owner of the view may drop it. The PostgreSQL command *DROP TABLE* also can be used to drops views.

FETCH

The *FETCH* command is one of four commands used in cursor processes. *FETCH* retrieves a specific row from a server-side cursor.

Vendor	Command
SQL Server	Supported
MySQL	Not supported
Oracle	Supported, with variations
PostgreSQL	Supported, with variations

SQL99 Syntax and Description

The *FETCH* command retrieves a record from the *cursor_name* (created by the *DECLARE CURSOR* statement), based on either the *NEXT, PRIOR, FIRST, LAST, ABSOLUTE,* or *RELATIVE* keyword. The values retrieved by the *FETCH* statement optionally may be stored in variables. The *FETCH* operations are:

NEXT

Tells the cursor to return the record immediately following the current row, and increments the current row to the row returned. *FETCH NEXT* is the default behavior for *FETCH* and retrieves the first record if it is performed as the first fetch against a cursor. (PostgreSQL uses the keyword *FORWARD* or the string *FETCH RELATIVE NEXT.*)

PRIOR

Tells the cursor to return the record immediately preceding the current row, and decrements the current row to the row returned. *FETCH PRIOR* does not retrieve a record if it is performed as the first fetch against the cursor. (PostgreSQL uses the keyword *BACKWARD* or the string *FETCH RELATIVE PRIOR.*)

FIRST

Tells the cursor to return the first record in the cursor and makes it the current row. (Not supported by PostgreSQL.)

LAST

Tells the cursor to return the last record in the cursor and makes it the current row. (Not supported by PostgreSQL.)

ABSOLUTE { n }

Tells the cursor to return the nth record from the cursor record set counting from the top (if n is positive), or nth record counting from the bottom (if n is negative), making the returned record the new current record of the cursor. If n is 0, no rows are returned. (Not supported by PostgreSQL.)

RELATIVE { n }

Tells the cursor to return the record n rows after the current record (if n is positive) or n rows before the current record (if n is negative), making the returned record the new current row of the cursor. If n is 0, the current row is returned. (Supported as described by PostgreSQL except where n is 0.)

The *INTO* keyword allows data from each column in the *FETCH* command to be placed into a local variable. Each column in the *FETCH* command must have a corresponding variable of a matching datatype in the *INTO* clause. (*INTO* is not supported by PostgreSQL.)

PostgreSQL cursors may be used only within explicitly declared transactions using *BEGIN, COMMIT,* or *ROLLBACK.* PostgreSQL allows either a specific number of records to be retrieved or all of them, using either a number or the keyword *ALL.*

Oracle Syntax and Variations

```
FETCH cursor_name
{INTO variable_name1 [,...n] ]
| BULK COLLECT INTO [collection_name [,...n] }
```

Oracle cursors are forward-scrolling cursors. They must either insert the retrieved values into matching variables, or using the *BULK COLLECT* clause, bulk-bind the output before passing it back to the PL/SQL parser. *FETCH* often is paired with a PL/SQL *FOR* loop to process all the rows in the cursor.

PostgreSQL Syntax and Variations

```
FETCH [ FORWARD | BACKWARD | RELATIVE [ { [ # | ALL | NEXT | PRIOR ] } ]   ]
[ count ]
FROM cursor_name
```

PostgreSQL cursors may be used only within explicitly declared transactions using *BEGIN, COMMIT,* or *ROLLBACK.*

The cursor can be *FORWARD* scrolling, *BACKWARD* scrolling, or *RELATIVE* scrolling. The *RELATIVE* clause may include either a number of records to retrieve or all of them, using either a number or the keyword *ALL.*

Examples

This Oracle example retrieves several elements of the **employee_new_hires_cursor** (refer to the example under *DECLARE CURSOR*) into some local variables:

```
FETCH FROM employee_new_hires_cursor
INTO : emp_id, :fname, :lname, :job_id
```

This PostgreSQL retrieves five records from the **employee** table:

```
FETCH FORWARD 5 IN employee_new_hires_cursor;
```

GRANT

In SQL99, the *GRANT* statement authorizes users and roles to access and use database objects. Most database vendors also use the *GRANT* statement to authorize users and roles to create database objects and execute stored procedures, functions, and so on.

Vendor	Command
SQL Server	Supported, with variations
MySQL	Supported, with variations
Oracle	Supported, with variations
PostgreSQL	Supported, with variations

SQL99 Syntax and Description

```
GRANT { ALL [PRIVILEGES] }
| SELECT
| INSERT [ (column_name [,...n]) ]
| DELETE
| UPDATE [ (column_name [,...n]) ]
| REFERENCES [ (column_name [,...n]) ]
| USAGE }[,...n]
ON { [TABLE] table_name
| DOMAIN domain_name
| COLLATION collation_name
| CHARACTER SET character_set_name
| TRANSLATION translation_name }
TO {grantee_name | PUBLIC}
[WITH GRANT OPTION]
```

The *GRANT* statement allows users to be authorized for one or more access privileges—*SELECT, INSERT, UPDATE, DELETE, REFERENCES,* or *USAGE*—by an authority who can grant those privileges. Each privilege allows the user to execute the specified command, while *REFERENCES* and *USAGE* provide other privileges. Multiple access privileges are specified by placing a comma between each privilege, or access to all privileges is granted with *ALL*. The *PRIVILEGES* keyword is entirely optional.

The *USAGE* privilege applies to any database object besides a table, while the others apply only to tables. The *USAGE* privilege lets users create objects based upon the definition of another, such as using a translation to construct a collation. The *REFERENCES* privilege enables a table in a constraint or foreign key to be used.

The *INSERT, UPDATE,* and *REFERENCES* privileges may be assigned against specific columns within a table. If no columns are specified, then all columns are assumed.

The *ON* clause declares the specific table or database object where the user is receiving privileges.

The *TO* clause tells exactly which user or role receives a given authorization. Alternately, privileges may be granted to *PUBLIC*, meaning that all users (including those that will be created in the future) have the specified privilege. Authorization may be granted to other users using *WITH GRANT OPTION*. In turn, this clause tells the database that users who receive an access privilege can then grant that same access privilege to other users.

 Depending on the specific database implementation, views may or may not have independent access privileges from their base tables.

Microsoft SQL Server Syntax and Variations

```
GRANT { ALL [PRIVILEGES] }
| SELECT
| INSERT
| DELETE
| UPDATE
| REFERENCES
| EXECUTE
| CREATE {DATABASE | DEFAULT | FUNCTION | PROCEDURE | RULE | TABLE | VIEW}
| BACKUP {DATABASE | LOG} } [,...n]
ON { {table_name | view_name} [(column [,...n])]
| stored_procedure_name
| extended_stored_procedure_name
| user_defined_function_name
| [(column [,...n] ON {table_name | view_name} }
TO {grantee_name | PUBLIC} [,...n]
[WITH GRANT OPTION]
[AS {group | role}]
```

Microsoft SQL Server allows the *SELECT, INSERT, UPDATE, DELETE,* and *REFERENCES* access permissions to be granted on a table. A column list may be identified only for *SELECT* and *UPDATE* access permissions. By default, all columns are granted *SELECT* and *UPDATE* access privileges.

Only the *EXECUTE* permission may be granted on stored procedures, extended stored procedures, and user-defined functions; a user must have the *REFERENCES* privilege to create a *FOREIGN KEY* constraint. This permission also is required when creating a function or view that depends upon an object with *SCHEMABINDING.*

The *AS* clause grants privileges as if under a different group or role context. Since groups and roles cannot execute the *GRANT* command, this is an easy way to grant privileges to someone outside of the group or role. Privileges may not be granted in a database other than the current database context.

Example

First, *CREATE DATABASE* and *CREATE TABLE* are used to grant permissions to the users Emily and Sarah. Next, numerous permissions are granted on the **titles** table to the editors group. The editors are then able to grant these permission to others:

```
GRANT CREATE DATABASE, CREATE TABLE TO emily, sarah
GO

GRANT SELECT, INSERT, UPDATE, DELETE ON titles
TO editors
WITH GRANT OPTION
GO
```

MySQL Syntax and Variations

```
GRANT { ALL PRIVILEGES
  | SELECT
  | INSERT [ (column_name [,...n]) ]
  | DELETE
  | UPDATE [ (column_name [,...n]) ]
  | REFERENCES [ (column_name [,...n]) ]
  | USAGE
  | ALTER
  | CREATE
  | DROP
  | FILE
  | INDEX
  | PROCESS
  | RELOAD
  | SHUTDOWN }[,...n]
ON {table_name | * | *.* | database_name.*}
TO grantee_name [IDENTIFIED BY 'password'] [,...n]
[WITH GRANT OPTION]
```

MySQL provides additional access privileges, primarily relating to object manipulation within a database. As with the other privileges, granting any of the access privileges (such as *ALTER, CREATE, INDEX,* or *RELOAD*) allows the user to execute the command. *REFERENCES* is supported, but has no functionality. *USAGE* actually *disables* a grantee's privileges.

The following are access privileges that are usable with tables: *SELECT, INSERT, UPDATE, DELETE, CREATE, DROP, GRANT, INDEX,* and *ALTER. INSERT, UPDATE,* and *SELECT* may be applied at the column level.

MySQL's implementation of the *ON* clause allows some interesting options. Global privileges can be set, applying to all databases on the server, by specifying *ON *.**. Database-wide privileges may be set by specifying *ON database_name.** or *ON ** within the current database. The host, table, database, and column name must be 60 or fewer characters.

MySQL supports the possibility of granting rights to a specific user on a specific host if the *grantee_name* is in the form *USER@HOST*. Wildcards can be included in a *grantee_name* to provide the access privilege to a large number of users at one time. The *grantee_name* must be 16 or fewer characters. When specifying the user, password protection may be enforced by including the *IDENTIFIED BY* clause.

Example

This example grants permissions to two users with passwords:

```
GRANT SELECT ON employee TO Dylan IDENTIFIED BY 'porsche',
    kelly IDENTIFIED BY 'mercedes',
    emily IDENTIFIED BY 'saab';
```

Oracle Syntax and Variations

```
GRANT { ALL [PRIVILEGES] }
{| GRANT ANY PRIVILEGE }
{| SELECT | INSERT  | DELETE | UPDATE | REFERENCES }
{| CREATE [ANY] {CLUSTER | CONTEXT | DATABASE| DATABASE LINK | DIMENSION
    | DIRECTORY | INDEXTYPE | INDEX | LIBRARY | OPERATOR | OUTLINE
    | PROCEDURE | PROFILE | ROLE | ROLLBACK SEGMENT | SEQUENCE | SESSION
    | SNAPSHOT | SYNONYM | TABLE | TABLESPACE | TRIGGER | TYPE |
    | USER | [MATERIALIZED] VIEW}
| DROP [ANY] {...as CREATE...}
| ALTER [ANYh] {...as CREATE...}
| AUDIT SYSTEM
| EXECUTE [ANY] {INDEXTYPE | OPERATOR | PROCEDURE | TYPE
| BACKUP [ANY] {TABLE | DATABASE | LOG} } [,...n] }
ON { [schema_name.]
{table_name | view_name} [ (column [,...n]) ]
| stored_procedure_name
| extended_stored_procedure_name
| user_defined_function_name
| DIRECTORY directory_name
| JAVA {SOURCE | RESOURCE} [schema_name.]object_name }
TO {{grantee_name | role_name} [,...n] | PUBLIC}
[WITH ADMIN OPTION];
```

It is plainly clear that Oracle has an exhaustive *GRANT* command. In fact, the syntax shown does not cover every permutation of the statement. Note that there are two general classes of privileges available under GRANT: object privileges (such as the privilege to *SELECT* or *DELETE* from a specific table) and system privileges (such as *CREATE CLUSTER* or *DROP ANY TABLE*).

 Oracle does not allow the combination of object and system privileges in a single *GRANT* command. Multiple object privileges or system privileges may be granted to a single user or role in a *GRANT* command, but a *GRANT* command may not grant both object and system privileges.

Nearly every supported Oracle feature is permitted under a *GRANT* command. Privileges can be granted not only on database objects (such as tables and views) and system commands (such as *CREATE ANY TABLE*), but also on schema objects (such as *DIRECTORY, JAVA SOURCE,* and *RESOURCE*).

The *ANY* option grants the privilege to execute a given statement against objects of a specific type owned by any user within the schema. A more complete list of Oracle system privileges is shown in Table 3-2.

Table 3-2: Oracle System Privileges

Category of Privilege	System Privilege	Description
CLUSTER	CREATE CLUSTER	Grants privilege to create a cluster in the grantee's own schema.
	CREATE ANY CLUSTER	Grants privilege to create a cluster in any schema.
	ALTER ANY CLUSTER	Grants privilege to alter clusters in any schema.
	DROP ANY CLUSTER	Grants privilege to drop clusters in any schema.
CONTEXT	CREATE ANY CONTEXT	Grants privilege to create any context namespace.
	DROP ANY CONTEXT	Grants privilege to drop any context namespace.
DATABASE	ALTER DATABASE	Grants privilege to alter the database.
	ALTER SYSTEM	Issues *ALTER SYSTEM* statements.
	AUDIT SYSTEM	Issues *AUDIT sql_statements* statements.
DATABASE LINKS	CREATE DATABASE LINK	Grants privilege to create private database links in grantee's own schema.
	CREATE PUBLIC DATABASE LINK	Grants privilege to create public database links.
	DROP PUBLIC DATABASE LINK	Grants privilege to drop public database links.
DIMENSIONS	CREATE DIMENSION	Grants privilege to create dimensions in the grantee's own schema.
	CREATE ANY DIMENSION	Grants privilege to create dimensions in any schema.
	ALTER ANY DIMENSION	Grants privilege to alter dimensions in any schema.
	DROP ANY DIMENSION	Grants privilege to drop dimensions in any schema.
DIRECTORIES	CREATE ANY DIRECTORY	Grants privilege to create directory database objects.
	DROP ANY DIRECTORY	Grants privilege to drop directory database objects.
INDEXTYPES	CREATE INDEXTYPE	Grants privilege to create an indextype in the grantee's own schema.
	CREATE ANY INDEXTYPE	Grants privilege to create an indextype in any schema.
	ALTER ANY INDEXTYPE	Modifies indextypes in any schema.
	DROP ANY INDEXTYPE	Grants privilege to drop an indextype in any schema.

Table 3-2: Oracle System Privileges (continued)

Category of Privilege	System Privilege	Description
	EXECUTE ANY INDEXTYPE	References an indextype in any schema.
INDEXES	CREATE ANY INDEX	Grants privilege to create a domain index in any schema or an index on any table in any schema.
	ALTER ANY INDEX	Grants privilege to alter indexes in any schema.
	DROP ANY INDEX	Grants privilege to drop indexes in any schema.
	QUERY REWRITE	Enables rewrite using a materialized view, or creates a function-based index, when materialized view or index references tables and views are in the grantee's own schema.
	GLOBAL QUERY REWRITE	Enables rewrite using a materialized view, or creates a function-based index, when materialized view or index references tables views are in any schema.
LIBRARIES	CREATE LIBRARY	Grants privilege to create external procedure/function libraries in grantee's own schema.
	CREATE ANY LIBRARY	Grants privilege to create external procedure/function libraries in any schema.
	DROP LIBRARY	Grants privilege to drop external procedure/function libraries in the grantee's own schema.
	DROP ANY LIBRARY	Grants privilege to drop external procedure/function libraries in any schema.
MATERIALIZED VIEWS (identical to SNAPSHOTS)	CREATE MATERIAL-IZED VIEW	Grants privilege to create a materialized view in the grantee's own schema.
	CREATE ANY MATERI-ALIZED VIEW	Grants privilege to create materialized views in any schema.
	ALTER ANY MATERIAL-IZED VIEW	Grants privilege to alter materialized views in any schema.
	DROP ANY MATERIAL-IZED VIEW	Grants privilege to drop materialized views in any schema.
	GLOBAL QUERY REWRITE	Enables rewrite using a materialized view, or creates a function-based index, when materialized view or index references tables or views are in any schema.
	QUERY REWRITE	Enables rewrite using a materialized view, or creates a function-based index, when that materialized view or index references tables and views that are in the grantee's own schema.
OPERATORS	CREATE OPERATOR	Grants privilege to create an operator and its bindings in the grantee's own schema.
	CREATE ANY OPERATOR	Grants privilege to create an operator and its bindings in any schema.

Table 3-2: Oracle System Privileges (continued)

Category of Privilege	System Privilege	Description
	DROP ANY OPERATOR	Grants privilege to drop an operator in any schema.
	EXECUTE ANY OPERATOR	References an operator in any schema.
OUTLINES	CREATE ANY OUTLINE	Grants privilege to create outlines that can be used in any schema that uses outlines.
	ALTER ANY OUTLINE	Modifies outlines.
	DROP ANY OUTLINE	Grants privilege to drop outlines.
PROCEDURES	CREATE PROCEDURE	Grants privilege to create stored procedures, functions, and packages in grantee's own schema.
	CREATE ANY PROCEDURE	Grants privilege to create stored procedures, functions, and packages in any schema.
	ALTER ANY PROCEDURE	Grants privilege to alter stored procedures, functions, or packages in any schema.
	DROP ANY PROCEDURE	Grants privilege to drop stored procedures, functions, or packages in any schema.
	EXECUTE ANY PROCEDURE	Executes procedures or functions (standalone or packaged).
PROFILES	CREATE PROFILE	Grants privilege to create profiles.
	ALTER PROFILE	Grants privilege to alter profiles.
	DROP PROFILE	Grants privilege to drop profiles.
ROLES	CREATE ROLE	Grants privilege to create roles.
	ALTER ANY ROLE	Grants privilege to alter any role in the database.
	DROP ANY ROLE	Grants privilege to drop roles.
	GRANT ANY ROLE	Grants any role in the database.
ROLLBACK SEGMENTS	CREATE ROLLBACK SEGMENT	Grants privilege to create rollback segments.
	ALTER ROLLBACK SEGMENT	Grants privilege to alter rollback segments.
	DROP ROLLBACK SEGMENT	Grants privilege to drop rollback segments.
SEQUENCES	CREATE SEQUENCE	Grants privilege to create sequences in grantee's own schema.
	CREATE ANY SEQUENCE	Grants privilege to create sequences in any schema.
	ALTER ANY SEQUENCE	Grants privilege to alter any sequence in the database.
	DROP ANY SEQUENCE	Grants privilege to drop sequences in any schema.
	SELECT ANY SEQUENCE	References sequences in any schema.
SESSIONS	CREATE SESSION	Connects to the database.
	ALTER RESOURCE COST	Sets costs for session resources.

Table 3-2: Oracle System Privileges (continued)

Category of Privilege	System Privilege	Description
	ALTER SESSION	Issues *ALTER SESSION* statements.
	RESTRICTED SESSION	Logs on after the instance is started using the SQL*Plus *STARTUP RESTRICT* statement.
SNAPSHOTS (identical to MATERIALIZED VIEWS)	CREATE SNAPSHOT	Grants privilege to create snapshots in grantee's own schema.
	CREATE ANY SNAPSHOT	Grants privilege to create snapshots in any schema.
	ALTER ANY SNAPSHOT	Grants privilege to alter any snapshot in the database.
	DROP ANY SNAPSHOT	Grants privilege to drop snapshots in any schema.
	GLOBAL QUERY REWRITE	Enables rewrite using a snapshot, or creates a function-based index, when that snapshot or index references tables and views in any schema.
	QUERY REWRITE	Enables rewrite using a snapshot, or creates a function-based index, when that snapshot or index references tables and views are in the grantee's own schema.
SYNONYMS	CREATE SYNONYM	Grants privilege to create synonyms in grantee's own schema.
	CREATE ANY SYNONYM	Grants privilege to create private synonyms in any schema.
	CREATE PUBLIC SYNONYM	Grants privilege to create public synonyms.
	DROP ANY SYNONYM	Grants privilege to drop private synonyms in any schema.
	DROP PUBLIC SYNONYM	Grants privilege to drop public synonyms.
TABLES	CREATE ANY TABLE	Grants privilege to create tables in any schema. The owner of the schema containing the table must have a space quota on the tablespace to contain the table.
	ALTER ANY TABLE	Grants privilege to alter any table or view in the schema.
	BACKUP ANY TABLE	Uses the Export utility to incrementally export objects from the schema of other users.
	DELETE ANY TABLE	Deletes rows from tables, table partitions, or views in any schema.
	DROP ANY TABLE	Grants privilege to drop or truncate tables or table partitions in any schema.
	INSERT ANY TABLE	Inserts rows into tables and views in any schema.
	LOCK ANY TABLE	Locks tables and views in any schema.
	UPDATE ANY TABLE	Updates rows in tables and views in any schema.

Table 3-2: Oracle System Privileges (continued)

Category of Privilege	System Privilege	Description
	SELECT ANY TABLE	Queries tables, views, or snapshots in any schema.
TABLESPACES	CREATE TABLESPACE	Grants privilege to create tablespaces.
	ALTER TABLESPACE	Grants privilege to alter tablespaces.
	DROP TABLESPACE	Grants privilege to drop tablespaces.
	MANAGE TABLESPACE	Takes tablespaces offline and online, and begins and ends tablespace backups.
	UNLIMITED TABLESPACE	Uses an unlimited amount of any tablespace. This privilege overrides any specific quotas assigned. If you revoke this privilege from a user, the user's schema objects remain, but further tablespace allocation is denied unless authorized by specific tablespace quotas. You cannot grant this system privilege to roles.
TRIGGERS	CREATE TRIGGER	Grants privilege to create a database trigger in grantee's own schema.
	CREATE ANY TRIGGER	Grants privilege to create database triggers in any schema.
	ALTER ANY TRIGGER	Enables, disables, or compiles database triggers in any schema.
	DROP ANY TRIGGER	Grants privilege to drop database triggers in any schema.
	ADMINISTER DATA-BASE TRIGGER	Grants privilege to create a trigger on *DATABASE.* (You also must have the *CREATE TRIGGER* or *CREATE ANY TRIGGER* privilege.)
TYPES	CREATE TYPE	Grants privilege to create object types and object-type bodies in grantee's own schema.
	CREATE ANY TYPE	Grants privilege to create object types and object-type bodies in any schema.
	ALTER ANY TYPE	Grants privilege to alter object types in any schema.
	DROP ANY TYPE	Grants privilege to drop object types and object-type bodies in any schema.
	EXECUTE ANY TYPE	Uses and references object types and collection types in any schema, and invokes methods of an object type in any schema *if you make the grant to a specific user.* If you grant *EXECUTE ANY TYPE* to a role, users holding the enabled role will not be able to invoke methods of an object type in any schema.
USERS	CREATE USER	Grants privilege to create users. This privilege also allows the creator to: • Assign quotas on *any* tablespace • Set default and temporary tablespaces • Assign a profile as part of a *CREATE USER* statement

Statements

Table 3-2: Oracle System Privileges (continued)

Category of Privilege	System Privilege	Description
	ALTER USER	Grants the privilege to alter any user. This privilege authorizes the grantee to: • Change another user's password or authentication method • Assign quotas on *any* tablespace • Set default and temporary tablespaces, and • Assign a profile and default roles
	BECOME USER	Becomes another user (required by any user performing a full database import).
	DROP USER	Grants privilege to drop users.
VIEWS	CREATE VIEW	Grants privilege to create views in grantee's own schema.
	CREATE ANY VIEW	Grants privilege to create views in any schema.
	DROP ANY VIEW	Grants privilege to drop views in any schema.
MISCELLANEOUS	ANALYZE ANY	Analyzes any table, cluster, or index in any schema.
	AUDIT ANY	Audits any object in any schema using *AUDIT schema_objects* statements.
	COMMENT ANY TABLE	Comments on any table, view, or column in any schema.
	FORCE ANY TRANSACTION	Forces the commit or rollback of any in-doubt distributed transaction in the local database; induces the failure of a distributed transaction.
	FORCE TRANSACTION	Forces the commit or rollback of grantee's own in-doubt distributed transactions in the local database.
	GRANT ANY PRIVILEGE	Grants any system privilege.
	SYSDBA	Authorizes the user to: • Performs *STARTUP* and *SHUTDOWN* operations • *ALTER DATABASE*: open, mount, back up, or change character set • *CREATE DATABASE* • *ARCHIVELOG* and *RECOVERY* • Includes the *RESTRICTED SESSION* privilege
	SYSOPER	Authorizes the user to: • Performs *STARTUP* and *SHUTDOWN* operations • *ALTER DATABASE OPEN/MOUNT/ BACKUP—ARCHIVELOG* and *RECOVERY* • Includes the *RESTRICTED SESSION* privilege

PostgreSQL Syntax and Variations

```
GRANT { ALL
| SELECT
```

```
| INSERT
| DELETE
| UPDATE
| RULE } [,...n]
ON { object_name }
TO {grantee_name | PUBLIC | GROUP group_name}
```

PostgreSQL does not support the *WITH GRANT OPTION* clause or column-level permissions. PostgreSQL's implementation of *GRANT* behaves as if *WITH GRANT OPTION* is always enabled. Any user granted a permission is able to grant that privilege to other users. PostgreSQL allows permissions to be assigned to a *GROUP*, provided it is a valid, preexisting *group_name*.

PostgreSQL does not support *GRANT* on system commands, but several other database vendors do.

Example

PostgreSQL support for the *GRANT* statement is elementary:

```
GRANT INSERT ON publishers TO PUBLIC;

GRANT SELECT, UPDATE ON sales TO emily;
```

INSERT

The *INSERT* statement adds rows of data to a table or view. The *INSERT* statement allows records to be entered into a table through one of several methods:

- The first method is to insert records using the *DEFAULT* values created on the columns given table via the *CREATE TABLE* or *ALTER TABLE* statements. (This method is not supported by Oracle.)

- The second and most common method is to declare the actual values to be inserted into each column of the record.

- The third method, which quickly populates a table with many records, is to insert the result set of a *SELECT* statement into a table.

Vendor	Command
SQL Server	Supported, with variations
MySQL	Supported, with variations
Oracle	Supported, with variations
PostgreSQL	Supported

SQL99 Syntax and Description

```
INSERT [INTO] [[database_name.]owner.] {table_name | view_name} [(column_
    list)]
{[DEFAULT] VALUES | VALUES (value[,...]) | SELECT_statement }
```

To use the *INSERT* statement, first declare the table (or view) where the data is to be inserted. The *INTO* keyword is optional. Specify the columns in the table that receives data by enclosing them in parentheses separated by commas in the *column_list*. The *column_list* can be left off, but all columns that are defined for the table are then assumed.

The *DEFAULT VALUES* method is mutually exclusive from the *list_of_values* and *SELECT_statement* methods.

The *INSERT . . . VALUES* statement adds a single row of data to a table using literal values supplied in the statement. The *INSERT* statement, combined with a nested *SELECT* statement, allows a table to be quickly populated with multiple rows. When using *INSERT . . . SELECT* between two tables, it is important to ensure that the tables possess compatible datatypes and structures, although any incompatibilities between the two tables can be compensated for in the *SELECT* statement. *INSERT . . . SELECT* also is supported by PostgreSQL.

Microsoft SQL Server Syntax and Description

```
INSERT [INTO] [[database_name.]owner.]
    {table_name | view_name} [(column_list)]
{[DEFAULT] VALUES | list_of_values | SELECT_statement |
 EXEC[UTE] { procedure_name }
    [[@parameter_name=] {value [OUTPUT] | DEFAULT}[,...]}
```

Microsoft SQL Server's implementation of the *INSERT* command differs in that it allows the *DEFAULT* keyword. *DEFAULT* tells the *INSERT* statement simply to create a new record using all of the default values declared for a given table.

The major difference in this vendor's implementation is the *EXECUTE* keyword. The *EXECUTE* clause tells SQL Server to store the result set returned by a dynamic Transact-SQL statement, a system-stored procedure, a user-stored procedure, a Remote Procedure Call (RPC), or extended stored procedure into a local table.

For example, the following *INSERT* retrieves the *C:\temp* directory and stores it in the temporary table called **#ins_exec_container**:

```
INSERT INTO #ins_exec_container
EXEC master..xp_cmdshell "dir c:\temp"
GO
```

MySQL Syntax and Variations

```
INSERT [LOW_PRIORITY | DELAYED] [IGNORE]
[INTO] [[database_name.]owner.] {table_name | view_name} [(column_list)]
{VALUES (value[,...]) | SELECT_statement | SET column=value[,...n]}
```

The option *LOW_PRIORITY* tells MySQL to defer the execution of *INSERT* until no other clients are reading from the table. This could result in a long wait. The *DELAYED* option allows the client to continue at once, even if the *INSERT* has not yet completed. The *IGNORE* keyword tells MySQL not to attempt to insert records that would duplicate a value in a primary key or unique key; otherwise, without this clause, the *INSERT* fails. The *SET column=value* syntax allows the columns of the table to be declared and the values to insert in them.

Oracle Syntax and Description

```
INSERT [INTO] [[database_name.]owner.] {table_name | view_name}
    [PARTITION partition_name | SUBPARTITION subpartition_name]
```

```
[(column_list)]
{VALUES (value1[,...n]) RETURNING expression1 [,...n] INTO variable1 [,...n]
    |
SELECT_statement
[WITH {READ ONLY | CHECK OPTION [CONSTRAINT constraint_name]} }
```

Oracle's implementation of the *INSERT* statement allows data insertion not only into a given table, view, or snapshot, but also into a given partition or subpartition within a table using the *PARTITION* and *SUBPARTITION* keywords.

When the *INSERT* statement is correlated with a *SELECT* clause, some new rules come into play. If the *SELECT* clause is coupled with a *VALUES* clause, only one row is inserted into the table—the first row returned by the *SELECT* clause. If *SELECT* is used without *VALUES*, then all rows returned by the query are inserted into the table.

The *RETURNING* clause is not used to insert the values into a table, but into variables instead. There must be a one-for-one match between the expressions and variables of the *RETURNING* clause. The expressions returned by the clause do not necessarily have to be those mentioned in the *VALUES* clause. For example, the following INSERT statement places a record into the **sales** table, but places a completely distinct value into a bind variable:

```
INSERT authors (au_id, au_lname, au_fname, contract )
VALUES ('111-11-1111', 'Rabbit', 'Jessica', 1)
RETURNING hire_date INTO :temp_hr_dt;
```

Notice that the *RETURNING* clause returns the **hire_date** even though **hire_date** is not one of the values listed in the *VALUES* clause. (In this example, it is reasonable to assume a default value was established for the **hire_date** column.) LONG datatypes may not be manipulated by *RETURNING*. *RETURNING* cannot be used on views with *INSTEAD OF* triggers.

Additionally, the *SELECT* clause may utilize the *WITH* option. *WITH READ ONLY* specifies that the result set retrieved by the *SELECT* clause cannot be altered by the *INSERT* statement. The *WITH CHECK OPTION* clause tells Oracle to prohibit any data change that would produce rows that are not included in the result set of the *SELECT* clause.

PostgreSQL Syntax and Description

PostgreSQL supports the SQL99 standard for the *INSERT* statement. Refer to the earlier section for the SQL99 syntax and usage.

Examples

In this example, a new row in the **authors** table is inserted for the author Jessica Rabbit on a Microsoft SQL Server database:

```
INSERT INTO authors (au_id, au_lname, au_fname, phone, address, city,
    state, zip, contract )
VALUES ('111-11-1111', 'Rabbit', 'Jessica', DEFAULT, '1717 Main St',
NULL,
    'CA', '90675', 1)
```

Every column is assigned a specific, literal value except the **phone** column, which is assigned the default value (as assigned during the *CREATE TABLE* or *ALTER TABLE* statement), and the **city** column, which is null.

Here is a partial *INSERT* on a Microsoft SQL Server database of the same data:

```
INSERT authors (au_id, au_lname, au_fname, phone, contract )
VALUES ('111-11-1111', 'Rabbit', 'Jessica', DEFAULT, 1)
```

To load data from **sales** table into the **new_sales** table, *INSERT . . . SELECT* can be used:

```
INSERT sales
    (stor_id,
    ord_num,
    ord_date,
    qty,
    payterms,
    title_id)
SELECT
    CAST(store_nbr AS CHAR(4)),
    CAST(order_nbr AS VARCHAR(20)),
    order_date,
    quantity,
    SUBSTRING(payment_terms,1,12),
    CAST(title_nbr AS CHAR(1))
FROM new_sales
WHERE order_date >= '01/01/2000'          -- retrieve only the newer
records
```

LIKE Operator

The *LIKE* operator enables specified string patterns in *SELECT, INSERT, UPDATE,* and *DELETE* statements to be matched. The specified pattern can even include special wildcard characters.

Vendor	Command
SQL Server	Supported, with variations
MySQL	Supported, with variations
Oracle	Supported, with variations
PostgreSQL	Supported, with variations

SQL99 Syntax and Description

```
WHERE expression [NOT] LIKE string_pattern
```

The usefulness of *LIKE* is based on the wildcard operators that it supports. *LIKE* returns a *TRUE* Boolean value when the comparison finds one or more matching values. Note that the default case sensitivity of the DBMS is very important to the behavior of *LIKE*. For example, Microsoft SQL Server is not case-sensitive by default (though it can be configured that way). So the query:

```
SELECT *
FROM authors
WHERE lname LIKE 'LARS%'
```

would find authors whose last names are stored as 'larson' or 'lars,' even though the search was for uppercase 'LARS%'. Oracle is case-sensitive to "%" and "_" pattern characters, and has other regular-expression pattern matching available using operators other than *LIKE*. The wildcard operators are as follows in Table 3-3.

Table 3-3: Wildcard Operators and Sample Code

Wildcard Operator	Example	Description

%	Retrieves any record of city with "ville" in its name. (Supported by all vendors.)
	
	`SELECT * FROM authors`
	`WHERE city LIKE '%ville%'`
		Matches any string; resembles * in DOS operations.

[]	Retrieves any author with a last name like Carson, Carsen, Karson, or Karsen. (Not supported by Oracle. Supported by Microsoft SQL Server.)
	
	`SELECT * FROM authors`
	`WHERE au_lname LIKE '[CK]ars[eo]n'`
		Matches any value in the specified set, as in [abc], or any range, as in [k-n].

[^]	Retrieves any author with a last name that ends in arson or arsen, *but not* Larsen or Larson. (Supported by Microsoft SQL Server.)
	
	`SELECT * FROM authors`
	`WHERE au_lname LIKE '[A-Z^L]ars[eo]n'`
		Matches any characters not in the specified set or range.

_ (underscore)	Retrieves any author with a first name *not* like Sheryl or Cheryl. (Supported by all vendors.)
	
	`SELECT * FROM authors`
	`WHERE au_fname NOT LIKE '_heryl'`
		Matches any single character.

When performing string comparisons with *LIKE*, all characters in the pattern string are significant, including all leading or trailing blank spaces.

OPEN

The *OPEN* command opens a server cursor created with a *DECLARE CURSOR* statement. MySQL does not support ANSI-style server-side cursors.

Vendor	Command
SQL Server	Supported
MySQL	Not supported
Oracle	Supported
PostgreSQL	Supported

SQL99 Syntax and Description

```
OPEN { cursor_name }
```

The *cursor_name* is the name of the cursor created with the *DECLARE CURSOR* command.

In addition to standard server cursors, Microsoft SQL Server allows global cursors to be declared (in the format *OPEN GLOBAL cursor_name*) that can be referenced by multiple users. Plus, Oracle allows parameters to be passed directly into the cursor when it is opened (in the format *OPEN cursor_name parameter1 [,...n]*).

Example

The following example from Microsoft SQL Server opens a cursor and fetches all the rows. The same functionality in Oracle and PostgreSQL could be accomplished without the final *DEALLOCATAE* clause:

```
DECLARE employee_cursor CURSOR FOR
  SELECT lname, fname
  FROM pubs.dbo.authors
  WHERE lname LIKE 'K%'

OPEN employee_cursor

FETCH NEXT FROM employee_cursor

WHILE @@FETCH_STATUS = 0
BEGIN
  FETCH NEXT FROM Employee_Cursor
END

CLOSE employee_cursor

DEALLOCATE employee_cursor
-- DEALLOCATE is specific to Microsoft SQL Server and non-ANSI
-- standard.
```

Operators

An operator is a symbol specifying an action that is performed on one or more expressions. Operators are used most often in *DELETE, INSERT, SELECT,* or *UPDATE* statements but also are used frequently in the creation of database objects, such as stored procedures, functions, triggers, and views.

Vendor	Command
SQL Server	Supported, with variations
MySQL	Supported, with variations
Oracle	Supported, with variations
PostgreSQL	Supported, with variations

Operators typically fall into these logical categories:

Arithmetic operators
  Supported by all databases

Assignment operators
  Supported by all databases

Bitwise operators
  Supported by Microsoft SQL Server

Comparison operators
  Supported by all databases

Logical operators
  Supported by Oracle, Microsoft SQL Server, and PostgreSQL

Unary operators
  Supported by Oracle

Arithmetic Operators

Arithmetic operators perform mathematical operations on two expressions of any datatypes in the numeric datatype category. See Table 3-4 for a listing of the arithmatic operators.

Table 3-4: Arithmetic Operators

Arithmetic Operator	Meaning
+	Addition
-	Subtraction
*	Multiplication
/	Division
%	Modula (SQL Server only); returns the remainder of a division operation as an integer value.

 In Oracle and SQL Server, the + and - operators also can be used to perform arithmetic operations on date values.

Assignment Operators

Except in Oracle, the assignment operator (=) assigns the value to a variable or the alias of a column heading. In Microsoft SQL Server, the keyword *AS* may be assigned as an operator for table- or column-heading aliases.

Bitwise Operators

Microsoft SQL Server provides bitwise operators as a shortcut to perform bit manipulations between two-integer expressions (see Table 3-5). Valid datatypes that are accessible to bitwise operators include *binary, bit, int, smallint, tinyint,* and *varbinary.*

Table 3-5: Bitwise Operators

Bitwise Operators	Meaning
&	Bitwise AND (two operands)
		Bitwise OR (two operands)
^	Bitwise exclusive OR (two operands)

Comparison Operators

Comparison operators test whether two expressions are equal or unequal. The result of a comparison operation is a Boolean value: *TRUE, FALSE,* or *UNKNOWN.* Also, note that the ANSI standard behavior for a comparison operation where one or more of the expressions are *NULL* is *NULL.* For example, the expression *23 + NULL* returns *NULL,* as does the expression *Feb 23, 2002 + NULL.* See Table 3-6 for a list of the comparison operators.

Table 3-6: Comparison Operators

Comparison Operators	Meaning
=	Equal to
>	Greater than
<	Less than
>=	Greater than or equal to
<=	Less than or equal to
<>	Not equal to
!=	Not equal to (not ANSI standard)
!<	Not less than (not ANSI standard)
!>	Not greater than (not ANSI standard)

Boolean comparison operators are used most frequently in a *WHERE* clause to filter the rows that qualify for the search conditions. The following Microsoft SQL Server example uses the greater than or equal to comparison operation:

```
SELECT *
    FROM Products
    WHERE ProductID >= @MyProduct
```

Logical Operators

Logical operators are commonly used in a *WHERE* clause to test for the truth of some condition. Logical operators return a Boolean value of either *TRUE* or *FALSE.* Logical operators also are discussed under the *SELECT* topic. Not all RDBMS support all operators. See Table 3-7 for a list of logical operators.

Table 3-7: Logical Operators

Logical Operators	Meaning
ALL	TRUE if all of a set of comparisons are TRUE
AND	TRUE if both Boolean expressions are TRUE
ANY	TRUE if any one of a set of comparisons is TRUE
BETWEEN	TRUE if the operand is within a range
EXISTS	TRUE if a subquery contains any rows
IN	TRUE if the operand is equal to one of a list of expressions
LIKE	TRUE if the operand matches a pattern
NOT	Reverses the value of any other Boolean operator
OR	TRUE if either Boolean expression is TRUE
SOME	TRUE if some of a set of comparisons are TRUE

Unary Operators

Unary operators perform an operation on only one expression of any of the datatypes of the numeric datatype category. Unary operators may be used on integer datatypes, though positive and negative may be used on any numeric datatype (see Table 3-8).

Table 3-8: Unary Operators

Unary Operators	Meaning
+	Numeric value is positive
-	Numeric value is negative
~	A bitwise NOT, returns the complement of the number (not in Oracle)

Operator Precedence

Sometimes operator expressions become rather complex. When an expression has multiple operators, *operator precedence* determines the sequence in which the operations are performed. The order of execution can significantly affect the resulting value.

Operators have the following precedence levels. An operator on higher levels is evaluated before an operator on a lower level:

- ( ) (parenthetical expressions)
- +, -, ~ (unary operators)
- *, /, % (mathematical operators)
- +, - (arithmetic operators)
- =, >, <, >=, <=, <>, !=, !>, !< (comparison operators)
- ^ (Bitwise Exclusive OR), & (Bitwise AND), | (Bitwise OR)
- NOT
- AND

- *ALL, ANY, BETWEEN, IN, LIKE, OR, SOME*

- = (variable assignment)

Operators are evaluated from left to right when they are of equal precedence. However, parentheses are used to override the default precedence of the operators in an expression. Expressions within a parentheses are evaluated first, while operations outside the parentheses are evaluated next.

For example, the following expressions in an Oracle query return very different results:

```
SELECT 2 * 4 + 5 FROM dual
-- Evaluates to 8 + 5 which yields an expression result of 13.

SELECT 2 * (4 + 5) FROM dual
-- Evaluates to 2 * 9 which yields an expression result of 18.
```

In expressions with nested parentheses, the most deeply nested expression is evaluated first.

This example contains nested parentheses, with the expression *5–3* in the most deeply nested set of parentheses. This expression yields a value of *2*. Then, the addition operator (+) adds this result to *4*, which yields a value of *6*. Finally, the *6* is multiplied by *2* to yield an expression result of *12*:

```
SELECT 2 * (4 + (5 - 3) ) FROM dual
-- Evaluates to 2 * (4 + 2) which further evaluates to 2 * 6, and
-- yields an expression result of 12.
```

RETURN

The *RETURN* statement terminates processing within a SQL-invoked function (as opposed to a host-invoked function) and returns the function's result value.

Vendor	Command
SQL Server	Supported
MySQL	Supported
Oracle	Supported
PostgreSQL	Supported

SQL99 Syntax and Description

```
RETURNS return_parameter_value | NULL
```

The *RETURN* function is used within a function to end its processing. Using the *NULL* clause terminates the function without returning an actual value. Otherwise, the parameter value specified is returned either as a variable or as a literal expression.

Although the *RETURN* statement is categorized as a separate command within SQL, it is deeply intertwined with the *CREATE FUNCTION* statement. Check the *CREATE FUNCTION* statement for a more complete understanding of each vendor's implementation of *RETURN*.

Examples

This example creates a function. The function returns the value that is stored in the *proj_rev* variable to the calling session:

```
CREATE FUNCTION project_revenue (project IN varchar2)
RETURN NUMBER
AS
    proj_rev NUMBER(10,2);
BEGIN
    SELECT SUM(DECODE(action,'COMPLETED',amount,0) -
           SUM(DECODE(action,'STARTED',amount,0)   +
           SUM(DECODE(action,'PAYMENT',amount,0)
    INTO proj_rev
    FROM construction_actions
    WHERE project_name = project;
    RETURN (proj_rev);
END;
```

This example creates a function that returns a calculated value to the calling session:

```
CREATE FUNCTION metric_volume -- Input dimensions in centimeters.
    (@length decimal(4,1),
     @width decimal(4,1),
     @height decimal(4,1) )
RETURNS decimal(12,3) -- Cubic Centimeters.
AS
BEGIN
    RETURN ( @length * @width * @height )
END
GO
```

REVOKE

The *REVOKE* statement removes permissions for a user, group, or role on a specific database object or system command.

Vendor	Command
SQL Server	Supported, with variations
MySQL	Supported, with variations
Oracle	Supported, with variations
PostgreSQL	Supported, with variations

SQL99 Syntax and Description

```
REVOKE [GRANT OPTION FOR]
{ ALL PRIVILEGES }
| SELECT
| INSERT
| DELETE
| UPDATE
| REFERENCES
| USAGE }[,...n]
```

```
ON { [TABLE] table_name
 | DOMAIN domain_name
 | COLLATION collation_name
 | CHARACTER SET character_set_name
 | TRANSLATION translation_name }
FROM {grantee_name | PUBLIC} [,...n]
{CASCADE | RESTRICT}
```

A specific privilege on a specific database object can be revoked for a single user using *REVOKE privilege_name ON object_name FROM grantee_name*. A specific privilege on a specific object may be revoked from all users via the *PUBLIC* clause. As an alternative, the *WITH GRANT OPTION* can be used to revoke permissions using the *REVOKE GRANT OPTION FOR* clause.

The *RESTRICT* option revokes only the specified privilege. The *CASCADE* option revokes the specified privilege and any privileges that are dependent upon the granted privilege. A cascading revocation may exhibit different behavior on different database platforms, so be sure to read the vendor documentation for the correct implementation of this option.

Microsoft SQL Server Syntax and Variations

```
REVOKE [GRANT OPTION FOR]
{ALL [ PRIVILEGES ]
 | SELECT
 | INSERT
 | DELETE
 | UPDATE
 | REFERENCES
 | EXECUTE
 | CREATE {DATABASE | DEFAULT | FUNCTION | PROCEDURE | RULE | TABLE | VIEW}
 | BACKUP {DATABASE | LOG} } [,...n]
ON { {table_name | view_name} [(column [,...n])]
 | stored_procedure_name
 | extended_stored_procedure_name
 | user_defined_function_name
 | [(column [,...n] ON {table_name | view_name} }
{TO | FROM} {grantee_name} [,...n]
[CASCADE]
[AS {group_name | role_name} ]
```

This command is essentially SQL99 compatible, with the exception of the augmentations introduced in the *GRANT* command.

If commands were granted to a user *WITH GRANT OPTION* enabled, the privilege should be revoked using both *WITH GRANT OPTION* and *CASCADE*.

REVOKE can only be used in the current database. *REVOKE* also is used to disable any *DENY* settings.

 Microsoft SQL Server additionally supports the *DENY* statement. *DENY* is syntactically similar to *REVOKE*. However, it is conceptually different in that *REVOKE* neutralizes a user's privileges while *DENY* explicitly prohibits a user's privileges. Use the *DENY* statement to keep a user or role from accessing a privilege.

Example

```
REVOKE CREATE DATABASE, CREATE TABLE FROM emily, sarah
GO

REVOKE GRANT OPTION FOR
SELECT, INSERT, UPDATE, DELETE ON titles
TO editors
GO
```

MySQL Syntax and Variations

```
REVOKE { ALL PRIVILEGES
  | SELECT
  | INSERT [ (column_name [,...n]) ]
  | UPDATE [ (column_name [,...n]) ]
  | REFERENCES [ (column_name [,...n]) ]
  | DELETE
  | USAGE
  | ALTER
  | CREATE
  | DROP
  | FILE
  | INDEX
  | PROCESS
  | RELOAD
  | SHUTDOWN } [,...n]
ON {table_name | * | *.* | database_name.*}
FROM user_name [,...n]
```

The *REVOKE* statement rolls back any permissions previously granted to one or more users. Permissions may be revoked globally, as described in the *GRANT* statement. Furthermore, MySQL's implementation of *REVOKE* does not explicitly roll back permissions on objects that are dropped. Thus, it is necessary to explicitly *REVOKE* permissions on a table, even if the table is dropped. MySQL otherwise conforms to the SQL99 standard for the *REVOKE* command.

Example

The first command revokes all privileges on the **sales** table for Emily and Dylan, while the second command revokes all privileges for the user Kelly in the current database:

```
REVOKE ALL PRIVILEGES ON sales FROM emily, dylan;

REVOKE * employee FROM kelly;
```

Oracle Syntax and Variations

```
REVOKE {ALL [PRIVILEGES] | [object_privilege] }
ON { [schema_name.][object] | [DIRECTORY directory_object_name] }
FROM {grantee_name | role | PUBLIC} [,...n]
[CASCADE [CONSTRAINTS] ] [FORCE];

REVOKE {system_privilege | role}
FROM {grantee_name | role | PUBLIC} [,...n];
```

The *REVOKE* command not only can revoke object and system privileges, it also can revoke a role from a given user or other role. Refer to the *GRANT* statement for more information on the specific object and system privileges supported by the *REVOKE* command.

 The two forms of the *REVOKE* command, *REVOKE object_privilege* and *REVOKE system_privilege*, are mutually exclusive. Do not attempt to do both operations in a single statement.

When a user's privileges are revoked, the privileges of all users who received their privileges from the revoked user also are revoked.

Users who are granted *GRANT ANY ROLE* system privilege also can revoke any role. The *REVOKE* command can only revoke privileges specifically granted with the *GRANT* command, not privileges available through roles or the operating system.

The *ON DIRECTORY* clause identifies a directory object where permissions are revoked. The *CASCADE CONSTRAINTS* clause drops any referential integrity constraints users create if their *REFERENCES* privilege is revoked. The *FORCE* clause revokes *EXECUTE* permissions on dependent user-defined table and type objects. Consequently, those objects are marked as invalid and unusable until they are recompiled.

Examples

To revoke a user from a role:

```
REVOKE read-only FROM sarah;
```

To revoke a system-command privilege:

```
REVOKE CREATE ANY SEQUENCE, CREATE ANY DIRECTORY FROM read_only;
```

To revoke a *REFERENCES* privilege:

```
REVOKE REFERENCES
ON pubs_new_york.emp
FROM dylan
CASCADE CONSTRAINTS;
```

PostgreSQL Syntax and Variations

```
REVOKE { ALL
  | SELECT
  | INSERT
  | DELETE
  | UPDATE
  | RULE
  | REFERENCES
  | USAGE} [,...n]
ON {object_name}
TO {grantee_name | PUBLIC | GROUP group_name}
{CASCADE | RESTRICT}
```

Access to tables, views, and sequences can be revoked in PostgreSQL. It is otherwise identical to the SQL99 command. Refer to the SQL99 *REVOKE* syntax discussion, as well as the SQL99 *GRANT* discussion.

ROLLBACK

The *ROLLBACK* statement undoes a transaction to its beginning or a previously declared *SAVEPOINT*. It closes open cursors and releases locks in the same way as *COMMIT*.

Vendor	Command
SQL Server	Supported, with variations
MySQL	Not supported
Oracle	Supported
PostgreSQL	Supported

SQL99 Syntax and Description

```
ROLLBACK [WORK]
[TO SAVEPOINT savepoint_name]
```

In addition to finalizing a single or group of data-manipulation operations, the *ROLLBACK* statement undoes transactions up to the last issued *BEGIN* or *SAVEPOINT* statement.

SQL99 offers the new, optional keywords *AND CHAIN*. None of the four vendors yet support this command. This new syntax is:

```
ROLLBACK [WORK] [AND [NO] CHAIN]
```

The *AND CHAIN* option tells the DBMS to end the current transaction, but to share the common transaction environment (such as transaction isolation level) with the next transaction. The *AND NO CHAIN* option simply ends the single transaction. The *ROLLBACK* command is functionally equivalent to the command, *ROLLBACK WORK AND NO CHAIN*.

Microsoft SQL Server Syntax and Variations

```
ROLLBACK [TRAN[SACTION] [transaction_name | @tran_name_variable |
savepoint_name | @savepoint_variable] ]
```

ROLLBACK clears all data modifications made to the current open transaction or to a specific, existing savepoint. If *ROLLBACK* is issued alone, it rolls back the current open transaction. *ROLLBACK* normally frees locks, but it does not free locks when rolling back to a savepoint. *ROLLBACK* behaves similarly to *COMMIT* with regards to nested triggers, decrementing the *@@TRANCOUNT* system variable by one.

ROLLBACK TRANSACTION, when issued in a trigger, undoes all data modifications, including those performed by the trigger, up to the point of the *ROLLBACK* statement. Nested triggers are not executed if they follow a *ROLLBACK* within a trigger; however, any statements within the trigger that follow the rollback are not impacted by the rollback.

Oracle Syntax and Variations

```
ROLLBACK [WORK] [TO savepoint_name] [FORCE text];
```

ROLLBACK clears all data modifications made to the current open transaction or to a specific, existing savepoint. Oracle's implementation closely follows the SQL standard with the exception of the *FORCE* option. *ROLLBACK FORCE* rolls back to an in-doubt distributed transaction. These transactions are described in the Oracle system view, *DBA_2PC_PENDING*.

PostgreSQL Syntax and Variations

```
{ROLLBACK | ABORT} [WORK | TRANSACTION];
```

ROLLBACK clears all data modifications made to the current open transaction or to a specific, existing savepoint. PostgreSQL supports both the SQL99 *WORK* option and the *TRANSACTION* option. It does not support rolling back to a savepoint. The *ABORT* option may be used as a full synonym of *ROLLBACK*.

Example

Here is a Transact-SQL batch using *COMMIT* and *ROLLBACK* in Microsoft SQL Server. It inserts a record into the **sales** table. If it fails, the transaction is rolled back; if the statement succeeds, the transaction is committed:

```
BEGIN TRAN -- initializes a transaction

-- the transaction itself
INSERT INTO sales
VALUES('7896','JR3435','Oct 28 1997',25,'Net 60','BU7832')

-- some error-handling in the event of a failure
IF @@ERROR <> 0
BEGIN
    -- raises an error in the event log and skips to the end
    RAISERROR 50000 'Insert of sales record failed'
    ROLLBACK WORK
    GOTO end_of_batch
END

-- the transaction is committed if no errors are detected
COMMIT TRAN

-- the GOTO label that enables the batch to skip to the end without
-- committing
end_of_batch:
GO
```

SAVEPOINT

This command creates a savepoint in the current transaction. Transactions can be divided into logical breakpoints using the *SAVEPOINT* command. Multiple savepoints may be specified within a single transaction. The main benefit of the

SAVEPOINT command is that transactions may be partially rolled back to a unique savepoint marker using the *ROLLBACK* command.

Vendor	Command
SQL Server	Supported, with variations
MySQL	Not supported
Oracle	Supported
PostgreSQL	Not supported

SQL99 Syntax and Description

```
SAVEPOINT savepoint_name
```

Some vendors allow duplicate savepoint names within a transaction, but this is not recommended. Substitute savepoint identifiers (in the format :X) also may be included to enable DBMS to track the savepoint with an integer rather than a name. Not all vendors support this approach, and it is not recommended as the best practice.

Note that SQL99 supports the statement *RELEASE SAVEPOINT savepoint_name*, enabling an existing savepoint to be eliminated. However, this statement is not supported by any of the vendors covered in this book.

Microsoft SQL Server Syntax and Variations

```
SAVE TRAN[SACTION] {savepoint_name | @savepoint_variable}
```

Microsoft SQL Server does not support the *SAVEPOINT* command. Instead, it uses the *SAVE* command. Rather than declaring the literal name of the savepoint, you can reference a variable containing the name of the savepoint.

When the *ROLLBACK TRAN savepoint_name* command is executed, SQL Server rolls the transaction back to the appropriate savepoint, then continues processing at the next valid Transact-SQL command following the *ROLLBACK* statement. Finally, the transaction must be concluded with a *COMMIT* or a final *ROLLBACK* statement.

Oracle Syntax and Variations

```
SAVEPOINT savepoint_name
```

Oracle fully supports the SQL99 implementation.

Example

This example performs several data modifications, rolls back to a savepoint, and then rolls back the transaction completely:

```
INSERT INTO sales VALUES('7896','JR3435','Oct 28 1997',25,'Net
60','BU7832');

SAVEPOINT after_insert;

UPDATE sales SET terms = 'Net 90'
WHERE sales_id = '7896';
```

```
SAVEPOINT after_update;

DELETE sales;

ROLLBACK TO after_insert;
ROLLBACK;
```

SELECT

The *SELECT* statement retrieves rows, columns, and derived values from one or many tables of a database.

Vendor	Command
SQL Server	Supported, with variations (ANSI joins supported)
MySQL	Supported, with variations (ANSI joins partially supported)
Oracle	Supported, with variations (ANSI joins not supported)
PostgreSQL	Supported, with variations (ANSI joins partially supported)

SQL99 Syntax and Description

The full syntax of the *SELECT* statement is powerful and complex, but can be broken down into these main clauses:

```
SELECT [ALL | DISTINCT] select_list
FROM table_name1 [,..., table_nameN]
[JOIN join_condition]
[WHERE search_condition]
[GROUP BY group_by_expression]
[HAVING search_condition]
[ORDER BY order_expression [ASC | DESC] ]
```

Each clause of the *SELECT* statement has a specific use. Thus, it is possible to speak individually of the *FROM* clause, the *WHERE* clause, or the *GROUP BY* clause. However, not every query needs every clause. At a minimum, a query needs a *SELECT* item list and a *FROM* clause. (Microsoft SQL Server and PostgreSQL both support certain types of queries that do not need a *FROM* clause. Refer to the examples below for more information.)

The SELECT item list

The *SELECT item list* basically includes all items of information a user wants to retrieve from the server. Different types of elements can appear in the select item list. It's possible to retrieve literal strings, aggregate functions, and mathematical calculations. In Microsoft SQL Server, the *SELECT* item list may contain a subquery.

ALL is the default, meaning all records are returned, including defaults. *DISTINCT* is a keyword that tells the query to filter out all duplicate records. Thus, the result set includes only one instance of identical records.

There are several other rules for what can appear in the *SELECT* item list:

- Most commonly, all the columns desired should be listed out using a comma between each one.

- An asterisk (*) serves as shorthand to retrieve all the columns in every table shown in the *FROM* clause, as they are listed in the *CREATE TABLE* statement.

- Column aliases are added in to replace the default column headings used in the results. Use the *format column AS "alias"* or *column alias*. This is especially useful when a column heading is too cryptic or lengthy to be readily understood. For example:

```
-- alias format
SELECT au_lname AS "Last Name"
FROM    authors

-- alternative alias format
SELECT au_lname "Last Name"
FROM    authors
```

- Local and global variables, where supported, may appear as a select list item.

- Comments may be dispersed throughout any SQL or Transact-SQL statement by using either the double-dash (--) or the slash-asterisk (/* ... */). The double-dash causes the query to ignore any text that follows the double-dash until the end of line. The slash causes the query to ignore any text within the slash-asterisk and inverse slash-asterisk.

- The table name should be prefixed to the column name in a query using multiple tables. Technically, the table name needs to apply to any column in *both* tables; it is commonly considered good practice to do so anyway. For example, both the **jobs** and **employee** tables contain the **job_id** column:

```
SELECT    employee.emp_id,
          employee.fname,
          employee.lname,
          jobs.job_desc
FROM      employee,
          jobs
WHERE     employee.job_id = jobs.job_id
ORDER BY  employee.fname,
          employee.lname
```

- The schema or owner name should be prefixed to a column when extracted from a context outside of the current user. If the table is owned by another username, then the username must be included in the column reference. For example, assume that this example query is run in the **PUBS** database but also retrieves data from the **SALES** database:

```
SELECT    employee.emp_id,
          salesadmin.sales_summary.total_amt
```

```
              -- the schema, table, and then column name must be listed!
FROM      employee,
          salesadmin.sales_summary
WHERE     employee.emp_id = salesadmin.sales_summary.emp_id
ORDER BY employee.emp_id;
```

- Literal expressions may be used as a select list item.

- Mathematics calculations can be entered as a select list item. In Microsoft SQL Server, no *FROM* statement is needed. In Oracle, the calculation should be executed against the system table called *DUAL*. The table allows the SELECT command to retrieve values where no table exists. For example:

```
--QUERY (Microsoft)
SELECT 2 + 2

--QUERY (Oracle)
SELECT 2 + 2
FROM dual

--RESULTS
4
```

The FROM clause

The *FROM* clause generally serves two purposes: to list the tables and views where a query retrieved its data (with a comma between each tablename); and to assign an alias for long table names, making coding lengthy queries a lot easier. An alias can be assigned in the *FROM* clause by two means: by typing the table-name, a space, and the alias; or by typing the tablename, **AS**, and the alias. The example below illustrates each of these techniques. An example of a query that extracts data from multiple tables might have a *FROM* and *WHERE* clause that is coded in the following manner:

```
SELECT    e.emp_id,
          e.fname,
          e.lname,
          j.job_desc
FROM      employee e,
          jobs AS  j
WHERE     e.job_id = j.job_id
ORDER BY e.fname,
          e.lname
```

 Once an alias has been assigned in a query, be sure to use it exclusively for table references within that query. Do *not* mix references to the full table name and the alias in a query.

This query retrieves the *emp_id* (first and last name of each employee stored in the **employee** table) and joins the *job_id* of the employee, which is a code number, with the full job description found in the *JOBS* table.

The JOIN clause

In non-ANSI standard implementations, the join operation is performed in the *WHERE* clause (described in the section on *WHERE* clauses). In the ANSI SQL-92 standards, joins are performed in the *JOIN* clause of the query. These join methods are known as the *theta style* and the *ANSI style* of joins, respectively.

To retrieve joined data from two or more tables, the tables first must share a meaningful relationship. *The tables to be joined must possess a column or columns that share a common set of values that allow the tables to be meaningfully linked.* This column, or columns, is called the *join key* or *common key*. Most—but not all —of the time, the join key is the primary key of one table and a foreign key in another table. As long as the data in the columns match, the join can be performed.

In the *PUBS* database, both the **employee** table and the **jobs** table contain a **job_id** column. Thus, **job_id** is the common key between the **employee** and **jobs** tables.

To perform a query using an ANSI-style join, list the first table and the keyword *JOIN*, followed by the table to be joined. Once the second table is typed in, type the keyword *ON* and the join condition that would have been used in the old style query. The following shows the original query now in ANSI style:

```
SELECT    e.emp_id,
          e.fname,
          e.lname,
          j.job_desc
FROM      employee AS e
JOIN      jobs AS j ON e.job_id = j.job_id
ORDER BY  e.fname,
          e.lname
```

Join types

These problems are solved by the use of join types in the ANSI style and the equal-asterisk ('=*') combination for Microsoft SQL Server or plus-asterisk ('+*') for Oracle in theta joins. The following list shows how to control this behavior in joins:

Cross Join

Specifies the complete cross product of two tables. For each record in the first table, all the records in the second table are joined, creating a *huge* result set. This command has the same effect as leaving off the join condition and is also know as a "Cartesian Product." Cross joins are not advisable or recommended (currently supported by Microsoft SQL Server):

```
-- theta style
SELECT e.emp_id,
       e.fname,
       e.lname,
       j.job_desc
FROM    employee e,
    Jobs j
```

```
-- ANSI style
SELECT e.emp_id,
       e.fname,
       e.lname,
       j.job_desc
FROM   employee e
CROSS JOIN jobs j
```

Inner Join

Specifies that unmatched rows in either table of the join should be discarded.
If no join type is explicitly defined in the ANSI style, then this is the default
(currently supported by Microsoft SQL Server, PostgreSQL and MySQL):

```
-- theta style
SELECT e.emp_id,
       e.fname,
       e.lname,
       j.job_desc
FROM   employee e,
       jobs j
WHERE  e.job_id = j.job_id

-- ANSI style
SELECT e.emp_id,
       e.fname,
       e.lname,
       j.job_desc
FROM   employee e
JOIN   jobs j ON e.job_id = j.job_id
```

Left [Outer] Join

Specifies that all records be returned from the table on the left side of the join
statement. If a record is returned from the left table has no matching record in
the table on the right side of the join, it is still returned. Columns from the
right table return NULL values. (In this case, all employees are returned
whether they have a job description or not.) Many professionals recommend
configuring outer joins as left joins wherever possible for consistency
(currently supported by Microsoft SQL Server):

```
-- Oracle theta style
SELECT e.emp_id,
       e.fname,
       e.lname,
       j.job_desc
FROM   employee e,
       jobs     j
WHERE  j.job_id (+) = e.job_id

-- ANSI style
SELECT e.emp_id,
       e.fname,
       e.lname,
       j.job_desc
FROM   employee e
LEFT JOIN jobs j ON e.job_id = j.job_id
```

Right [Outer] Join

Specifies that all records be returned from the table on the right side of the join statement, even if the table on the left has no matching record. Columns from the left table return NULL values. (In the example, all records in the **jobs** table are returned with or without a matching record in the **employee** table (currently supported by Microsoft SQL Server):

```
-- Oracle theta style
SELECT e.emp_id,
       e.fname,
       e.lname,
       j.job_desc
FROM   employee e,
       jobs j
WHERE  j.job_id = (+) e.job_id

-- ANSI style
SELECT e.emp_id,
       e.fname,
       e.lname,
       j.job_desc
FROM   employee e
RIGHT JOIN jobs j ON e.job_id = j.job_id
```

Full Join

Specifies that all rows from either table be returned, regardless of matching records in the other table. The result set shows NULL values where no data exists in the join (currently supported by Microsoft SQL Server):

```
-- theta style does not support this
-- function

-- ANSI style
SELECT e.emp_id,
       e.fname,
       e.lname,
       j.job_desc
FROM   employee e
FULL JOIN jobs j ON e.job_id = j.job_id
```

Joins in the ANSI style are actually easier to understand than those in theta style, since the query itself clearly indicates which table is on the left in a *LEFT JOIN* and which table is on the right in a *RIGHT JOIN*.

The syntax to perform a similar query with multipart keys and multiple tables joined together is largely an extension of the same technique.

Multi-table Join Example

```
--theta style query with multiple tables
SELECT   a.au_lname,
         a.au_fname,
         t2.title
FROM     authors a,
         titleauthor t1,
         titles t2
```

```
WHERE      a.au_id      = t1.au_id
   AND     t1.title_id = t2.title_id
ORDER BY t2.title

-- ANSI style query with multiple tables
SELECT    a.au_lname,
          a.au_fname,
          t2.title
FROM      authors a
JOIN      titleauthor AS t1 ON a.au_id      = t1.au_id
JOIN      titles      AS t2 ON t1.title_id = t2.title_id
ORDER BY t2.title
```

Multi-key Join Example:

```
--theta style query with multipart key
SELECT    s1.store_id,
          s1.title_id,
          s2.qty
FROM      sales s1,
          sales_projections s2
WHERE     s1.store_id = s2.store_id
   AND  s1.title_id = s2.title_id
ORDER BY s1.store_id, s2.title_id

-- ANSI style query with multipart key
SELECT    s1.store_id,
          s1.title_id,
          s2.qty
FROM      sales s1
JOIN      sales_projections s2 ON s1.store_id = s2.store_id
    AND   s1.title_id = s2.title_id
ORDER BY s1.store_id, s2.title_id
```

The WHERE clause

The *WHERE* clause is an extremely potent component of the *SELECT* statement. The *WHERE* clause provides most of the search conditions that cull unwanted data from the query; the remaining search conditions are satisfied by the *HAVING* clause (explained later in this section).

A poorly written *WHERE* clause can ruin an otherwise beautiful *SELECT* statement, so the nuances of the *WHERE* clause *must be mastered* thoroughly. This is an example of a typical query and a multipart *WHERE* clause:

```
SELECT    a.au_lname,
          a.au_fname,
          t2.title,
          convert(char,t2.pubdate)
FROM      authors a
JOIN      titleauthor t1 ON a.au_id = t1.au_id
JOIN      titles t2 ON t1.title_id = t2.title_id
WHERE     (t2.type = 'business' OR t2.type = 'popular_comp')
   AND    t2.advance > $5500
ORDER BY t2.title
```

In examining the query, note that parentheses impact the order in which *WHERE* criteria are processed according to *Operators Precedence*.

The database's default *sort order* determines how the *WHERE* clause retrieves results sets for a query. For example, Microsoft SQL Server is (by default) *dictionary-order* and *case-insensitive*, making no differentiation between "Smith", "smith", and "SMITH". But Oracle uses *dictionary-order* and *case-sensitive*, finding the values "Smith", "smith", and "SMITH" to be unequal.

There are more specific capabilities of the *WHERE* clause than what is illustrated in the example. Table 3-9 helps provide a quick summary of the common capabilities of the *WHERE* clause.

Table 3-9: Search Conditions Using the WHERE Clause

Search Condition Shorthand	Syntax	Example	Usage & Description
Simple Boolean check	WHERE [NOT] expression comparison_operator expression	SELECT au_id FROM authors WHERE au_id = '172-32-1176' SELECT au_id FROM authors WHERE au_lname NOT LIKE 'John%'	The operators <, >, <>, >=, <=, and = can be used when comparing expressions. There are also a number of special comparison operators, such as *LIKE*, described later in this table. The keyword *NOT* checks for the inverse of any Boolean check based on the regular operators <, >, <>, <=, and =, in addition to special operators such as *LIKE*, *NULL*, *BETWEEN*, *IN*, *EXISTS*, *ANY*, and *ALL*.
Multiple search conditions	WHERE [NOT] expression comparison_operator expression {AND | OR} expression comparison_operator expression	SELECT au_id FROM authors WHERE au_id = '172-32-1176' AND au_lname = 'White'	*AND* merges multiple conditions and returns results when *both* conditions are true. *AND* takes priority over other operators. Parentheses in the *WHERE* clause further affect the priority of operators. *OR* merges multiple conditions and returns results when *either* condition is true. *OR* takes priority after *AND*.
NULL check	WHERE [NOT] column_name IS [NOT] NULL	SELECT * FROM titles WHERE price IS NULL	*IS NULL* and *IS NOT NULL* tell the query to check for null values (or all values except null values).

Table 3-9: Search Conditions Using the WHERE Clause (continued)

Search Condition Shorthand	Syntax	Example	Usage & Description

JOIN check	WHERE [NOT] column_value(s) [(+)]=[(+)] column_value(s)
	
	Or
	
	WHERE [NOT] column_value(s) [*]=[*] column_value(s)
		SELECT a.au_lname,
		    a.au_fname,
		    t2.title
		FROM authors a,
		    titleauthor t1,
		    titles t2
		WHERE a.au_id = t1.au_id
		    AND t1.title_id = t2.title_id
		ORDER BY t2.title
			JOIN checks can be performed by evaluating the common key between two or more tables. Outer joins are accomplished in PostgreSQL by adding the asterisk to the side where all records should be retrieved. Outer joins in Oracle are accomplished by adding the plus sign in parentheses (+) to the side where null values are allowed (basically, the opposite of the asterisk method). Refer to the previous section on JOINs for more information.

LIKE check	WHERE [NOT] column_name [NOT] LIKE 'match_string'	/* get any phone number starting with 415 */ SELECT * FROM authors WHERE phone LIKE '415%'	LIKE tells the query to use pattern matching on the string in quotation marks. The wildcard symbols are detailed under the LIKE entry.

EXISTence check	WHERE [NOT] EXISTS (subquery)	SELECT p1.pub_name
		FROM publishers p1
		WHERE EXISTS
		  (SELECT *
		  FROM titles t1
		  WHERE pub_id =p1.pub_id
		  AND type =
		  'psychology')
			EXISTS is always used in conjunction with a subquery; rather than returning data, the subquery is a Boolean test of whether the data exists. This example will return all publishers of psychology books.

BETWEEN range check	WHERE [NOT] expression [NOT] BETWEEN expression AND expression	SELECT * FROM titles WHERE ytd_sales BETWEEN 4000 AND 9000	BETWEEN performs an inclusive range check. It is the same as WHERE (expression >= x and expression <= y).

Table 3-9: Search Conditions Using the WHERE Clause (continued)

Search Condition Shorthand	Syntax	Example	Usage & Description
IN range check	WHERE [NOT] expression [NOT] IN (value_list | subquery)	SELECT * FROM stores WHERE state IN ('WA','IL','NY') SELECT * FROM stores WHERE stor_id IN (SELECT stor_id FROM sales WHERE ord_date LIKE 'Oct%')	*IN* returns a result set that matches any of a list of values or returns a result set of the outer query whose value matches those values returned by a subquery. The *value_list* or subquery should be enclosed in parentheses.

Table 3-9: Search Conditions Using the WHERE Clause (continued)

Search Condition Shorthand	Syntax	Example	Usage & Description

SOME | ALL range check	WHERE [NOT] expression comparison_operator {[ANY | SOME] | ALL} (subquery)	-- to duplicate the functionality of IN
		
		SELECT au_lname,
		       au_fname
		FROM authors
		WHERE city = ANY
		    (SELECT city
		     FROM publishers)
		
		-- to duplicate the functionality of NOT IN
		
		SELECT au_lname,
		       au_fname
		FROM authors
		WHERE city <> ALL
		    (SELECT city
		     FROM publishers)
		
		/* to find the titles that got an advance larger than the minimum advance amount paid New Moon Books*/
		SELECT title
		FROM titles
		WHERE advance > ANY
		    (SELECT advance
		    FROM publishers,
		     titles
		    WHERE titles.pub_id =
		      publishers.pub_id
		    AND pub_name = 'New
		     Moon Books')
			ALL and SOME are always used with a subquery and a comparison operator, such as <, >, <>, >=, or <=. A query of the ALL type evaluates either TRUE or FALSE when all values retrieved by the subquery match the value in the WHERE (or HAVING) clause, or when the subquery returns no rows of the outer statement.
			
			SOME has the same functionality as EXISTS. It works the same as ALL, except that it evaluates to TRUE when any value retrieved in the subquery satisfies the comparison predicate in the WHERE clause of the outer statement.

As mentioned in Table 3-9, wildcard characters can augment the search options, especially with the *LIKE* operator. Refer to the *LIKE* topic for more information on types of wildcard operations.

Aggregates and the GROUP BY clause

The *GROUP BY* clause (and the *HAVING* clause) are needed only in queries that utilize *aggregate functions* (discussed earlier in this chapter). Queries using aggregate functions provide many types of summary information. The most common aggregate functions include:

- *AVG* returns the average of all non-NULL values in the specified column(s).
- *COUNT* counts the occurrences of all non-NULL values in the specified column(s).
- *COUNT DISTINCT* counts the occurrences of all unique, non-null values in the specified column(s).
- *COUNT(*)* counts every record in the table.
- *MAX* returns the highest non-NULL value in the specified column(s).
- *MIN* returns the lowest non-NULL value in the specified column(s).
- *SUM* totals all non-NULL values in the specified column(s).

The aggregate functions are limited by the datatypes on which they may be used. Only *COUNT* and *COUNT DISTINCT* can be used on a column of any datatype. *MIN* and *MAX* operate on numeric columns (of any type), as well as date and character columns. The *SUM* and *AVG* functions may operate only on numeric column datatypes.

 If it is necessary to perform aggregate functions on columns containing null values, use the *ISNULL( )* function in SQL Server or the *NVL* function in Oracle to assign a value to the null columns.

Queries that return a sole value are known as a *scalar aggregate* values. Scalar aggregates do not need a *GROUP BY* clause. For example:

```
--Query
SELECT AVG(price)
FROM titles

--Results
14.77
```

Queries that return both regular column values and aggregate functions are commonly called *vector aggregates*. Vector aggregates use the *GROUP BY* clause and return one or many rows. There are a few rules to follow when using *GROUP BY*:

- Place *GROUP BY* in the proper clause order—after the *WHERE* clause and before the *ORDER BY* clause.
- Include all non-aggregate columns in the *GROUP BY* clause.
- Do not use a column alias in the *GROUP BY* clause, though table aliases are acceptable.

Suppose it is necessary to know how many employees occupy each type of job within the firm:

```
--Query
SELECT   j.job_desc AS "Job Description",
         COUNT(e.job_id) AS "Nbr in Job"
FROM     employee e
JOIN     jobs j ON e.job_id = j.job_id
GROUP BY j.job_desc
```

```
--Results
Job Description                                    Nbr in Job
-------------------------------------------------- -----------
Acquisitions Manager                               4
Business Operations Manager                        1
Chief Executive Officer                            1
Chief Financial Officer                            1
Designer                                           3
Editor                                             3
Managing Editor                                    4
Marketing Manager                                  4
Operations Manager                                 4
Productions Manager                                4
Public Relations Manager                           4
Publisher                                          7
Sales Representative                               3
```

The HAVING clause

The *HAVING* clause adds search conditions on the result of the *GROUP BY* clause. *HAVING* does not affect the rows used to calculate the aggregates; it affects only the rows returned by the query.

HAVING works very much like the *WHERE* clause. The *HAVING* clause uses all the same search conditions as the WHERE clause detailed in Table 3-9.

For example, to find out which jobs have more than three people:

```
--Query
SELECT   j.job_desc "Job Description",
         COUNT(e.job_id) "Nbr in Job"
FROM     employee e
JOIN     jobs j ON e.job_id = j.job_id
GROUP BY j.job_desc
HAVING   COUNT(e.job_id) > 3
```

```
--Results
Job Description                                    Nbr in Job
-------------------------------------------------- -----------
Acquisitions Manager                               4
Managing Editor                                    4
Marketing Manager                                  4
Operations Manager                                 4
Productions Manager                                4
Public Relations Manager                           4
Publisher                                          7
```

HAVING should not be used to eliminate rows that can be eliminated using the *WHERE* clause. *HAVING* conditions should always involve aggregate values.

The ORDER BY clause

A result set can be sorted through the *ORDER BY* clause, in accordance with the database's sort order. The result set may be sorted in either ascending (*ASC*) or descending (*DESC*) order. (Ascending order is the default.) For example:

```
--QUERY
SELECT   e.emp_id "Emp ID",
         rtrim(e.fname) || " " || rtrim(e.lname) "Name",
         j.job_desc "Job Desc"
FROM     employee e,
         jobs j
WHERE    e.job_id = j.job_id
  AND    j.job_desc = 'Acquisitions Manager'
ORDER BY e.fname DESC,
         e.lname ASC


--RESULTS
Emp ID     Name                             Job Desc
---------  -------------------------------  --------------------
M-R38834F  Martine Rancé                    Acquisitions Manager
MAS70474F  Margaret Smith                   Acquisitions Manager
KJJ92907F  Karla Jablonski                  Acquisitions Manager
GHT50241M  Gary Thomas                      Acquisitions Manager
```

After the result set is pared down to meet the search conditions, the result set is sorted by the authors' last names in descending order. Where the authors' last names are equal, the authors' first names are sorted in ascending order.

All implementations discussed here also allow the use of ordinal positions in the *ORDER_BY* clause. The order of the result set may be ordered by specifying the integer of the column_position rather than the column name or alias. For example, to order by the *au_id*, *au_fname*, and finally by the *au_lname*:

```
SELECT au_fname, au_lname, au_id
FROM authors
ORDER BY 3, 1, 2
```

In general, use an ORDER BY clause to control the order of the query result set. If no *ORDER BY* clause is specified, most implementations return the data according to the physical order of data within the table or according to the order of an index utilized by the query. This can cause problems if the index or physical sort order of the data is ever changed. Instead, explicitly state the order.

Microsoft SQL Server Syntax and Variations

Microsoft offers several variations on the *SELECT* statement, including optimizer hints, the *INTO* clause, the *TOP* clause, *GROUP BY* variations, *COMPUTE*, and *WITH OPTIONS*.

SELECT . . . INTO

```
SELECT  select_list
INTO    new_table_name
FROM    table_source
WHERE   clause
```

The *SELECT . . . INTO* feature is a somewhat controversial command option found only in SQL Server. The *SELECT . . . INTO* command quickly copies the rows and columns queried from other table(s) into a new table using a non-logged operation.

This example creates a table called **non_mgr_employees** using *SELECT . . . INTO*. The table contains the *emp_id*, first name, and last name of each non-manager from the **employee** table, joined with their job description taken from the **jobs** table:

```
--QUERY
SELECT  e.emp_id "emp_id",
        convert(char(25),rtrim(e.fname) + " " + rtrim(e.lname)) "name",
        substring(j.job_desc,1,30) "job_desc"
INTO    non_mgr_employee
FROM    employee e
   JOIN jobs AS j ON e.job_id = j.job_id
WHERE   j.job_desc NOT LIKE '%MANAG%'
ORDER BY 2,3,1
```

The newly created and loaded table **non_mgr_employee** now can be queried. A simple query returns that data:

```
--QUERY
SELECT  emp_id,
        name,
        job_desc
FROM    non_mgr_emp
ORDER BY 3,2,1
```

```
--RESULTS
emp_id    name                     job_desc
--------- ------------------------ -----------------------------
PTC11962M Philip Cramer            Chief Executive Officer
F-C16315M Francisco Chang          Chief Financial Officer
<...edited for brevity...>
PMA42628M Paolo Accorti            Sales Representative
TPO55093M Timothy O'Rourke         Sales Representative
```

SELECT . . . INTO should be used only in development or non-production code.

The TOP clause

The *TOP* clause follows this syntax:

```
SELECT [TOP n [PERCENT] [WITH TIES]] select list
FROM table_name
```

This command specifies that only the first *n* rows are to be retrieved in the query result set. If a percentage also is specified, only the first *n* percent of the rows are retrieved. The *WITH TIES* keyword can be used only on queries with an *ORDER BY* clause. This variation specifies that additional rows are returned from the base result set using the same value in the *ORDER BY* clause, appearing as the last of the *TOP* rows.

GROUP BY Variations

GROUP BY in Microsoft SQL Server supports the *ALL*, *WITH CUBE*, and *WITH ROLLUP* variations:

```
[ GROUP BY [ALL] group_by_expression [, ...n]
[ WITH { CUBE | ROLLUP } ] ]
```

The *ALL* variation forces the result set to include all groups, even those that do not have any rows matching the filters in the *WHERE* clause. *ALL* cannot be used with *CUBE* or *ROLLUP*. *CUBE* specifies that additional summary rows for every combination of group and subgroup should be retrieved with the result set. *ROLLUP* functions similarly to *CUBE* except that it returns groups in a summarized hierarchical order—from lowest level to highest level in the group.

The COMPUTE Clause

The *COMPUTE* clause generates totals that appear as additional summary columns at the end of the result set. The *COMPUTE BY* clause generates control breaks and subtotals in the result set. Both *COMPUTE BY* and *COMPUTE* can be specified in the same query:

```
[ COMPUTE { { AVG | COUNT | MAX | MIN | STDEV | STDEVP |VAR | VARP | SUM }
(expression) } [, ...n]
[ BY expression [, ...n] ] ]
```

The arguments (*AVG, COUNT, MAX, MIN, STDEV, STDEVP, VAR, VARP, SUM*) specify the aggregation to be performed by the *COMPUTE* clause. The *expression* value is typically a column name. The *BY expression* value can be one or more columns shown in the queries' *ORDER BY* clause. *COMPUTE* appears in a query after the *ORDER BY* clause.

The OPTION Clause

The *OPTION* clause is the last clause that may appear in a Microsoft SQL Server query. It specifies that a *query hint* should be used throughout the entire query. Query hints are a non-ANSI-standard method of overriding the default processing of a query. Query hints and the complete syntax and usage of *OPTION* are beyond the scope of this book, but may be found in SQL Server documentation.

MySQL Syntax and Variations

```
SELECT [STRAIGHT_JOIN][SQL_SMALL_RESULT][SQL_BIG_RESULT][HIGH_PRIORITY]
[INTO {OUTFILE | DUMPFILE} 'file_name' options]
FROM...
JOIN...
[LIMIT [[offset_record,] number_of_rows]];
```

MySQL extensions include changes to the default *SELECT* keyword, partial *JOIN* support, the *LIMIT* clause, and the *PROCEDURE* clause.

The first extension to the default *SELECT* clause is *STRAIGHT_JOIN. STRAIGHT_JOIN* forces the optimizer to join tables in the exact order they appear in the FROM clause. *SQL_SMALL_RESULT* and *SQL_BIG_RESULT* can be used when the query has a *GROUP BY* clause or a *DISTINCT* clause to tell the optimizer to expect a small or large result set, respectively. Since MySQL builds a temporary table when a query has a *DISTINCT* or *GROUP BY* clause, these optional clauses tell MySQL to build a fast temporary table in memory (for *SQL_SMALL_RESULT*) and a slower, disk-based temporary table (for *SQL_BIG_RESULT*) to process the work-table. *HIGH_PRIORITY* gives the query a higher priority than statements that modify data within the table. It should only be used for special, high-speed queries. The *LIMIT* clause constrains the number of rows returned by the query, starting at the *offset_record* and *returning number_of_rows*. If only one integer is supplied, this number is assumed to be the number of records wanted, and a default offset of 0 is assumed.

The *SELECT . . . INTO OUTFILE 'file_name'* clause writes the result set of the query to a file on the host filesystem. The file_name must not already exist. The syntax *SELECT . . . INTO DUMPFILE* writes a single continuous line of data without column terminations, line terminations, or escape characters. This option is used mostly for blob files.

MySQL supports only these types of *JOIN* syntax:

```
[CROSS JOIN]
INNER JOIN
STRAIGHT_JOIN
LEFT [OUTER] JOIN
NATURAL LEFT [OUTER] JOIN
```

Oracle Syntax and Variations

```
SELECT {[ALL] [DISTINCT] | [UNIQUE]}...
{columns_and_expressions_list} [,...n] AS alias
[INTO {variable[,...n] | record}]
FROM {[table_name [@database_link]| view_name | snapshot_name]
   | subquery [WITH {READ ONLY | CHECK OPTION [CONSTRAINT constraint_name]}]
   | TABLE {(nested_tbl_column)}
     [PARTITION {partition_name}]
     [SUBPARTITION {subpartition_name}
        [SAMPLE [BLOCK] [sample_percentage]}
WHERE
[[START WITH clause] CONNECT BY clause]
```

```
GROUP BY...
[ORDER BY... [NULLS FIRST | NULLS LAST] |
 FOR UPDATE [OF [schema.]table[,...n]] [NOWAIT] ]
```

Oracle allows several extensions to *SELECT* support-added functionality within the server. For example, since nested tables and partitioned tables both can be created (see *CREATE TABLE*), the *SELECT* statement allows queries from those specifically named structures. (The *PARTITION* clause is not needed to query from the default partition.)

The *SAMPLE* clause tells Oracle to select records from a random sampling of rows within the result set, rather than from the entire table. The *SAMPLE BLOCK* clause tells Oracle to use block sampling rather than row sampling. The sampling percentage, telling Oracle the total block or row count to be included in the sample, may be anywhere between .000001 to 99. Sampling may be used only on single-table queries.

 The *SELECT . . . INTO* syntax is usable only in PL/SQL code and allows the *SELECT* statement to assign values to variables.

When querying a nested table, the *FROM TABLE nested_table_column* clause must be used. The *@database_link* clause allows the query to access tables stored in other databases and on other servers when those databases and servers have been declared as a *db_link*. (Refer to the vendor documentation for more information on db_link.)

The *NULL FIRST* and *NULL LAST* options to the *ORDER BY* clause specify that the result set order rows containing nulls end should appear either first or last, respectively.

Oracle allows the specification of result sets in a hierarchical order. These so-called *hierarchical queries* have a number of rules and unique behaviors. Refer to the vendor documentation for complete rules on using this type of query. The *START WITH* clause is essential for hierarchical queries and specifies the root rows of a hierarchy. The *CONNECT BY* clause describes the relationship between parent and child rows in the hierarchy.

The *FOR UPDATE OF* clause exclusively locks the row returned by the query. It should be followed immediately by an *UPDATE . . . WHERE* command, *COMMIT,* or *ROLLBACK.* The *NOWAIT* option tells Oracle not to wait if that record is already locked. Instead, the query terminates and immediately returns to the user.

PostgreSQL Syntax and Variations

```
SELECT...
[INTO [TEMPORARY | TEMP] [TABLE] new_table_name]
FROM...
WHERE...
[FOR UPDATE [OF class_name[,...n]]
[LIMIT {count | ALL} [offset [,number_of_records]] ]
```

PostgreSQL allows the creation of a new table using the *SELECT . . . INTO* syntax, which is essentially the same as that supported by Microsoft SQL Server. It helps the *FOR UPDATE* clause to exclusively lock records selected by the query. It also supports the *LIMIT* clause, similar to that of MySQL, to constrain the number of rows returned by the query.

SET CONNECTION

The *SET CONNECTION* statement allows users to switch between several open connections on one or more database servers.

Vendor	Command
SQL Server	Supported, with limitations
MySQL	Not supported
Oracle	Not supported
PostgreSQL	Not supported

SQL99 Syntax and Description

```
SET CONNECTION {DEFAULT | connection_name}
```

This command does not end a connection. Instead, it switches from the current connection to the connection named in the command, or to the current connection using the *DEFAULT* clause. When switching between connections, the old connection becomes dormant (without committing any changes), while the new connection becomes active.

The *CONNECT* command must be used to create a new connection; the *DISCONNECT* command is used to terminate one.

Microsoft SQL Server Syntax and Variations

Microsoft SQL Server supports *SET CONNECTION* only in Embedded-SQL (ESQL), but not within its ad hoc querying tool, SQL Query Analyzer. It supports the full SQL99 syntax.

Example

Here is a full ESQL program in SQL Server that shows *CONNECT, DISCONNECT,* and *SET CONNECTION*:

```
EXEC SQL CONNECT TO chicago.pubs AS chicago1 USER sa;
EXEC SQL CONNECT TO new_york.pubs AS new_york1 USER read-only;
// opens connections to the servers named "chicago" //
//   and "new_york"//

EXEC SQL SET CONNECTION chicago1;
EXEC SQL SELECT name FROM employee INTO :name;
// sets the chicago1 connection as active and performs work //
//   within that session //

EXEC SQL SET CONNECTION new_york1;
EXEC SQL SELECT name FROM employee INTO :name;
```

```
// sets the new_york1 connection as active and performs work //
//   within that session //

EXEC SQL DISCONNECT ALL;
// Terminates all sessions.  You could alternately use two //
//   DISCONNECT commands, one for each named connection. //
```

SET ROLE

The *SET ROLE* command enables and disables specific security roles for the current session. Sessions are created using the *CONNECT* statement, while roles are created using the *CREATE ROLE* statement.

Vendor	Command
SQL Server	Not supported
MySQL	Not supported
Oracle	Supported, with variations
PostgreSQL	Not supported

SQL99 Syntax and Description

```
SET ROLE {NONE | role_name}
```

The session is opened using the *CONNECT* statement. Once a user session is initiated, issuing the *SET ROLE* statement grants that session a set of privileges associated with a role. The *SET ROLE* command can be issued only outside of a transaction.

SET ROLE NONE assigns the current session to a *NULL* role.

When a role is assigned to the currently active user session, a character string, database variable, or even a system function such as *CURRENT_ROLE* or *SYSTEM_ROLE* may be used. In any case, the value specified must be a valid role name.

Oracle Syntax and Variations

```
SET ROLE {role_name [IDENTIFIED BY password] [,...n]
| [ALL [EXCEPT role_name [,...]]
| NONE;
```

When a user initiates a connection, Oracle explicitly assigns the privileges that are roles to the user. The role(s) under which the session is operating can be changed with the *SET ROLE* command. Oracle uses the *MAX_ENABLED_ROLES* initialization parameter to control the maximum number of roles that can be opened concurrently.

The *role_name* specified must be a valid role name already created within Oracle. Any roles not specified are unavailable for the current session. If the *role_name* has a password, it must be listed using the *IDENTIFIED BY password* clause. Multiple roles are identified by placing a comma between each.

The *SET ROLE ALL* statement enables all roles that are granted to the current session, including roles that are granted through other roles; other roles may be exempted using the *EXCEPT* clause. *SET ROLE ALL* cannot be used when a password must be specified. Roles with passwords may be accessed only through the statement *SET ROLE role_name IDENTIFIED BY password*.

The *SET ROLE NONE* statement disables all roles, including the default role.

Examples

To enable the specific roles **read_only** and **updater**, identified by the passwords **editor** and **red_marker**, respectively, for the current session:

```
SET ROLE read_only IDENTIFIED BY editor, updater IDENTIFIED BY red_marker;
```

To enable all roles, except the **read_write** role:

```
SET ROLE ALL EXCEPT read_write;
```

SET TIME ZONE

The *SET TIME ZONE* statement changes the current session's time zone if it needs to be different from the default time zone.

Vendor	Command
SQL Server	Not supported
MySQL	Not supported
Oracle	Not supported
PostgreSQL	Supported, with variations

SQL99 Syntax and Description

```
SET TIME ZONE {LOCAL | INTERVAL {+ | -}'00:00' HOUR TO MINUTE}
```

Like most *SET* commands, *SET TIME ZONE* can be executed only outside of an explicit transaction. The *LOCAL* clause resets the current-session time values to those of the default time zone for the server. Otherwise, an interval value can be set to increase (with +) or decrease (with -) over the default time.

PostgreSQL Syntax and Variations

```
SET TIME ZONE {'timezone' | LOCAL | DEFAULT
| INTERVAL {+ | -}'00:00' HOUR TO MINUTE};
```

PostgreSQL allows a session's time value to be set to the server default by using either the *LOCAL* or *DEFAULT* clause.

The value specified for time zone is dependent on the operating system. For example, 'PST8PDT' is a valid time zone for California on Linux systems, while 'Europe/Rome' is a valid time zone for Italy on Linux and other systems. If an invalid time zone is specified, the command sets the time zone to Greenwich Mean Time (GMT).

The time zone also may be set as an interval of the default server time zone.

Examples

In the following example, the time zone is advanced three hours over the current default time zone:

```
SET TIME ZONE INTERVAL +'03:00' HOUR TO MINUTE;
```

Next, the current time for the current session is set back by four-and-a-half hours:

```
SET TIME ZONE INTERVAL -'04:30' HOUR TO MINUTE;
```

Finally, the time for the current session is returned to the default:

```
SET TIME ZONE LOCAL;
```

SET TRANSACTION

The *SET TRANSACTION* statement controls many characteristics of a data modification, such as read/write or its isolation level.

Vendor	Command
SQL Server	Supported, with variations
MySQL	Not supported
Oracle	Supported, with limitations
PostgreSQL	Supported

SQL99 Syntax and Description

```
SET [LOCAL] TRANSACTION { {READ ONLY | READ WRITE}[,...]
 | ISOLATION LEVEL
   {READ COMMITTED
   | READ UNCOMMITTED
   | REPEATABLE READ
   | SERIALIZABLE}[,...]
 | DIAGNOSTIC SIZE INT};
```

When issued, this command is outside the context of a transaction but applies to the next valid transaction. More than one option may be applied with this command, each separated by a comma.

The transaction settings may be applied only to the local server via the *LOCAL* command. Otherwise, the transaction settings are assumed to apply regardless of where the transaction is run. This option is new to SQL99.

A transaction also can be specified as *READ ONLY* or *READ WRITE*. The *DIAGNOSTIC SIZE* clause, followed by an integer, designates the specific number of error messages to capture for a transaction. The *GET DIAGNOSTICS* statement retrieves this information.

The *ISOLATION LEVEL* clause controls a number of behaviors in a transaction concerning concurrent transactions. Isolation levels control how transactions behave with regards to *dirty reads, non-repeatable reads*, and *phantom records*.

Dirty reads

    Occur when a transaction reads the altered records of another transaction before the other transaction has completed. This allows a data modification to occur on a record that might not be committed to the database.

Non-repeatable reads

    Occur when one transaction reads a record while another modifies it. So, if the first transaction attempts to reread the record, it can't find it.

Phantom records

    Occur when a transaction reads a group of records, but a data modification adds or changes the data so that more records satisfy the first transaction.

Setting the isolation level impacts these anomalies as depicted in Table 3-10.

Table 3-10: Isolation Level and Anomaly Impact

Isolation Level	Dirty Reads	Non-Repeatable Reads	Phantom Records
READ COMMITTED	No	Yes	Yes
READ UNCOMMITTED	Yes	Yes	Yes
REPEATABLE READ	No	No	Yes
SERIALIZABLE	No	No	No

For SQL99, *SERIALIZABLE* is the default isolation level. *READ WRITE* transactions may not be *READ UNCOMMITTED*.

Microsoft SQL Server Syntax and Variations

```
SET TRANSACTION ISOLATION LEVEL
{READ COMMITTED
| READ UNCOMMITTED
| REPEATABLE READ
| SERIALIZABLE}
```

READ COMMITTED is the SQL Server default, as opposed to serializable as the default in SQL99. The isolation level is established for the duration of the entire session, not just the transaction as in SQL99.

Oracle SQL Server Syntax and Variations

```
SET TRANSACTION READ ONLY;
```

Oracle does not support the full syntax of the *SET TRANSACTION* statement, and its implementation of *READ ONLY* differs somewhat as well. Oracle only supports *READ COMMITTED* and *SERIALIZABLE*. *READ COMMITTED* is the default behavior. In Oracle, this command starts a transaction in *SERIALIZABLE* isolation level. Oracle allows only the *SELECT* commands when the following commands are set: *READ ONLY, ALTER SESSION, ALTER SYSTEM, LOCK TABLE,* and *SET ROLE.*

PostgreSQL Syntax and Variations

```
SET TRANSACTION ISOLATION LEVEL {READ COMMITTED | SERIALIZABLE};
```

PostgreSQL does not support the full syntax of the *SET TRANSACTION* statement. In PostgreSQL, *SET TRANSACTION ISOLATION LEVEL READ COMMITTED* specifies that the current transaction's read-only rows committed before the transaction began. This is the default. *SERIALIZABLE*, which is the ANSI-default isolation level, specifies that the current transaction's read-only rows committed before the first data modification in the batch is executed.

START TRANSACTION

New in SQL99, the *START TRANSACTION* statement allows all the functions of *SET TRANSACTION* to be performed and allows a new transaction to be initiated.

Vendor	Command
SQL Server	Not supported; see *BEGIN TRAN* later
MySQL	Not supported
Oracle	Not supported
PostgreSQL	Not supported; see *BEGIN TRAN* later

SQL99 Syntax and Description

```
START TRANSACTION { {READ ONLY | READ WRITE}[,...]
| ISOLATION LEVEL
  {READ COMMITTED
  | READ UNCOMMITTED
  | REPEATABLE READ
  | SERIALIZABLE}[,...]
| DIAGNOSTIC SIZE INT};
```

The only difference between *SET* and *START* is that *SET* is considered outside of the current transaction, while *START* is considered the marking of a new transaction.

BEGIN TRANSACTION

The command *BEGIN TRANSACTION* provides similar functionality to *START TRANSACTION*. Both Microsoft SQL Server and PostgreSQL support *BEGIN TRANSACTION*, though they have slight variations in their syntax. Oracle supports implicit, but not explicit, transactions. MySQL doesn't support atomic transactions at all. *BEGIN TRANSACTION* declares an explicit transaction, but it does not set isolation levels.

The Microsoft SQL Server syntax is:

```
BEGIN TRAN[SACTION] [transaction_name | @transaction_variable
[WITH MARK [ 'log_description' ] ] ]
```

Microsoft SQL Server allows a name to be assigned to a transaction or to reference transactions using a variable. It does not affect or add to functionality. When nesting transactions, only the outermost *BEGIN . . . COMMIT* or *BEGIN . . . ROLLBACK* pair should reference the transaction name (if it has one).

The *WITH MARK* option logs the transaction to the SQL Server event log. By specifying *WITH MARK 'log_description'*, a descriptive string may be added for the event to be logged.

The PostgreSQL syntax is:

```
BEGIN [ WORK | TRANSACTION ]
```

PostgreSQL normally runs in autocommit mode where each data modification or query is its own transaction. PostgreSQL normally applies an implicit *COMMIT* or *ROLLBACK* at the end of the transaction. Using the *BEGIN* statement allows the next *COMMIT* or *ROLLBACK* to be declared explicitly.

Be sure to issue *BEGIN* in a pair with either *COMMIT* or *ROLLBACK*. Otherwise, the DBMS does not complete the command(s) until it encounters *COMMIT* or *ROLLBACK*. This could lead to potentially huge transactions with unpredictable results on the data.

Manually coded transactions are much faster in PostgreSQL than are autocommitted transactions. The *SET TRANSACTION ISOLATION LEVEL* should be set to *SERIALIZABLE* just after the *BEGIN* statement to bolster the transaction isolation. There could be many data-modification statements (*INSERT, UPDATE, DELETE*) within a *BEGIN . . . COMMIT* block. When the *COMMIT* command is issued, either all or none of the transactions takes place, depending on the success or failure of the command.

Example

In the following example, the three *INSERT* statements all be treated as a single transaction:

```
BEGIN TRANSACTION
    INSERT INTO sales VALUES('7896','JR3435','Oct 28 2001',25,
    'Net 60','BU7832')

    INSERT INTO sales VALUES('7901','JR3435','Oct 28 2001',17,
    'Net 60','BU7832')

    INSERT INTO sales VALUES('7907','JR3435','Oct 28 2001',6,
    'Net 60','BU7832')

COMMIT
GO
```

However, the entire group of transactions would fail, for example, if a primary key restraint is in any one of the *INSERT* statements.

TRUNCATE TABLE

The *TRUNCATE TABLE* command is a non-ANSI statement that removes all rows from a table without logging the individual row deletes. It is a very handy command because it quickly erases all the records in a table without altering the table structure, while taking very little space in the redo logs or transaction logs. However, it has a dark side; since it is not logged, it cannot be recovered or backed up.

Vendor	Command
SQL Server	Supported
MySQL	Not supported
Oracle	Supported
PostgreSQL	Supported

SQL99 Syntax and Description

```
TRUNCATE TABLE name
```

The *TRUNCATE TABLE* statement has the same effect as a *DELETE* statement with no *WHERE* clause; both erase all rows in a given table. However, there are two important differences. *TRUNCATE TABLE* is faster, and it is non-logged, meaning it cannot roll back if issued in error.

Typically, *TRUNCATE TABLE* does not activate triggers and does not function when foreign keys are in place on a given table.

Example

This example removes all data from the **publishers** table:

```
TRUNCATE TABLE publishers
```

Oracle Syntax and Variations

```
TRUNCATE { CLUSTER [owner.]cluster
    | TABLE [owner.]table [{PRESERVE | PURGE} SNAPSHOT LOG]}
  [{DROP | REUSE} STORAGE]
```

Oracle allows a table or an indexed cluster (but not a hash cluster) to be truncated.

When truncating a table, Oracle allows the option of preserving or purging the snapshot log, if one is defined on the table. *PRESERVE* maintains the snapshot log when the master table is truncated, while *PURGE* clears out the snapshot log.

If the *DROP STORAGE* clause is added, the disk space freed by the deleted rows is deallocated. If the *REUSE STORAGE* clause is added, the space of the deleted rows allocated to the table or cluster is left in place.

Microsoft SQL Server and PostgreSQL Note

Both of these implementations support the SQL99 default syntax.

UPDATE

The *UPDATE* command changes existing data in a table.

Vendor	Command
SQL Server	Supported, with variations
MySQL	Supported, with variations
Oracle	Supported, with variations
PostgreSQL	Supported

SQL99 Syntax and Description

```
UPDATE {table_name | view_name}
SET {column_name | variable_name} = {DEFAULT | expression} [,...n]
WHERE conditions
```

As with the *DELETE* statement, an *UPDATE* command is seldom issued without a *WHERE* clause, since the statement affects every row in the entire table.

 It is good practice to issue a *SELECT* command using the same *WHERE* clause before issuing the actual *UPDATE* statement. This checks all rows in the result set before actually performing the *UPDATE*. Whatever rows are returned by the *SELECT* are modified by the *UPDATE*.

Examples

A basic *UPDATE* statement without a *WHERE* clause looks like this:

```
UPDATE authors
SET contract = 0
```

Without a *WHERE* clause, all authors in the **authors** table have their contract status set to 0 (meaning they don't have a contract any more). Similarly, values can be adjusted mathematically with an *UPDATE* statement:

```
UPDATE titles
SET price = price * 1.1
```

This *UPDATE* statement would increase all book prices by 10%.

Adding a *WHERE* clause to an *UPDATE* statement allows records in the table to be modified selectively:

```
UPDATE titles
SET    type  = 'pers_comp',
       price = (price * 1.15)
WHERE  type  = 'popular_com'
```

This query makes two changes to any record of the type *'popular_com'*. The command increases their price by 15% and alters their type to *'pers_comp'*.

There are times when it's required to update values in a given table based on the values stored in another table. For example, if it is necessary to update the publication date for all the titles written by a certain author, it is also necessary to find the author and list of titles first through subqueries:

```
UPDATE titles
SET    pubdate = 'Jan 01 2002'
WHERE  title_id IN
    (SELECT title_id
     FROM   titleauthor
     WHERE  au_id IN
         (SELECT au_id
          FROM   authors
          WHERE  au_lname = 'White'))
```

Microsoft Syntax and Variations

```
UPDATE {table_name | view_name} [WITH (table_hint [,...n])]
SET {column_name | variable_name} = {DEFAULT | expression | NULL} [,...n]
[FROM {table [,...n]}]
WHERE {conditions | CURRENT OF [GLOBAL] cursor_name}
[OPTION (query_hint [,...n])]
```

Microsoft SQL Server is capable of updating both views and tables. Table- and query-level optimizer hints may be declared using the *WITH table_hint* and *OPTION* clauses. Optimizer hints override the default functionality of the query optimizer. Consult the vendor documentation for a full discussion of optimizer hints.

Microsoft SQL Server supports the *FROM* clause in an *UPDATE* statement. The chief benefit of this variation is much easier multitable joins. The following is a sample of table joins using both styles of syntax:

```
-- ANSI style
UPDATE titles
SET    pubdate = GETDATE()
WHERE  title_id IN
    (SELECT title_id
     FROM   titleauthor
     WHERE  au_id IN
         (SELECT au_id
          FROM   authors
          WHERE  au_lname = 'White'))

-- Microsoft Transact-SQL style
UPDATE  titles
SET     pubdate = GETDATE()
FROM    authors a,
        titleauthor t2
WHERE   a.au_id    = t2.au_id
    AND t2.title_id = titles.title_id
    AND a.au_lname  = 'White'
```

To perform the update using the Transact-SQL style is simply a matter of three table joins between **authors**, **titles**, and **titleauthor**. But to perform the same operation using ANSI-compliant code, first the **au_id** in **author** must be found and passed up to the **titleauthors** table, where the **title_id** must be identified and then passed up to the main update statement.

The clause *WHERE CURRENT OF cursor_name* tells SQL Server, when used in combination with a cursor, to update only the single record where the cursor is currently positioned. The cursor may be a global or local cursor as designated by the keyword *GLOBAL.*

This example updates the **state** column for the first 10 authors from the **authors** table:

```
UPDATE authors
SET state = 'ZZ'
FROM (SELECT TOP 10 * FROM authors ORDER BY au_lname) AS t1
WHERE authors.au_id = t1.au_id
```

MySQL Syntax and Variations

```
UPDATE [LOW PRIORITY] table_name
SET {column_name | variable_name} = {DEFAULT | expression}
WHERE conditions
[LIMIT integer]
```

MySQL supports the SQL99 standard with two variations: the *LOW PRIORITY* clause and the *LIMIT* clause. The *LOW PRIORITY* clause tells MySQL to delay the execution of the *UPDATE* statement until no other client is reading from the table. The *LIMIT* clause restricts the *UPDATE* action to a specific number of rows as designated by the integer value.

Oracle Syntax and Variations

```
UPDATE [schema.]{view_name | snapshot_name
  | table_name [@database_link]
    {[PARTITION partition_name] | [SUBPARTITION subpartition_name]}
  | subquery [WITH {[READ ONLY]
    | [CHECK OPTION [CONSTRAINT constraint_name] ]
SET {column [,...] = {expression [,...n] | subquery} | VALUE value}
WHERE conditions | CURRENT OF cursor_name}
RETURNING expression [,...n] INTO variable [,...n];
```

The Oracle implementation of *UPDATE* allows updates against views, snapshots, and tables in an allowable schema. When updating tables, the table can be a local table or one made available via *@dblink.* Updates always occur against the partition; however, the *UPDATE* command supports updates against a named *PARTITION* or *SUBPARTITION,* if preferred.

When updating against a subquery, the *WITH* clause becomes available. The *WITH READ ONLY* clause specifies that the subquery cannot be updated. The *WITH CHECK OPTION* tells Oracle to abort any changes to the updated table that would not appear in the result set of the subquery. The *CONSTRAINT* subclause tells Oracle to further restrict changes based upon a specific constraint.

The *SET VALUE* clause allows the user to set the entire row value for any table datatype values.

In Oracle, the *WHERE CURRENT OF* clause indicates that the *UPDATE* should be performed only on the current record within the cursor context.

RETURNING retrieves the rows affected by the command. When used for a single-row update, the values of the row can be stored in PL/SQL variables and bind variables. When used for a multirow delete, the values of the rows are stored in bind arrays. The *INTO* keyword indicates that the updated values should be stored in the variables list.

PostgreSQL Notes

PostgreSQL supports the SQL99 standard. Refer to the earlier section, "SQL99 Syntax and Description," for a full description of the *UPDATE* command.

Conclusion

The breadth and scope of the SQL commands provide the capability to create and manipulate a wide variety of database objects using the various *CREATE, ALTER,* and *DROP* commands. Those database objects then can be loaded with data using commands such as *INSERT.* The data can be manipulated using a wide variety of commands, such as *SELECT, DELETE,* and *TRUNCATE,* as well as the cursor commands, *DECLARE, OPEN, FETCH,* and *CLOSE.* Transactions to manipulate the data are controlled through the *SET* command, plus the *COMMIT* and *ROLLBACK* commands. And finally, other commands covered in this chapter include those that control a user's access to database resources through commands such as *GRANT* and *REVOKE.*

CHAPTER 4

SQL Functions

A *function* is a special type of command word in the SQL99 command set. In effect, functions are one-word commands that return a single value. The value of a function can be determined by input parameters, as with a function that averages a list of database values. But many functions do not use any type of input parameter, such as the function that returns the current system time, *CURRENT_TIME.*

The SQL99 standard supports a number of useful functions. This chapter covers those functions, providing detailed descriptions and examples. In addition, each database vendor maintains a long list of their own internal functions that are outside of the scope of the SQL standard. Lists and descriptions are provided for each database implementation's internal functions.

In addition, most database vendors support the ability to create user-defined functions (UDF). For more information on UDFs, refer to the *CREATE FUNCTION* command in Chapter 3, *SQL Statements Command Reference.*

Deterministic and Nondeterministic Functions

Functions can be either deterministic or nondeterministic. A *deterministic* function always returns the same results if given the same input values. A *nondeterministic* function returns different results every time it is called, even when the same input values are provided.

Why is this important? It is important because of how functions may be used within views, user-defined functions, and stored procedures. The restrictions vary across implementations, but these objects sometimes allow only deterministic functions within their defining code. For example, Microsoft SQL Server allows the creation of an index on a column expression—as long as the expression does not contain nondeterministic functions. Rules and restrictions vary between the vendors, so check their documentation when using functions.

Types of Functions

There are several basic types and categories of functions in SQL99 and vendor implementations of SQL. The basic types of functions are:

Aggregate functions
> Operate against a collection of values, but return a single, summarizing value.

Scalar functions
> Operate against a single value, and return a single value based on the input value. Some scalar functions, *CURRENT_TIME* for example, do not require any arguments.

Aggregate Functions

Aggregate functions return a single value based upon a set of other values. If used among many other expressions in the item list of a *SELECT* statement, the *SELECT* must have a *GROUP BY* clause. No *GROUP BY* clause is required if the aggregate function is the only value retrieved by the *SELECT* statement. The supported aggregate functions and their syntax are listed in Table 4-1.

Table 4-1: SQL99 Aggregate Functions

Function	Usage
AVG(expression)	Computes the average value of a column by the expression
COUNT(expression)	Counts the rows defined by the expression
COUNT(*)	Counts all rows in the specified table or view
MIN(expression)	Finds the minimum value in a column by the expression
MAX(expression)	Finds the maximum value in a column by the expression
SUM(expression)	Computes the sum of column values by the expression

Technically speaking, *ANY, EVERY,* and *SOME* are considered aggregate functions. However, they have been discussed as range search criteria since they are most often used that way. Refer to the *SELECT . . . WHERE* topic in the previous chapter for more information on these functions.

The number of values processed by an aggregate varies depending on the number of rows queried from the table. This behavior makes aggregate functions different from scalar functions, which require a fixed number and fixed type of parameters.

The general syntax of an aggregate function is:

```
aggregate_function_name ( [ALL | DISTINCT] expression )
```

The aggregate function name may be *AVG, COUNT, MAX, MIN,* or *SUM.* The *ALL* clause, which is the default behavior and does not actually need to be specified, evaluates all rows when aggregating the value of the function. The *DISTINCT* clause uses only distinct values when evaluating the function.

AVG and SUM

The *AVG* function computes the average of values in a column or an expression. *SUM* computes the sum. Both functions work with numeric values and ignore

NULL values. They also can be used to compute the average or sum of all *distinct* values of a column or expression.

AVG and *SUM* are supported by Microsoft SQL Server, MySQL, Oracle, and PostgreSQL.

Example

The following query computes average year-to-date sales for each type of book:

```
SELECT   type, AVG( ytd_sales ) AS "average_ytd_sales"
FROM     titles
GROUP BY type;
```

This query returns the sum of year-to-date sales for each type of book:

```
SELECT   type, SUM( ytd_sales )
FROM     titles
GROUP BY type;
```

COUNT

The *COUNT* function has three variations. *COUNT(*)* counts all the rows in the target table whether they include nulls or not. *COUNT(expression)* computes the number of rows with non-NULL values in a specific column or expression. *COUNT(DISTINCT expression)* computes the number of distinct non-NULL values in a column or expression.

Examples

This query counts all rows in a table:

```
SELECT COUNT(*) FROM publishers;
```

The following query finds the number of different countries where publishers are located:

```
SELECT COUNT(DISTINCT country) "Count of Countries"
FROM    publishers
```

MIN and MAX

MIN(expression) and MAX(expression) find the minimum and maximum value (string, datetime, or numeric) in a set of rows. *DISTINCT* or *ALL* may be used with these functions, but they do not affect the result.

MIN and *MAX* are supported by Microsoft SQL Server, MySQL, Oracle, and PostgreSQL.

MySQL also supports the functions *LEAST( )* and *GREATEST( )*, providing the same capabilities.

Examples

The following query finds the best and worst sales for any title on record:

```
SELECT  'MIN' = MIN(ytd_sales), 'MAX' = MAX(ytd_sales)
FROM    titles;
```

Aggregate functions are used often in the *HAVING* clause of queries with *GROUP BY*. The following query selects all categories (types) of books that have an average price for all books in the category higher than $15.00:

```
SELECT  type 'Category', AVG( price ) 'Average Price'
FROM    titles
GROUP BY type
HAVING AVG(price) > 15
```

Scalar Functions

Scalar functions fall into the categories listed in Table 4-2.

Table 4-2: Categories of Scalar Functions

Function Category	Explanation
Built-in	Performs operations on values or settings built into the database.
	Oracle uses the term "built-in" to describe all the specialty functions that are provided by Oracle, and thus "built into" their DBMS. This is a distinct and separate usage from the built-in functions described here.
Date & Time	Performs operations on datetime fields and returns values in datetime format.
Numeric	Performs operations on numeric values and returns numeric values.
String	Performs operations on character values (*char, varchar, nchar, nvarchar, and CLOB*) and returns a string or numeric value.

Note that *CASE* and *CAST* are both functions. However, they are detailed in Chapter 3 because of their complexity and frequent usage in SQL-data statements.

Built-in Scalar Functions

SQL99 built-in scalar functions identify the current user session, and also character-istics of the current user session, such as the current session privileges. Built-in scalar functions are almost always nondeterministic. The first three functions listed in Table 4-3 are built-in functions that fall into the date-and-time category of func-tions. Although the four vendors provide many additional functions beyond these SQL built-ins, the SQL standard declares only those listed in Table 4-3.

Table 4-3: SQL99 Built-in Scalar Functions

Function	Usage
CURRENT_DATE	Identifies the current date.
CURRENT_TIME	Identifies the current time.
CURRENT_TIMESTAMP	Identifies the current date and time.
CURRENT_USER	Identifies the currently active user within the database server.
SESSION_USER	Identifies the currently active Authorization ID, if it differs from the user.
SYSTEM_USER	Identifies the currently active user within the host operating system.

Microsoft SQL Server supports all the built-in scalar functions. Oracle does not support the built-in scalar functions shown above; however, it supports *USER* as a synonym of *CURRENT_USER* and *SYSDATE* as a synonym of *CURRENT_TIMESTAMP*. MySQL supports all the SQL99 built-in scalar functions, plus both of Oracle's variants. PostgreSQL supports *USER*, as defined in SQL99, as a synonym for *CURRENT_USER*. In addition, MySQL supports *NOW()* and *UNIX_TIMESTAMP()* as synonyms of the function *CURRENT_TIMESTAMP*. PostgreSQL supports all the SQL99 built-in scalar functions except *SESSION_USER*.

Example

The following queries retrieve the values from built-in functions. Notice that the various vendors return dates in their native formats:

```
/* On MySQL */
SELECT CURRENT_TIMESTAMP;
-> '2001-12-15 23:50:26'

/* On Microsoft SQL Server */
SELECT CURRENT_TIMESTAMP
GO
-> 'Dec 15,2001 23:50:26'

/* On Oracle */
SELECT USER FROM dual;
-> dylan
```

Numeric Scalar Functions

The list of official SQL99 numeric functions is rather small. The various vendors provide quite a large supplement of mathematical and statistical functions. MySQL supports many of these commands in its SQL99 incarnations. The other database products offer the same capabilities of numeric scalar functions through their own internally defined functions, but they do not share the same name as those declared by the SQL standard. The supported numeric functions and syntax are listed in Table 4-4.

Table 4-4: SQL99 Numeric Functions

Function	Usage
BIT_LENGTH(expression)	Returns an integer value representing the number of bits in an expression.
CHAR_LENGTH(expression)	Returns an integer value representing the number of characters in an expression.
EXTRACT(datetime_expression datepart FROM expression)	Allows the datepart to be extracted (*YEAR, MONTH, DAY, HOUR, MINUTE, SECOND, TIMEZONE_HOUR,* or *TIMEZONE_MINUTE*) from an expression.
OCTET_LENGTH(expression)	Returns an integer value representing the number of octets in an expression. This value is the same as BIT_LENGTH/8.
POSITION(starting_string IN search_string)	Returns an integer value representing the starting position of a string within the search string.

BIT_LENGTH, CHAR_LENGTH, and OCTET_LENGTH

The closest any of the vendors get to the *BIT_LENGTH* function is Oracle. Oracle supports the *LENGTHB* function, which returns an integer value representing the number of bytes in an expression.

MySQL and PostgreSQL support *CHAR_LENGTH* and the SQL99 synonym *CHARACTER_LENGTH( )*. PostgreSQL also supports *EXTRACT( )*, *OCTET_LENGTH( )*, and *POSITION( )* as per the SQL99 standard. The other two vendors each have a similar function that provides identical functionality. SQL Server provides the *LEN* function and Oracle provides the *LENGTH* function.

MySQL and PostgreSQL also fully support the *OCTET_LENGTH* function.

Example

The following example determines the length of a string and a value retrieved from a column:

```
/* On MySQL and PostgreSQL */
SELECT CHAR_LENGTH('hello');
SELECT OCTET_LENGTH(book_title) FROM titles;

/* On Microsoft SQL Server */
SELECT DATALENGTH(title)
FROM titles
WHERE type = 'popular_comp'
GO

/* On Oracle */
SELECT LENGTH('HORATIO') "Length of characters"
FROM dual;
```

EXTRACT

The *EXTRACT* function is not supported by the database vendors, except for PostgreSQL and MySQL.

Each vendor supports a separate command to accomplish the same functionality. Oracle uses the *TO_CHAR* function to extract a portion of a date into a character string. SQL Server uses the *CONVERT* function to extract a portion of a date.

MySQL implementation is extended somewhat beyond the SQL99 standard. The SQL99 standard does not have a provision for returning multiple fields in the same call to *EXTRACT( )* (e.g., "DAY_HOUR"). The MySQL extensions try to accomplish what the combination *DATE_TRUNC( )* and *DATE_PART( )* do in PostgreSQL. MySQL supports the dateparts listed in Table 4-5.

Table 4-5: MySQL Dateparts

Type value	Meaning	Expected format
SECOND	Seconds	SECONDS
MINUTE	Minutes	MINUTES

Table 4-5: MySQL Dateparts (continued)

Type value	Meaning	Expected format
HOUR	Hours	HOURS
DAY	Days	DAYS
MONTH	Months	MONTHS
YEAR	Years	YEARS
MINUTE_SECOND	Minutes and seconds	"MINUTES:SECONDS"
HOUR_MINUTE	Hours and minutes	"HOURS:MINUTES"
DAY_HOUR	Days and hours	"DAYS HOURS"
YEAR_MONTH	Years and months	"YEARS-MONTHS"
HOUR_SECOND	Hours, minutes, seconds	"HOURS:MINUTES:SECONDS"
DAY_MINUTE	Days, hours, minutes	"DAYS HOURS:MINUTES"
DAY_SECOND	Days, hours, minutes, seconds	"DAYSHOURS:MINUTES:SECONDS"

Example

This example extracts dateparts from several datetime values:

```
/* On MySQL */
SELECT EXTRACT(YEAR FROM "2013-07-02");
-> 1999
SELECT EXTRACT(YEAR_MONTH FROM "2013-07-02 01:02:03");
-> 199907
SELECT EXTRACT(DAY_MINUTE FROM "2013-07-02 01:02:03");
-> 20102
```

POSITION

The *POSITION* function returns an integer that indicates the starting position of a string within the search string. MySQL and PostgreSQL support the *POSITION* function with no variation from the SQL99 syntax. PostgreSQL has a synonymous function, *TEXTPOS,* while MySQL has the synonymous function, *LOCATE.*

Oracle's equivalent function is called *INSTR.* Microsoft SQL Server has both *CHARINDEX* and *PATINDEX.* The *CHARINDEX* and *PATINDEX* are very similar, except that *PATINDEX* allows the use of wildcard characters in the search criteria. For example:

```
/* On MySQL */
SELECT LOCATE('bar', 'foobar');
-> 4

/* On MySQL and PostgreSQL */
SELECT POSITION('fu' IN 'snafhu');
-> 0

/* On Microsoft SQL Server */
SELECT CHARINDEX( 'de', 'abcdefg' )
GO
-> 4
```

```
SELECT PATINDEX( '%fg', 'abcdefg' )
GO
-> 6
```

String Functions

Basic string functions offer a number of capabilities and return a string value as a result set. Some string functions are dyadic, indicating that they operate on two strings at once. SQL99 supports the string functions listed in Table 4-6.

Table 4-6: SQL String Functions

Function	Usage
CONCATENATE (expression || expression)	Appends two or more literal expressions, column values, or variables together into one string.
CONVERT	Converts a string to a different representation within the same character set.
LOWER	Converts a string to all lowercase characters.
SUBSTRING	Extracts a portion of a string.
TRANSLATE	Converts a string from one character set to another.
TRIM	Removes leading characters, trailing characters, or both from a character string.
UPPER	Converts a string to all uppercase characters.

CONCATENATE

SQL99 defines a concatenation operator (\|\|), which joins two distinct strings into one string value. The *CONCATENATE* function appends two or more strings together, producing a single output string. PostgreSQL and Oracle support the double-pipe concatenation operator. Microsoft SQL Server uses the plus sign (+) concatenation operator.

MySQL supports a similar function, *CONCAT()*. Refer to the "Concatenation Operators" section Chapter 3, *SQL Statements Command Reference*, for more information on concatenation within Oracle, PostgreSQL, and Microsoft SQL Server.

SQL99 Syntax

```
CONCATENATE('string1' || 'string2')
```

MySQL Syntax

```
CONCAT(str1, str2, [,...n])
```

If any of the concatenation values are null, the entire returned string is null. Also, if a numeric value is concatenated, it is implicitly converted to a character string:

```
SELECT CONCAT('My ', 'bologna ', 'has ', 'a ', 'first ', 'name...');
-> 'My bologna has a first name...'
SELECT CONCAT('My ', NULL, 'has ', 'first ', 'name...');
-> NULL
```

CONVERT and TRANSLATE

The *CONVERT* function alters the representation of a character string within its character set and collation. For example, *CONVERT* might be used to alter the number of bits per character.

TRANSLATE alters the character set of a string value from one base-character set to another. Thus, *TRANSLATE* might be used to translate a value from the English character set to a Kanji (Japanese) or Russian character set. The translation must already exist, either by default or having been created using the *CREATE TRANSLATION* command.

SQL99 Syntax

```
CONVERT (char_value target_char_set USING form_of_use source_char_name)

TRANSLATE(char_value target_char_set USING translation_name)
```

Among the database vendors, only Oracle supports *CONVERT* and *TRANSLATE* with the same meaning as SQL99. Oracle's implementation of *TRANSLATE* is very similar to SQL99, but not identical. In its implementation, Oracle accepts only two arguments and allows translating only between the database character set or the national language support character set.

MySQL's implementation of the *CONVERT* function only translates numbers from one base to another. In contrast, Microsoft SQL Server's implementation of *CONVERT* is a very rich utility that alters the base datatype of an expression, but is otherwise dissimilar to the SQL99 *CONVERT* function. PostgreSQL does not support *CONVERT*, and its implementation of *TRANSLATE* serves to morph any occurrence of a character string to any other character string.

MySQL Syntax and Variations

```
CONV(int, from_base, to_base)
```

MySQL does not support *TRANSLATE*. This implementation of *CONVERT* returns a string value representing the number as it is converted from the *from_base* value to the *to_base* value. If any of the numbers are NULL, then the function returns NULL. Following are some examples:

```
SELECT CONV("a",16,2);
-> '1010'
SELECT CONV("6E",18,8);
-> '172'
SELECT CONV(-17,10,-18);
-> '-H'
```

Microsoft SQL Server Syntax and Variations

```
CONVERT (data_type[(length) | (precision,scale)], expression[,style])
```

Microsoft SQL Server does not support *TRANSLATE*. Microsoft's implementation of the *CONVERT* function does not follow the SQL99 specification. Instead, it is functionally equivalent to the *CAST* function. The *style* clause is used to define the format of a date conversion. Refer to the vendor documentation for more information. Following is an example:

```
SELECT title, CONVERT(char(7), ytd_sales)
FROM titles
ORDER BY title
GO
```

Oracle Syntax and Variations

```
CONVERT('char_value', target_char_set, source_char_set)

TRANSLATE('char_value', 'from_text', 'to_text')
```

Under Oracle's implementation, the *CONVERT* function returns the *char_value* in the target character set. The *char_value* is the string being converted, while the *target_char_set* is the name of the character set where the *char_value* is converted. *Source_char_set* is the name of the character set where the *char_value* was originally stored.

Both the target and source character set can be either literals strings, variables, or columns containing the name of the character set. Note that inadequate replacement characters might be substituted when converting from or to a character set that does not support a representation of all the characters used in the conversion.

Oracle supports several common character sets including *US7ASCII*, *WE8DECDEC*, *WE8HP*, *F7DEC*, *WE8EBCDIC500*, *WE8PC850*, and *WE8ISO8859P1*. For example:

```
SELECT CONVERT('Groß', 'US7ASCII', 'WE8HP')
FROM DUAL;
->Gross
```

PostgreSQL Syntax and Variations

```
TRANSLATE (character_string, from_text, to_text)
```

PostgreSQL does not support *CONVERT*. PostgreSQL's implementation of the *TRANSLATE* function offers a large superset of functions compared to that found in the SQL99 specification. Instead, it converts any occurrence of one text string to another within another specified string. Here is an example:

```
SELECT TRANSLATE('12345abcde', '5a', 'XX');
-> 1234XXbcde

SELECT TRANSLATE(title, 'Computer', 'PC')
FROM  titles
WHERE type = 'Personal_computer'
```

LOWER and UPPER

The functions *LOWER* and *UPPER* allow the case of a string to be altered quickly and easily, so that all the characters are lower- or uppercase, respectively. These functions are supported in all the database implementations covered in this book.

Example

```
SELECT LOWER('You Talkin To ME?'), UPPER('you talking to me?!');
-> you talking to me?, YOU TALKIN TO ME?!
```

The various database vendors also support a variety of other text formatting functions that are specific to their implementation.

SUBSTRING

The *SUBSTRING* function allows one character string to be extracted from another.

SQL99 Syntax

```
SUBSTRING(extraction_string FROM starting_position [FOR length]
[COLLATE collation_name])
```

If any of the inputs are NULL, the *SUBSTRING* function returns a NULL. The *extraction_string* is where the character value is extracted from. It may be a literal string, a column in a table with a character datatype, or a variable with a character datatype. The *starting_position* is an integer value telling the function at which position to perform the extract. The optional *length* is an integer value that tells the function how many characters to extract, starting at the *starting_position*.

MySQL Syntax and Variations

```
SUBSTRING(extraction_string FROM starting_position)
```

MySQL's implementation assumes that the characters are to be extracted from the starting position continuing to the end of the character string.

Microsoft SQL Server Syntax and Variations

```
SUBSTRING(extraction_string [FROM starting_position] [FOR length])
```

Microsoft SQL Server largely supports the SQL99 standard, except that it does not allow the *COLLATE* clause. Microsoft allows this command to be applied to text, image, and binary datatypes; however, the *starting_position* and *length* represent the number of bytes rather than the number of characters to count.

Oracle Syntax and Variations

```
SUBSTR(extraction_string, starting_position [, length])
```

Oracle's implementation, *SUBSTR*, largely functions the same way as SQL99. It does not support the *COLLATE* clause. When a *starting_value* is a negative number, Oracle counts from the end of the *extraction_string*. If *length* is omitted, the remainder of the string (starting at *starting_position*) is returned.

PostgreSQL Syntax and Variations

```
SUBSTRING(extraction_string [FROM starting_position] [FOR length])
```

PostgreSQL largely supports the SQL99 standard, except that it does not accept the *COLLATE* clause.

Examples

These examples generally work on any one of the four database vendors profiled in this book. Only the second Oracle example, with a negative starting position, fails on the others (assuming, of course, that Oracle's *SUBSTR* is translated into *SUBSTRING*):

```
/* On Oracle, counting from the left */
SELECT SUBSTR('ABCDEFG',3,4) FROM DUAL;
-> CDEF

/* On Oracle, counting from the right */
SELECT SUBSTR('ABCDEFG',-5,4) FROM DUAL;
-> CDEF

/* On MySQL */
SELECT SUBSTRING('Be vewy, vewy quiet',5);
-> 'wy, vewy quiet''

/* On PostgreSQL or SQL Server */
SELECT au_lname, SUBSTRING(au_fname, 1, 1)
FROM authors
WHERE au_lname = 'Carson'
-> Carson      C
```

TRIM

The *TRIM* function removes leading spaces, trailing characters, or both from a specified character string. This function also removes other types of characters from a specified character string. The default function is to trim the specified character from both sides of the character string. If no removal string is specified, *TRIM* removes spaces by default.

SQL99 Syntax

```
TRIM( [ [{LEADING | TRAILING | BOTH}] [removal_string] FROM ]
   target_string
   [COLLATE collation_name])
```

The *removal_string* is the character string to be stripped out. The *target_string* is the character string from which characters are to be taken. If a *removal_string* is not specified, then *TRIM* strips out spaces. The *COLLATE* clause forces the result set of the function into another preexisting collation set.

MySQL, PostgreSQL, and Oracle support the SQL99 syntax of *TRIM*.

Microsoft SQL Server (and the other vendors for that matter) provide the functions *LTRIM* and *RTRIM* to trim off leading spaces or trailing spaces, respectively. *LTRIM* and *RTRIM* cannot be used to trim other types of characters.

Examples

```
SELECT TRIM('  wamalamadingdong  ');
-> 'wamalamadingdong'
```

```
SELECT TRIM(LEADING '19' FROM '1976 AMC GREMLIN');
-> '76 AMC GREMLIN'

SELECT TRIM(BOTH 'x' FROM 'xxxWHISKEYxxx');
-> 'WHISKEY'

SELECT TRIM(TRAILING 'snack' FROM 'scooby snack');
-> 'scooby '
```

Vendor Extensions

The following section provides a full listing and description of each vendor-supported function. These functions are vendor-specific. Thus, a MySQL function, for example, is not guaranteed to be supported by any other vendor. MySQL functions are provided to give an idea of the capabilities available within the various products. Refer to the vendor's documentation for exact syntax usage.

Microsoft SQL Server-Supported Functions

Table 4-7 provides an alphabetical listing of Microsoft SQL Server–supported functions.

Table 4-7: Microsoft SQL Server–Supported Functions

Function	Description
abs(numeric_expression)	Returns absolute value.
acos(float_expression)	Returns angle (in radians) whose cosine is the specified argument.
app_name()	Returns application name for current session; set by application.
ascii(character_ expression)	Converts character to a numeric ASCII code.
asin(float_expression)	Returns angle (in radians) whose sine is the specified argument.
atan(float_expression)	Returns angle (in radians) whose tangent is the specified argument.
atn2(float_expression, float_expressioin)	Returns angle (in radians) whose tangent is argument1/argument1.
avg([All | Distinct] Expression)	Computes average of a column.
binary_checksum(* | expression [,...n])	Returns binary checksum for list of expressions or row of a table.
cast(Expression as Data Type)	Converts a valid SQL Server expression to the specified datatype.
ceiling(numeric_ expression)	Returns smallest integer greater than or equal to the argument.
char(integer_expression)	Converts a numeric ASCII code to a character.
charindex(expression1, expression2 [, start_ location])	Returns position of the first occurrence of a substring in a string.
checksum(* | expression [,...n])	Returns checksum value (computed over row values or expressions provided).

Table 4-7: Microsoft SQL Server–Supported Functions (continued)

Function	Description
checksum_agg([ALL | Distinct] expression)	Returns checksum of the values in group.
coalesce(expression [,...n])	Returns the first non-NULL argument from a list of arguments.
col_length('table', 'column')	Returns column length in bytes.
col_name(table_id, column_id)	Returns column name, given table ID and column ID.
contains([column |], 'contains_search_ condition'])	Searches columns on exact or "fuzzy" matches of *contains_ seach_criteria*. It is an elaborate function used to perform full-text searches. Refer to the vendor documentation for more information.
containsable(table, column, contains_ search_condition)	Returns a table with exact and "fuzzy" matches of *contains_ search_condition*. It is an elaborate function used to perform full-text searches. Refer to the vendor documentation for more information.
convert(data_type [(length)], expression [, style])	Converts data from one datatype to another.
cos(float_expression)	Returns cosine.
cot(float_expression)	Returns cotangent.
*count([[All | Distinct] expression] | *])*	Counts rows.
count(*)	Computes the number of rows, including those with NULL values.
count(DISTINCT expression)	Calculates the number of distinct non-NULL values in a column or expression. Each group of rows with the same value of *expression* adds 1 to the result.
count(expression)	Returns the number of rows with non-NULL values in a certain column or expression.
count_big([All | Distinct] expression)	Same as *count* except returns big integer.
current_timestamp	Returns current date and time.
current_user	Returns username in the current database of the current session.
datalength(expression)	Returns number of bytes in a character or binary string.
databasepropertyex(data base, property)	Returns database option or property
dateadd(datepart, number, date)	Adds a number of dateparts (e.g., days) to a datetime value.
datediff(datepart, startdate, enddate)	Calculates difference between two datetime values expressed in certain dateparts.
datename(datepart, date)	Returns name of a datepart (e.g., month) of a datetime argument.
datepart(datepart, date)	Returns value of a datepart (e.g., hour) of a datetime argument.
day(date)	Returns an integer value representing the day of the date provided as a parameter.
db_id('[database_ name]')	Returns database ID and given name.
db_name(database_id)	Returns the database name.

Table 4-7: Microsoft SQL Server–Supported Functions (continued)

Function	Description
degrees(numeric_ expression)	Converts radians to degrees.
difference(character_ expression, character_ expression)	Compares how two arguments sound and returns a number from 0 to 4. Higher result indicates better phonetic match.
exp(float_expression)	Returns exponential value.
floor(numeric_ expression)	Returns largest integer less than or equal to the argument.
file_id('file_name')	Returns the file ID for the logical filename.
file_name(file_id)	Returns the logical filename for file ID.
filegroup_id ('filegroup_name')	Returns filegroup ID for the logical filegroup name.
filegroup_name (filegroup_id)	Returns the logical filegroup name for filegroup ID.
filegroupproperty (filegroup_name, property)	Returns filegroup property value for the specified property.
fileproperty (file, property)	Returns file property value for the specified property.
fulltextcatalog property(catalog_name, property)	Returns full-text catalog properties.
fulltextservice property(property)	Returns full-text service level properties.
formatmessage (msg_number, param_ value [,... n])	Constructs a message from an existing message in **SYSMESSAGES** table (similar to RAISERROR).
freetexttable(table { column |}, 'freetext_ string'[, top_n_by_rank])*	Used for full-text search; returns a table with columns that match the meaning but don't exactly match value of *freetext_ string*.
getdate( )	Returns current date and time.
getansinull(['database'])	Returns default nullability setting for new columns.
getutcdate( )	Returns Universal Time Coordinate (UTC) date.
grouping(column_ name)	Returns 1 when the row is added by CUBE or ROLLUP; otherwise, returns 0.
host_id( )	Returns workstation ID of a given process.
host_name( )	Returns process hostname.
ident_incr ('table_or_view')	Returns identity-column increment value.
ident_seed ('table_or_view')	Returns identity seed value.
ident_current ('table_name')	Returns the last identity value generated for the specified table.
identity(data_type [, seed, increment]) As column_name	Used in *SELECT INTO* statement to insert an identity column into the destination table.
index_col('table', index_id, key_id)	Returns index column name, given table ID, index ID, and column sequential number in the index key.
indexproperty(table_id, index, property)	Returns index property (such as Fillfactor).

Table 4-7: Microsoft SQL Server–Supported Functions (continued)

Function	Description
isdate(expression)	Validates if a character string can be converted to DATETIME.
is_member('group' | 'role')	Returns true or false (1 or 0) depending on whether user is a member of NT group or SQL Server role.
is_srvrolemember ('role' [, 'login'])	Returns true or false (1 or 0) depending on whether user is a member of specified server role.
isnull(check_expression, replacement_value)	Returns the first argument if it is not NULL; otherwise, returns the second argument.
isnumeric(expression)	Validates if a character string can be converted to NUMERIC.
left(character_ expression, integer_ expression)	Returns a portion of a character expression, starting at integer_expression from left.
len(string_expression)	Returns the number of characters in the expression.
log(float_expression)	Returns natural logarithm.
log10(float_expression)	Returns base-10 logarithm.
lower(character_ expression)	Converts a string to lowercase.
ltrim(character_ expression)	Trims leading-space characters.
max([All | Distinct] expression)	Finds maximum value in a column.
min([All | Distinct] expression)	Finds minimum value in a column.
month(date)	Returns month part of the date provided.
nchar(integer_ expression)	Returns the unicode character with the given integer code.
newid()	Creates a new unique identifier of type *uniqueidentifier*.
nullif(expression, expression)	Returns NULL if two specified expressions are equivalent.
object_id('object')	Returns object ID and given name.
object_name(object_id)	Returns object name and given ID.
objectproperty (id, property)	Returns properties of objects in the current database.

MySQL-Supported Functions

Table 4-8 provides an alphabetical listing of MySQL-supported functions.

Table 4-8: MySQL-Supported Functions

Function	Description
abs(X)	Returns the absolute value of X.
acos(X)	Returns the arc cosine of X, i.e., the value whose cosine is X; returns NULL if X is not in the range −1 to 1.
ascii(str)	Returns the ASCII code value of the leftmost character of the string *str*; returns 0 if *str* is the empty string; returns NULL if *str* is NULL.
asin(X)	Returns the arc sine of X, i.e., the value whose sine is X; returns NULL if X is not in the range −1 to 1.

Table 4-8: MySQL-Supported Functions (continued)

Function	Description
atan(X)	Returns the arctangent of *X*, i.e., the value whose tangent is *X*.
atan2(X, Y)	Returns the arctangent of the two variables *X* and *Y*.
avg(expr)	Returns the average value of *expr*.
benchmark(count, expr)	Executes the expression *expr count* times. It may be used to time how fast MySQL processes the expression. The result value is always 0.
binary	Casts the string following it to a binary string.
bin(N)	Returns a string representation of the binary value of *N*, where *N* is a long (*BIGINT*) number.
bit_count(N)	Returns the number of bits that are set in the argument *N*.
bit_and(expr)	Returns the bitwise *AND* of all bits in *expr*. The calculation is performed with 64-bit (*BIGINT*) precision.
bit_or(expr)	Returns the bitwise *OR* of all bits in *expr*. The calculation is performed with 64-bit (*BIGINT*) precision.
CASE value WHEN [compare-value] THEN result [WHEN [compare-value] THEN result ...] [ELSE result] END *CASE WHEN [condition] THEN result [WHEN [condition] THEN result .. .] [ELSE result] END*	The first version returns the result where *value=compare-value*. The second version returns the result for the first condition that is true. If there is no matching result value, then the result after *ELSE* is returned. If there is no *ELSE* part, NULL is returned.
ceiling(X)	Returns the smallest integer value not less than *X*.
char(N,...)	Interprets the arguments as integers and returns a string consisting of the characters given by the ASCII code values of those integers. NULL values are skipped.
coalesce(list)	Returns first non-NULL element in the list.
concat(str1,str2,...)	Returns the string that results from concatenating the arguments.
concat_ws(separator, str1, str2,...)	Stands for CONCAT With Separator and is a special form of *CONCAT( )*. The first argument is the separator for the rest of the arguments. The separator and the rest of the arguments can be a string. If the separator is NULL, the result is NULL. The function skips any NULLs and empty strings after the separator argument. The separator is added between the strings to be concatenated.
connection_id( )	Returns the connection ID (*thread_id*) for the connection. Every connection has its own unique ID.
conv(N,from_base,to_ base)	Converts numbers between different number bases; returns a string representation of the number *N*, converted from base *from_base* to base *to_base*; returns NULL if any argument is NULL.
cos(X)	Returns the cosine of *X*, where *X* is given in radians.
cot(X)	Returns the cotangent of *X*.
count(DISTINCT expr,[expr...])	Returns a count of the number of different values.
count(expr)	Returns a count of the number of non-NULL values in the rows retrieved by a *SELECT* statement.
curdate( ) *current_date*	Returns today's date as a value in 'YYYY-MM-DD' or YYYYMMDD format, depending on whether the function is used in a string or numeric context.

Functions

Table 4-8: MySQL-Supported Functions (continued)

Function	Description
curtime() current_time	Returns the current time as a value in 'HH:MM:SS' or HHMMSS format, depending on whether the function is used in a string or numeric context.
database()	Returns the current database name.
date_ add(date,INTERVAL expr type) date_sub(date,INTERVAL expr type) adddate(date,INTERVAL expr type) subdate(date,INTERVAL expr type)	These functions perform date arithmetic. *ADDDATE()* and *SUBDATE()* are synonyms for *DATE_ADD()* and *DATE_SUB()*. *date* is a *DATETIME* or *DATE* value specifying the starting date. *expr* is an expression specifying the interval value to be added or subtracted from the starting date. *expr* may start with a - for negative intervals. *type* indicates how the expression should be interpreted.
date_format (date,format)	Formats the date value according to the format string.
dayname(date)	Returns the name of the weekday for date.
dayofmonth(date)	Returns the day of the month for date, in the range 1 to 31.
dayofweek(date)	Returns the weekday index for date (1 = Sunday, 2 = Monday, . . . 7 = Saturday).
dayofyear(date)	Returns the day of the year for date, in the range 1 to 366.
decode(crypt_str, pass_str)	Decrypts the encrypted string *crypt_str* using *pass_str* as the password. *crypt_str* should be a string returned from *ENCODE()*.
degrees(X)	Returns the argument *X*, converted from radians to degrees.
elt(N,str1,str2,str3,...)	Returns *str1* if *N* = 1, *str2* if *N* = 2, and so on. Returns NULL if *N* is less than 1 or greater than the number of arguments. *ELT()* is the complement of *FIELD()*.
encode(str,pass_str)	Encrypts *str* using *pass_str* as the password. To decrypt the result, use *DECODE()*. The result is a binary string the same length as the string.
encrypt(str[,salt])	Encrypts *str* using the Unix *crypt()* system call. The *salt* argument should be a string with two characters.
exp(X)	Returns the value of *e* (the base of natural logarithms) raised to the power of *X*.
export_set (bits,on,off,[separator, [number_of_bits]])	Returns a string where every bit set in 'bit' gets an 'on' string and every reset bit gets an 'off' string. Each string is separated with 'separator' (default ',') and only 'number_of_bits' (default 64) of 'bits' is used.
field(str,str1,str2,str3,...)	Returns the index of *str* in the *str1, str2, str3,* . . . list. Returns 0 if *str* is not found. *FIELD()* is the complement of *ELT()*.
find_in_set(str,strlist)	Returns a value 1 to *N* if the string *str* is in the list *strlist* consisting of *N* substrings. A string list is a string composed of substrings separated by ',' characters. Returns 0 if *str* is not in *strlist* or if *strlist* is the empty string. Returns NULL if either argument is NULL. This function does not work properly if the first argument contains a ','.
floor(X)	Returns the largest integer value not greater than *X*.
format(X,D)	Formats the number *X* to a format like '#,###,###.##', rounded to *D* decimals. If *D* is 0, the result has no decimal point or fractional part.
from_days(N)	Given a daynumber *N*, returns a *DATE* value. Not intended for use with values that precede the advent of the Gregorian calendar (1582), due to the days lost when the calendar was changed.

Table 4-8: MySQL-Supported Functions (continued)

Function	Description
from_unixtime(unix_ timestamp)	Returns a representation of the *unix_timestamp* argument as a value in 'YYYY-MM-DD HH:MM:SS' or YYYYMMDDH-HMMSS format, depending on whether the function is used in a string or numeric context.
from_unixtime(unix_ timestamp,format)	Returns a string representation of the *unix_timestamp*, formatted according to the format string. Format may contain the same specifiers as those listed in the entry for the *DATE_ FORMAT()* function.
get_lock(str,timeout)	Tries to obtain a lock with a name given by the string *str*, with a timeout of *timeout* seconds. Returns 1 if the lock is obtained successfully, 0 if the attempt times out, or NULL if an error occurs.
greatest(X,Y,...)	Returns the largest (maximum-valued) argument.
hex(N)	Returns a string representation of the hexadecimal value of *N*, where *N* is a long (*BIGINT*) number. This is equivalent to *CONV(N,10,16)*. Returns NULL if *N* is NULL.
interval(N,N1,N2,N3,...)	Returns 0 if $N < N1$, 1 if $N < N2$, and so on. All arguments are treated as integers. It is required that $N1 < N2 < N3 < \ldots < Nn$ for this function to work correctly.
hour(time)	Returns the hour for time, in the range 0 to 23.
if(expr1,expr2,expr3)	If *expr1* is TRUE (*expr1* <> 0 and *expr1* <> NULL), then *IF()* returns *expr2*, else it returns *expr3*. *IF()* returns a numeric or string value, depending on the context in which it is used.
ifnull(expr1,expr2)	If *expr1* is not NULL, *IFNULL()* returns *expr1*; otherwise it returns *expr2*. *IFNULL()* returns a numeric or string value, depending on the context in which it is used.
isnull(expr)	If *expr* is NULL, *ISNULL()* returns 1; otherwise it returns 0.
insert(str,pos,len,newstr)	Returns the string *str*. The substring begins at position *pos* and is 10 characters long, replaced by the string *newstr*.
instr(str,substr)	Returns the position of the first occurrence of substring *substr* in string *str*.
last_insert_id([expr])	Returns the last automatically generated value that was inserted into an *AUTO_INCREMENT* column.
lcase(str) *lower(str)*	Returns the string *str* with all characters changed to lowercase according to the current character-set mapping (default is ISO-8859-1 Latin1).
least(X,Y,...)	With two or more arguments, returns the smallest (minimum-valued) argument.
left(str,len)	Returns the leftmost *len* characters from the string *str*.
length(str) *octet_length(str)* *char_length(str)* *character_length(str)*	These functions return the length of the string *str*.
load_file(file_name)	Reads the file and returns the file contents as a string. The file must be on the server, and the user must specify the full path-name to the file and have the file privilege.
locate(substr,str) *position(substr IN str)*	Returns the position of the first occurrence of substring *substr* in string *str*. Returns 0 if *substr* is not in *str*.
locate(substr,str,pos)	Returns the position of the first occurrence of substring *substr* in string *str*, starting at position *pos*; returns 0 if *substr* is not in *str*.

Functions

Table 4-8: MySQL-Supported Functions (continued)

Function	Description
log(X)	Returns the natural logarithm of *X*.
log10(X)	Returns the base-10 logarithm of *X*.
lpad(str,len,padstr)	Returns the string *str*, left-padded with the string *padstr* until *str* is 10 characters long.
ltrim(str)	Returns the string *str* with leading-space characters removed.
make_set(bits,str1,str2, . . .)	Returns a set (a string containing substrings separated by ',' characters) consisting of the strings that have the corresponding bits in bit set. *str1* corresponds to bit 0, *str2* to bit 1, etc. NULL strings in *str1, str2, . . .* are not appended to the result.
md5(string)	Calculates a MD5 *checksum* for the string. Value is returned as a 32-long hex number.
min(expr) max(expr)	Returns the minimum or maximum value of *expr*. *MIN()* and *MAX()* may take a string argument; in such cases they return the minimum or maximum string value.
minute(time)	Returns the minute for time, in the range 0 to 59.
mod(N,M)	% Modulo (like the % operator in C); returns the remainder of *N* divided by *M*.
month(date)	Returns the month for date, in the range 1 to 12.
monthname(date)	Returns the name of the month for date.
now() sysdate() current_timestamp	Returns the current date and time as a value in 'YYYY-MM-DD HH:MM:SS' or YYYYMMDDHHMMSS format, depending on whether the function is used in a string or numeric context.
nullif(expr1,expr2)	If *expr1* = *expr2* is true, returns NULL; otherwise returns *expr1*.
oct(N)	Returns a string representation of the octal value of *N*, where *N* is a long number. This is equivalent to *CONV(N,10,8)*. Returns NULL if *N* is NULL.
ord(str)	If the leftmost character of the string *str* is a multibyte character, returns the code of multibyte character by returning the ASCII code value of the character in the format of: `((first byte ASCII code)*256+(second byte ASCII code))[*256+third byte ASCII code...]` If the leftmost character is not a multibyte character, returns the same value as the *ASCII()* function does.
password(str)	Calculates a password string from the plain-text password *str*. This is the function that is used for encrypting MySQL passwords for storage in the **Password** column of the user grant table.
period_add(P,N)	Adds *N* months to period *P* (in the format YYMM or YYYYMM). Returns a value in the format YYYYMM. Note that the period argument *P* is not a date value.
period_diff(P1,P2)	Returns the number of months between periods *P1* and *P2*. *P1* and *P2* should be in the format YYMM or YYYYMM. Note that the period arguments *P1* and *P2* are not date values.
pi()	Returns the value of _π.
pow(X,Y) power(X,Y)	Returns the value of *X* raised to the power of *Y*.
quarter(date)	Returns the quarter of the year for date, in the range 1 to 4.
radians(X)	Returns the argument *X*, converted from degrees to radians.

Table 4-8: MySQL-Supported Functions (continued)

Function	Description
rand( ) *rand(N)*	Returns a random floating-point value in the range 0 to 1.0. If an integer argument *N* is specified, it is used as the seed value.
release_lock(str)	Releases the lock named by the string *str* that was obtained with *GET_LOCK( )*. Returns 1 if the lock is released, 0 if the lock isn't locked by this thread (in which case the lock is not released), and NULL if the named lock doesn't exist.
repeat(str,count)	Returns a string consisting of the string *str* repeated *count* times. If *count* <= 0, returns an empty string. Returns NULL if *str* or *count* are NULL.
replace(str,from_str,to_str)	Returns the string *str* with all occurrences of the string *from_str* replaced by the string *to_str*.
reverse(str)	Returns the string *str* with the order of the characters reversed.
right(str,ten)	Returns the rightmost 10 characters from the string *str*.
round(X)	Returns the argument *X*, rounded to an integer.
round(X,D)	Returns the argument *X*, rounded to a number with *D* decimals. If *D* is 0, the result has no decimal point or fractional part.
rpad(str,len,padstr)	Returns the string *str*, right-padded with the string *padstr* until *str* is ten characters long.
rtrim(str)	Returns the string *str* with trailing space characters removed.
sec_to_time(seconds)	Returns the seconds argument, converted to hours, minutes, and seconds, as a value in 'HH:MM:SS' or HHMMSS format, depending on whether the function is used in a string or numeric context.
second(time)	Returns the second for time, in the range 0 to 59.
sign(X)	Returns the sign of the argument as −1, 0, or 1, depending on whether *X* is negative, zero, or positive.
sin(X)	Returns the sine of *X*, where *X* is given in radians.
soundex(str)	Returns a *soundex* string from *str*. Two strings that sound "about the same" should have identical *soundex* strings. A "standard" *soundex* string is four characters long, but the *SOUNDEX( )* function returns an arbitrarily long string. A *SUBSTRING( )* can be used on the result to get a "standard" *soundex* string. All non-alphanumeric characters are ignored in the given string. All international alphabetic characters outside the A–Z range are treated as vowels.
space(N)	Returns a string consisting of *N* space characters.
sqrt(X)	Returns the nonnegative square root of *X*.
std(expr) *stddev(expr)*	Returns the standard deviation of *expr*. The *STDDEV( )* form of this function is provided for Oracle compatability.
strcmp(expr1,expr2)	*STRCMP( )* returns 0 if the strings are the same, −1 if the first argument is smaller than the second according to the current sort order, and 1 otherwise.
substring(str,pos,len) *substring(str FROM pos FOR len)* *mid(str,pos,len)*	Returns a substring 10 characters long from string *str*, starting at position *pos*. The variant form that uses *FROM* is ANSI SQL92 syntax.

Functions

Table 4-8: MySQL-Supported Functions (continued)

Function	Description
substring_index (str,delim,count)	Returns the substring from string *str* after *count* occurrences of the delimiter *delim*. If *count* is positive, everything to the left of the final delimiter (counting from the left) is returned. If *count* is negative, everything to the right of the final delimiter (counting from the right) is returned.
substring(str,pos) substring(str FROM pos)	Returns a substring from string *str* starting at position *pos*.
sum(expr)	Returns the sum of *expr*. Note that if the return set has no rows, it returns NULL.
tan(X).	Returns the tangent of *X*, where *X* is given in radians.
time_format (time,format)	This is used like *DATE_FORMAT()*, but the format string may contain only those format specifiers that handle hours, minutes, and seconds. Other specifiers produce a NULL value or 0.
time_to_sec(time)	Returns the time argument, converted to seconds.
to_days(date)	Given a date, returns a daynumber (the number of days since year 0).
trim([[BOTH | LEADING | TRAILING] [remstr] FROM] str)	Returns the string *str* with all *remstr* prefixes and/or suffixes removed. If none of the specifiers *BOTH, LEADING,* or *TRAILING* are given, *BOTH* is assumed. If *remstr* is not specified, spaces are removed.
truncate(X,D)	Returns the number *X*, truncated to *D* decimals. If *D* is 0, the result has no decimal point or fractional part.
ucase(str) upper(str)	Returns the string *str* with all characters changed to uppercase according to the current character set mapping (default is ISO-8859-1 Latin1).
unix_timestamp() unix_timestamp(date)	If called with no argument, returns a Unix timestamp (seconds since '1970-01-01 00:00:00' GMT). If *UNIX_TIMESTAMP()* is called with a date argument, it returns the value of the argument as seconds since '1970-01-01 00:00:00' GMT.
user() system_user() session_user()	These functions return the current MySQL username.
version()	Returns a string indicating the MySQL server version.
week(date) week(date,first)	With a single argument, returns the week for date, in the range 0 to 53. (The beginning of a week 53 is possible during some years.) The two-argument form of *WEEK()* allows the user to specify whether the week starts on Sunday (0) or Monday (1).
weekday(date)	Returns the weekday index for date (0 = Monday, 1 = Tuesday, . . . 6 = Sunday).
year(date)	Returns the year for date, in the range 1000 to 9999.
yearweek(date) yearweek(date,first)	Returns year and week for a date. The second argument works exactly like the second argument to *WEEK()*. Note that the year may be different from the year in the date argument for the first and the last week of the year.

Oracle SQL-Supported Functions

Table 4-9 provides an alphabetical listing of the SQL functions specific to Oracle.

Table 4-9: Oracle-Supported Functions

Function	Description
abs(number)	Returns the absolute value of *number*.
acos(number)	Returns the arc cosine of *number* ranging from −1 to 1. The result ranges from 0 to π and is expressed in radians.
add_months(date, int)	Returns the date *date* plus *int* months.
ascii(string)	Returns the decimal value in the database character set of the first character of *string*; returns an ASCII value when the database character set is 7-bit ASCII; returns EBCDIC values if the database character set is EBCDIC Code Page 500.
asin(number)	Returns the arc sine of *number* ranging from −1 to 1. The resulting value ranges from $-\pi/2$ to $\pi/2$ and is expressed in radians.
atan(number)	Returns the arctangent of any *number*. The resulting value ranges from $-\pi/2$ to $p/2$ and is expressed in radians.
atan2(number,nbr)	Returns the arctangent of *number* and *nbr*. The values for *number* and *nbr* are not restricted, but the results range from $-\pi$ to π and are expressed in radians.
avg([DISTINCT] expression) over (analytics)	Returns the average value of *expr*. It can be used as an aggregate or analytic function (analytic functions are beyond the scope of this text).
bfilename('directory','file name')	Returns a *BFILE* locator associated with a physical LOB binary *filename* on the server's filesystem in *directory*.
ceil(number)	Returns smallest integer greater than or equal to *number*.
chartorowid(char)	Converts a value from a character datatype (*CHAR* or *VARCHAR2* datatype) to *ROWID* datatype.
chr(number [USING NCHAR_CS])	Returns the character having the binary equivalent to *number* in either the database character set (if *USING NCHAR_CS* is not included) or the national character set (if *USING NCHAR_CS* is included).
concat(string1, string2)	Returns *string1* concatenated with *string2*. It is equivalent to the concatenation operator (| |).
convert(char_value, target_char_set, source_char_set)	Converts a character string from one character set to another; returns the *char_value* in the *target_char_set* after converting *char_value* from the *source_char_set*.
corr(expression1, expression2) over (analytics)	Returns the correlation coefficient of a set of numbered pairs (*expressions* 1 and 2). It can be used as an aggregate or analytic function (analytic functions are beyond the scope of this text).
cos(number)	Returns the cosine of *number* as an angle expressed in radians.
cosh(number)	Returns the hyperbolic cosine of *number*.
count	Returns the number of rows in the query; refer to the earlier section on *COUNT* for more information.
covar_pop(expression1, expression2) over (analytics)	Returns the population covariance of a set of number pairs (*expressions* 1 and 2). It can be used as an aggregate or analytic function (analytic functions are beyond the scope of this text).
covar_samp(expression1, expression2) over(analytics)	Returns the sample covariance of a set of number pairs (*expressions* 1 and 2). It can be used as an aggregate or analytic function (analytic functions are beyond the scope of this text).
cume_dist( ) ([OVER (query)] ORDER BY...)	The cumulative distribution function computes the relative position of a specified value in a group of values.

Table 4-9: Oracle-Supported Functions (continued)

Function	Description
decode(expr search , result [,. n] [,default])	Compares *expr* to the search value; if *expr* is equal to a search, returns the result. Without a match, *DECODE* returns default, or *NULL* if default is omitted. Refer to Oracle documentation for more details.
dense_rank( ) ([OVER (query)] ORDER BY...)	Computes the rank of each row returned from a query with respect to the other rows, based on the values of the *value_ exprs* in the *ORDER_BY_clause*.
deref(expression)	Returns the object reference of *expression*, where *expression* must return a *REF* to an object.
dump(expression [,return_format [, starting_at [,length]]])	Returns a *VARCHAR2* value containing a datatype code, length in bytes, and internal representation of *expression*. The resulting value is returned in the format of *return_format*.
*empth[B	C]lob( )*	Returns an empty LOB locator that can be used to initialize a LOB variable. It can also be used to initialize a LOB column or attribute to empty in an *INSERT* or *UPDATE* statement.
exp(number)	Returns *E* raised to the *number*ed power, where E = 2.71828183.
first_value(expression) over (analytics)	Returns the first value in an ordered set of values.
floor(number)	Returns largest integer equal to or less than *number*.
greatest(expression [,...n])	Returns the greatest of the list of *expressions*. All *expressions* after the first are implicitly converted to the datatype of the first *expression* before the comparison.
grouping(expression)	Distinguishes null cause by a super-aggregation in *GROUP BY* extension from an actual null value.
hextoraw(string)	Converts *string* containing hexadecimal digits into a raw value.
initcap(string)	Returns *string*, with the first letter of each word in uppercase and all other letters in lowercase.
instr(string1, string2, start_at, occurrence)	Searches one character string for another character string. *INSRT* search *char1* with a starting position of *start_at* (an integer) looking for the numeric *occurrence* within *string2*. Returns the position of the character in *string1* that is the first character of this occurrence.
instrb(string1, string2, [start_a[t, occurrence]])	The same as *INSTR*, except that *start_at* and the return value are expressed in bytes instead of characters.
lag(expression [,offset][,default]) over(analytics)	Provides access to more than one row of a table at the same time without a self join; refer to the vendor documentation for more information.
last_day(date)	Returns the date of the last day of the month that contains *date*.
last_value(expression) over (analytics)	Returns the last value in an ordered set of values; refer to the vendor documentation for more information.
lead(expression [,offset][,default]) over(analytics)	Provides access to more than one row of a table at the same time without a self join. Analytic functions are beyond the scope of this text.
least(expression [,...n])	Returns the least of the list of *expressions*.
length(string)	Returns the integer length of *string*, or null if *string* is null.
lengthb(string)	Returns the length of *char* in bytes; otherwise, the same as *LENGTH*.
ln(number)	Returns the natural logarithm of *number*, where the *number* is greater than 0.

Table 4-9: Oracle-Supported Functions (continued)

Function	Description
log(base_number, number)	Returns the logarithm of any *base_number* of *number*.
lower(string)	Returns *string* in the same datatype as it was supplied with all characters lowercase.
lpad(string1, number [,string2])	Returns *string1*, left-padded to length *number* using characters in *string2*; *string2* defaults to a single blank.
ltrim(string[, set])	Removes all characters in *set* from the left of *string. Set* defaults to a single blank.
make_ref({table_name | view_name}, key [,...n])	Creates a reference (*REF*) to a row of an object view or a row in an object table whose object identifier is primary key-based.
max([DISTINCT] expression) over (analytics)	Returns maximum value of *expression*. It can be used as an aggregate or analytic function (analytic functions are beyond the scope of this text).
min([DISTINCT] expression) over (analytics)	Returns minimum value of *expression*. It can be used as an aggregate or analytic function (analytic functions are beyond the scope of this text).
mod(dividend, divider)	Returns remainder of *dividend* divided by *divider*; returns the *dividend* if *divider* is 0.
months_between (date1, date2)	Returns number of months between dates *date1* and *date2*. When *date1* is later than *date2*, the result is positive. If it is earlier, the result is negative.
new_time(date, time_ zone1, time_zone2)	Returns the date and time in *time_zone2* when date and time in *time_zone1* are *date. Time_zones* 1 and 2 may be any of these text strings: • AST, ADT: Atlantic Standard or Daylight Time • BST, BDT: Bering Standard or Daylight Time • CST, CDT: Central Standard or Daylight Time • EST, EDT: Eastern Standard or Daylight Time • GMT: Greenwich Mean Time • HST, HDT: Alaska-Hawaii Standard Time or Daylight Time • MST, MDT: Mountain Standard or Daylight Time • NST: Newfoundland Standard Time • PST, PDT: Pacific Standard or Daylight Time • YST, YDT: Yukon Standard or Daylight Time
next_day(date, string)	Returns the date of the first weekday named by *string* that is later than *date*. The argument *string* must be either the full name or the abbreviation of a day of the week in the date language of the session.
nls_charset_decl_ len(bytecnt, csid)	Returns the declaration width (*bytecnt*) of an *NCHAR* column using the character set ID (*csid*) of the column.
nls_charset_id(text)	Returns the NLS character set ID number corresponding to *text*.
nls_charset_ name(number)	Returns the *VARCHAR2* name for the NLS character set corresponding to the ID *number*.
nls_initcap(string [,'nlsparameter'])	Returns *string* with the first letter of each word in uppercase and all other letters in lowercase. The *nlsparameter* offers special linguistic sorting features.
nls_lower(string, [,'nlsparameter'])	Returns *string* with all letters lowercase. The *nlsparameter* offers special linguistic sorting features.
nlssort(string [,'nlsparameter'])	Returns the string of bytes used to sort *string*. The *nlsparameter* offers special linguistic sorting features.
nls_upper string [,'nlsparameter'])	Returns *string* with all letters uppercase. The *nlsparameter* offers special linguistic sorting features.

Table 4-9: Oracle-Supported Functions (continued)

Function	Description
ntile(expression) over (query_partition ORDER BY...)	Divides an ordered data set into a number of buckets numbered 1 to *expression* and assigns the appropriate bucket number to each row.
numtodsinterval (number, 'string')	Converts *number* to an *INTERVAL DAY TO SECOND* literal, where *number* is a number or an expression resolving to a number, such as a numeric datatype column.
numtoyminterval (number, 'string')	Converts *number* to an *INTERVAL DAY TO MONTH* literal, where *number* is a number or an expression resolving to a number, such as a numeric datatype column.
nvl(expression1, expression2)	If *expression1* is null, *expression2* is returned in the place of a null value. Otherwise, *expression1* is returned. The expressions may be any datatype.
nvl2(expression1, expression2, expression3)	Similar to *NLV*, except that if *expression1* is not null, *expression2* is returned. If *expression1* is null, *expression3* is returned. The expressions may be any datatype, except *LONG*.
percent_rank( ) over (query_partition ORDER BY...)	Similar to the *CUME_DIST* analytical function. Rather than return the cumulative distribution, it returns the percentage rank of a row compared to the others in its result set. Refer to the vendor documentation for more assistance.
power(number, power)	Returns *number* raised to the nth *power*. The base and the exponent can be any numbers, but if *number* is negative, *power* must be an integer.
rank (value_expression) over (query_partition ORDER BY ...)	Computes the rank of each row returned from a query with respect to the other rows returned by the query, based on the values of the *value_expression* in the *ORDER_BY_clause*.
ratio_to_report (value_exprs) over (query_partition)	Computes the ratio of a value to the sum of a set of values. If *values_expr* is null, the ratio-to-report value also is null.
rawtohex(raw)	Converts a *raw* value to a string (character datatype) of its hexadecimal equivalent.
ref(table_alias)	*REF* takes a table alias associated with a row from a table or view. A special reference value is returned for the object instance that is bound to the variable or row.
reftohex(expression)	Converts argument *expression* to a character value containing its hexadecimal equivalent.
regr_ xxx(expression1, expression2) over (analytics)	Linear regression functions fit an ordinary-least-squares regression line to a set of number pairs where *expression1* is the dependent variable and *expression2* is the independent variable. The linear regression functions are: • REGR_SLOPE: returns the slope of the line • REGR_INTERCEPT: returns the y-intercept of the regression line • REGR_COUNT: returns the number of non-null pairs fitting the regression line • REGR_R2: returns the coefficient of determination for the regression • REGR_AVGX: returns the average of the independent variable • REGR_AVGY: returns the average of the dependent variable • REGR_SXX: calculates *REGR_COUNT(exp1, exp2) * VAR_POP(exp2)* • REGR_SYY: calculates *REGR_COUNT(exp1, exp2) * VAR_POP(exp1)* • REGR_SXY: calculates *REGR_COUNT(exp1, exp2) * COVAR_POP(exp1, exp2)* These can be used as aggregate or analytic functions.

Table 4-9: Oracle-Supported Functions (continued)

Function	Description
replace(string, search_string [,replacement_string])	Returns *string* with every occurrence of *search_string* replaced with *replacement_string*.
round (number, decimal)	Returns *number* rounded to *decimal* places right of the decimal point. When *decimal* is omitted, *number* is rounded to 0 places. Note that *decimal*, an integer, can be negative to round off digits left of the decimal point.
round (date[, format])	Returns the *date* rounded to the unit specified by the format model *format*. When *format* is omitted, *date* is rounded to the nearest day.
row_number ( ) over (query_partition ORDER BY ...)	Assigns a unique number to each row where it is applied in the ordered sequence of rows specified by the *ORDER_BY_ clause*, beginning with 1.
rowidtochar(rowid)	Converts a *rowid* value to *VARCHAR2* datatype, 18 characters long.
rpad(string1, number [, string2])	Returns *string1*, right-padded to length *number* with the value of *string2*, repeated as needed. *String2* defaults to a single blank.
rtrim(string[,set])	Returns *string*, with all the rightmost characters that appear in *set* removed; *set* defaults to a single blank.
sign(number)	When *number* < 0, returns –1. When *number* = 0, returns 0. When *number* > 0, returns 1.
sin(number)	Returns the sine of *number* as an angle expressed in radians.
sinh(number)	Returns the hyperbolic sine of *number*.
soundex(string)	Returns a character string containing the phonetic representation of *string*. This function allows words that are spelled differently but sound alike in English to be compared for equality.
sqrt(number)	Returns square root of *number*, a nonnegative number.
stddev([DISTINCT] expression) over (analytics)	Returns sample standard deviation of a set of numbers shown as *expression*.
stdev_pop(expression) over (analytics)	Computes the population standard deviation and returns the square root of the population variance.
seddev_samp(expression) over (analytics)	Computes the cumulative sample standard deviation and returns the square root of the sample variance.
substr(extraction_string [FROM starting_position] [FOR length])	Refer to the earlier section on *SUBSTR*.
substrb(extraction_string [FROM starting_position] [FOR length])	*SUBSTRB* is the same as *SUBSTR*, except that the arguments *m starting_position* and *length* are expressed in bytes, rather than in characters.
sum([DISTINCT] expression) over (analytics)	Returns sum of values of *expr*; refer to vendor documentation for assistance with analytics and the *OVER* subclause.
sys_context ('namespace','attribute' [,length])	Returns the value of *attribute* associated with the context *namespace*, usable in both SQL and PL/SQL statements.
sys_guid( )	Generates and returns a globally unique identifier (*RAW* value) made up of 16 bytes.
sysdate	Returns the current date and time, requiring no arguments.
tan(number)	Returns the tangent of *number* as an angle expressed in radians.

Functions

Table 4-9: Oracle-Supported Functions (continued)

Function	Description
tanh(number)	Returns the hyperbolic tangent of *number*
to_char (date [, format [, 'nls_parameter']])	Converts *date* to a *VARCHAR2* in the format specified by the date format *format*. When *fmt* is omitted, *date* is converted to the default date format. The *nls_parameter* option offers additional control over formatting options.
to_char (number [, format [, 'nls_parameter']])	Converts *number* to a *VARCHAR2* in the format specified by the number format *format*. When *fmt* is omitted, *number* is converted to a string long enough to hold the *number*. The *nls_parameter* option offers additional control over formatting options.
to_date(string [, format [, 'nls_parameter']])	Converts *string* (in *CHAR* or *VARCHAR2*) to a *DATE* datatype. The *nls_parameter* option offers additional control over formatting options.
to_lob(long_column)	Usable only by *LONG* or *LONG RAW* expressions, it converts *LONG* or *LONG RAW* values in the column *long_column* to LOB values. It is usable only in the *SELECT* list of a subquery in an *INSERT* statement.
to_multi_byte(string)	Returns *string* with all of its single-byte characters converted to their corresponding multi-byte characters.
to_number(string [, format [,'nls_parameter']])	Converts a numeric *string* (of *CHAR* or *VARCHAR2* datatype) to a value of a NUMBER datatype in the format specified by the optional format model *format*. The *nls_parameter* option offers additional control over formatting options.
to_single_byte(string)	Returns *string* with all of its multi-byte characters converted to their corresponding single-byte characters.
translate('char_value', 'from_text', 'to_text')	Returns *char_value* with all occurrences of each character in *from_text* replaced by its corresponding character in *to_text*; refer to the section "CONVERT and TRANSLATE" earlier in this chapter for more information on *TRANSLATE*.
translate (text USING [CHAR_CS | NCHAR_CS])	Converts *text* into the character set specified for conversions between the database character set or the national character set.
trim([[LEADING | TRAILING | BOTH] trim_char | trim_char] FROM trim_source])	Enables leading or trailing characters (or both) to be trimmed from a character string.
trunc (base [, number])	Returns *base* truncated to *number* decimal places. When *number* is omitted, *base* is truncated to 0 places. *Number* can be negative to truncate (make zero) *number* digits left of the decimal point.
trunc (date [, format])	Returns *date* with any time data truncated to the unit specified by *format*. When *format* is omitted, *date* is truncated to the nearest whole day.
uid	Returns an integer that uniquely identifies the session user who logged on. No parameters are needed.
upper(string)	Returns *string* with all letters in uppercase.
user	Returns the name of the session user who logged on in *VARCHAR2*.
userenv(option)	Returns information about the current session in *VARCHAR2*.
value(table_alias)	Takes as a table alias associated with a row in an object table and returns object instances stored within the object table.
var_pop(expression) over (analytics)	Returns the population variance of a set of numbers after discarding the nulls in the *expression* number set. Analytic functions are covered in the vendor documentation.

Table 4-9: Oracle-Supported Functions (continued)

Function	Description
var_samp(expression) over (analytics)	Returns the sample variance of a set of numbers after discarding the nulls in the *expression* number set. Analytic functions are covered in the vendor documentation.
variance([DISTINCT] expression) over (analytics)	Returns variance of *expression* calculated as follows: • 0 if the number of rows in *expression* = 1 • *VAR_SAMP* if the number of rows in *expression* > 1
vsize(expression)	Returns the number of bytes in the internal representation of *expression*. When *expression* is null, it returns null.

PostgreSQL-Supported Functions

Table 4-10 lists the functions specific to PostgreSQL.

Table 4-10: PostgreSQL–Supported Functions

Function	Description
abstime(timestamp)	Converts to abstime
abs(float8)	Returns absolute value
acos(float8)	Returns arccosine
age(timestamp)	Preserves months and years
age(timestamp, timestamp)	Preserves months and years
area(object)	Returns area of item
asin(float8)	Returns arcsine
atan(float8)	Returns arctangent
atan2(float8,float8)	Returns arctangent
box(box,box)	Returns intersection box
box(circle)	Converts circle to box
box(point,point)	Returns points to box
box(polygon)	Converts polygon to box
broadcast(cidr)	Constructs broadcast address as text
broadcast(inet)	Constructs broadcast address as text
CASE WHEN expr THEN expr [...] ELSE expr END	Returns expression for first true *WHEN* clause
cbrt(float8)	Returns cube root
center(object)	Returns center of item
char(text)	Converts text to char type
char(varchar)	Converts varchar to char type
char_length(string)	Returns length of string
character_length(string)	Returns length of string
circle(box)	Converts to circle
circle(point,float8)	Converts point to circle
COALESCE(list)	Returns first non-NULL value in list
cos(float8)	Returns cosine
cot(float8)	Returns cotangent

Table 4-10: PostgreSQL–Supported Functions (continued)

Function	Description
date_part(text,timestamp)	Returns portion of date
date_part(text,interval)	Returns portion of time
date_trunc(text,timestamp)	Truncates date
degrees(float8)	Converts radians to degrees
diameter(circle)	Returns diameter of circle
exp(float8)	Raises *e* to the specified exponent
float(int)	Converts integer to floating point
float4(int)	Converts integer to floating point
height(box)	Returns vertical size of box
host(inet)	Extracts host address as text
initcap(text)	Converts first letter of each word to uppercase
interval(reltime)	Converts to interval
integer(float)	Converts floating point to integer
isclosed(path)	Returns a closed path
isopen(path)	Returns an open path
isfinite(timestamp)	Returns a finite time
isfinite(interval)	Returns a finite time
length(object)	Returns length of item
ln(float8)	Returns natural logarithm
log(float8)	Returns base-10 logarithm
lower(string)	Converts string to lowercase
lseg(box)	Converts box diagonal to lseg
lseg(point,point)	Converts points to lseg
lpad(text,int,text)	Returns left-pad string to specified length
ltrim(text,text)	Returns left-trim characters from text
masklen(cidr)	Calculates netmask length
masklen(inet)	Calculates netmask length
netmask(inet)	Constructs netmask as text
npoint(path)	Returns number of points
NULLIF(input,value)	Returns NULL if input = value, else returns input
octet_length(string)	Returns storage length of string
path(polygon)	Converts polygon to path
pclose(path)	Converts path to closed
pi()	Returns fundamental constant
polygon(box)	Returns 12-point polygon
polygon(circle)	Returns 12-point polygon
polygon(npts,circle)	Returns npts polygon
polygon(path)	Converts path to polygon
point(circle)	Returns center
point(lseg,lseg)	Returns intersection
point(polygon)	Returns center

Table 4-10: PostgreSQL–Supported Functions (continued)

Function	Description
position(string in string)	Returns location of specified substring
pow(float8,float8)	Raises a number to the specified exponent
popen(path)	Converts path to open path
reltime(interval)	Converts to reltime
radians(float8)	Converts degrees to radians
radius(circle)	Returns radius of circle
round(float8)	Rounds to nearest integer
rpad(text,int,text)	Converts right pad string to specified length
rtrim(text,text)	Converts right trim characters from text
sin(float8)	Returns sine
sqrt(float8)	Returns square root
substring(string [from int] [for int])	Extracts specified substring
substr(text,int[,int])	Extracts specified substring
tan(float8)	Returns tangent
text(char)	Converts char to text type
text(varchar)	Converts varchar to text type
textpos(text,text)	Locates specified substring
timestamp(date)	Converts to timestamp
timestamp(date,time)	Converts to timestamp
to_char(timestamp, text)	Converts timestamp to string
to_char(int, text)	Converts int4/int8 to string
to_char(float, text)	Converts float4/float8 to string
to_char(numeric, text)	Converts numeric to string
to_date(text, text)	Converts string to date
to_number(text, text)	Converts string to numeric
to_timestamp(text, text)	Converts string to timestamp
translate(text,from,to)	Converts character in string
trim([leading |trailing | both] [string] from string)	Trims characters from string
trunc(float8)	Truncates (towards zero)
upper(text)	Converts text to uppercase
varchar(char)	Converts char to varchar type
varchar(text)	Converts text to varchar type
width(box)	Returns horizontal size

Functions

CHAPTER 5

Unimplemented SQL99 Commands

The SQL92 and SQL99 standards specify many commands. However, RMBDS vendors are not able to implement all of them immediately. In fact, many commands specified in the new SQL99 standard are nowhere near being implemented by any of the database vendors covered in *SQL in a Nutshell*. In effect, these commands exist because the standard says they exist, but they cannot currently be executed anywhere. As a result, these commands are described only briefly in Table 5-1.

Nonetheless, it should be noted that although these commands are not implemented yet, they could be eventually. Consequently, it is important to check vendor documentation to see if the newest version has implemented any of these commands.

Table 5-1: Unimplemented SQL99 Commands

Commands	Description
ALLOCATE CURSOR	The *ALLOCATE CURSOR* statement is used in Dynamic SQL to link a *SELECT* statement initialized with the *PREPARE* statement. This statement differs from *DECLARE CURSOR* in that *ALLOCATE CURSOR* creates multiple precompiled cursor statements while *DECLARE CURSOR* is created and compiled dynamically each time it is run.
ALLOCATE DESCRIPTOR	This statement prepares a dynamic area that stores information about the parameters in a dynamically generated SQL statement. In effect, this command allows the amount of space set aside for dynamic SQL statements to be controlled precisely.

Table 5-1: Unimplemented SQL99 Commands (continued)

Commands	Description
ALTER DOMAIN	A domain is generally a user-defined datatype. According to the SQL99 standard, the *ALTER DOMAIN* command allows the definition of a domain to be changed by adding or dropping a default or constraint. Typically, only the owner of the schema that contains the domain may alter it. Any changes specified with the command instantly affect all columns based on the domain.
CREATE ASSERTION	An assertion is a generic *CHECK* constraint that may be applied over and over again. Thus, a check constraint that controls the **emp_id** column can be applied as an assertion in every table that holds **emp_id**. This command is not supported by the database vendors covered in this book; however, Microsoft SQL Server supports the *CREATE RULE* statement, which is functionally equivalent.
CREATE CHARACTER SET	This statement creates individualized character sets for improved internationalization of a database platform. However, most vendors ship their products with a wide range of character sets. Although some make it possible to create or change character sets, they do not support this command.
CREATE COLLATION	A collating sequence determines the order in which text strings are sorted. Like character sets, the database platform normally ships with one or more collations. This command creates new sorting sequences for a given character set.
CREATE TRANSLATION	A translation is a descriptor that translates strings from one character set to another. Character strings then can be translated using the *TRANSLATE* command. New translations based upon old ones can be built using this command.
DEALLOCATE DESCRIPTOR	This statement removes a previously declared descriptor created using *ALLOCATE DESCRIPTOR*.
DEALLOCATE PREPARE	This statement destroys a previously prepared SQL statement created using the *PREPARE* statement.
DESCRIBE	This command stores parameterized information about a SQL statement held in the named descriptor area created using the *ALLOCATE DESCRIPTOR* statement. Note: Oracle possesses a *DESCRIBE* command that is used to report information on a table, describing its columns, datatypes, and so on.
DROP ASSERTION	This statement removes an assertion from the database that was previously created using the *CREATE ASSERTION* statement.
DROP CHARACTER SET	This command removes a character set from the database that was previously created using the *CREATE CHARACTER SET* statement.
DROP COLLATION	This statement removes a collation from the database that was previously created using the *CREATE COLLATION* statement.
DROP TRANSLATION	This command removes a translation from the database that was previously created using the *CREATE TRANSLATION* statement.
GET DESCRIPTOR	The *GET DESCRIPTOR* statement retrieves information from the descriptor areas, primarily about input and output parameters used in Dynamical SQL statements.
GET DIAGNOSTICS	The *GET DIAGNOSTICS* command provides information (taken from the diagnostics area) about the last SQL statement executed or about a specific error message encountered while processing a SQL statement.

New
Commands

Table 5-1: Unimplemented SQL99 Commands (continued)

Commands	Description
PREPARE	The *PREPARE* statement creates a Dynamic SQL from a text variable so that it can be executed many times using the *EXECUTE* command.
SET CATALOG	This command defines the current catalog, which holds the current schema, used by the current session.
SET CONSTRAINTS MODE	This statement determines whether constraints are checked immediately upon completion of a transaction or deferred until the end of the transaction. Constraints also might be checked immediately, meaning after each statement. Many vendors offer alternative methods for achieving this sort of functionality. For example, Oracle offers this functionality through the command *ALTER SESSION SET CONSTRAINTS*. Research the vendor documentation for other possible alternatives.
SET DESCRIPTOR	The *SET DESCRIPTOR* statement places values into previously allocated cursors or alters the behavior of a descriptor.
SET NAMES	This command sets the default character set for a session.
SET SESSION AUTHORIZATION	The *SET SESSION AUTHORIZATION* statement alters the authorization under which statements are processed.
SET SESSION CHARACTERISTICS	The *SET SESSION CHARACTERISTICS* statement allows the same properties to be set for all of the transactions processed in an entire session, just like using other *SET* statements for a single transaction.

APPENDIX

SQL99 and Vendor-Specific Keywords

The tables below display the keywords in the SQL99 standard and in the four vendor implementations of SQL that are discussed in this book. SQL keywords are described in more detail in Chapter 2, *Foundational Concepts*.

Table A-1: SQL Keywords

ABSOLUTE	ACTION	ADD	ADMIN
AFTER	AGGREGATE	ALIAS	ALL
ALLOCATE	ALTER	AND	ANY
ARE	ARRAY	AS	ASC
ASSERTION	AT	AUTHORIZA-TION	BEFORE
BEGIN	BINARY	BIT	BLOB
BOOLEAN	BOTH	BREADTH	BY
CALL	CASCADE	CASCADED	CASE
CAST	CATALOG	CHAR	CHARACTER
CHECK	CLASS	CLOB	CLOSE
COLLATE	COLLATION	COLUMN	COMMIT
COMPLETION	CONDITION	CONNECT	CONNECTION
CONSTRAINT	CONSTRAINTS	CONSTRUCTOR	CONTAINS
CONTINUE	CORRE-SPONDING	CREATE	CROSS
CUBE	CURRENT	CURRENT_DATE	CURRENT_PATH
CURRENT_ROLE	CURRENT_TIME	CURRENT_TIMESTAMP	CURRENT_USER
CURSOR	CYCLE	DATA	DATALINK
DATE	DAY	DEALLOCATE	DEC
DECIMAL	DECLARE	DEFAULT	DEFERRABLE
DELETE	DEPTH	DEREF	DESC
DESCRIPTOR	DIAGNOSTICS	DICTIONARY	DISCONNECT
DO	DOMAIN	DOUBLE	DROP
END-EXEC	EQUALS	ESCAPE	EXCEPT
EXCEPTION	EXECUTE	EXIT	EXPAND
EXPANDING	FALSE	FIRST	FLOAT

Table A-1: SQL Keywords (continued)

FOR	FOREIGN	FREE	FROM
FUNCTION	GENERAL	GET	GLOBAL
GOTO	GROUP	GROUPING	HANDLER
HASH	HOUR	IDENTITY	IF
IGNORE	IMMEDIATE	IN	INDICATOR
INITIALIZE	INITIALLY	INNER	INOUT
INPUT	INSERT	INT	INTEGER
INTERSECT	INTERVAL	INTO	IS
ISOLATION	ITERATE	JOIN	KEY
LANGUAGE	LARGE	LAST	LATERAL
LEADING	LEAVE	LEFT	LESS
LEVEL	LIKE	LIMIT	LOCAL
LOCALTIME	LOCALTIME-STAMP	LOCATOR	LOOP
MATCH	MEETS	MINUTE	MODIFIES
MODIFY	MODULE	MONTH	NAMES
NATIONAL	NATURAL	NCHAR	NCLOB
NEW	NEXT	NO	NONE
NORMALIZE	NOT	NULL	NUMERIC
OBJECT	OF	NUMERIC	OBJECT
OF	OFF	OLD	ON
ONLY	OPEN	OPERATION	OPTION
OR	ORDER	ORDINALITY	OUT
OUTER	OUTPUT	PAD	PARAMETER
PARAMETERS	PARTIAL	PATH	PERIOD
POSTFIX	PRECEDES	PRECISION	PREFIX
PREORDER	PREPARE	PRESERVE	PRIMARY
PRIOR	PRIVILEGES	PROCEDURE	PUBLIC
READ	READS	REAL	RECURSIVE
REDO	REF	REFERENCES	REFERENCING
RELATIVE	REPEAT	RESIGNAL	RESTRICT
RESULT	RETURN	RETURNS	REVOKE
RIGHT	ROLE	ROLLBACK	ROLLUP
ROUTINE	ROW	ROWS	SAVEPOINT
SCHEMA	SCROLL	SEARCH	SECOND
SECTION	SELECT	SEQUENCE	SESSION
SESSION_USER	SET	SETS	SIGNAL
SIZE	SMALLINT	SPECIFIC	SPECIFICTYPE
SQL	SQLEXCEPTION	SQLSTATE	SQLWARNING
START	STATE	STATIC	STRUCTURE
SUCCEEDS	SUM	SYSTEM_USER	TABLE
TEMPORARY	TERMINATE	THAN	THEN
TIME	TIMESTAMP	TIMEZONE_HOUR	TIMEZONE_MINUTE
TO	TRAILING	TRANSACTION	TRANSLATION
TREAT	TRIGGER	TRUE	UNDER
UNDO	UNION	UNIQUE	UNKNOWN
UNTIL	UPDATE	USAGE	USER
USING	VALUE	VALUES	VALUES
VARIABLE	VARYING	VIEW	WHEN
WHENEVER	WHERE	WHILE	WITH
WRITE	YEAR	ZONE	

Table A-2: Microsoft SQL Server Keywords

ADD	ALL	ALTER	AND
ANY	AS	ASC	AUTHORIZATION
BACKUP	BEGIN	BETWEEN	BREAK
BROWSE	BULK	BY	CASCADE
CASE	CHECK	CHECKPOINT	CLOSE
CLUSTERED	COALESCE	COLLATE	COLUMN
COMMIT	COMPUTE	CONSTRAINT	CONTAINS
CONTAINSTABLE	CONTINUE	CONVERT	CREATE
CROSS	CURRENT	CURRENT_DATE	CURRENT_TIME
CURRENT_TIMES-TAMP	CURRENT_USER	CURSOR	DATABASE
DBCC	DEALLOCATE	DECLARE	DEFAULT
DELETE	DENY	DESC	DISK
DISTINCT	DISTRIBUTED	DOUBLE	DROP
DUMMY	DUMP	ELSE	END
ERRLVL	EXCEPT	EXEC	EXECUTE
EXISTS	EXIT	FETCH	FILE
FILLFACTOR	FOR	FOREIGN	FREETEXT
FREETEXTTABLE	FROM	FULL	FUNCTION
GOTO	GRANT	GROUP	HAVING
HOLDLOCK	IDENTITY	IDENTITY_INSERT	IDENTITY_INSERT
IF	IN	INDEX	INNER
INSERT	INTERSECT	INTO	IS
JOIN	KEY	KILL	LEFT
LIKE	LINENO	LOAD	NATIONAL
NOCHECK	NONCLUSTERED	NONCLUSTERED	NULL
NULLIF	OF	OF	OFFSETS
ON	OPEN	OPENDATA-SOURCE	OPENQUERY
OPENROWSET	OPENXML	OPTION	OR
ORDER	OUTER	PERCENT	PLAN
PRECISION	PRIMARY	PRINT	PROC
READTEXT	RECONFIGURE	REFERENCES	REPLICATION
RESTORE	RESTRICT	RETURN	REVOKE
RIGHT	ROLLBACK	ROWCOUNT	ROWGUID-COL
RULE	SAVE	SCHEMA	SELECT
SESSION_USER	SET	SETUSER	SHUTDOWN
SOME	STATISTICS	SYSTEM_USER	TABLE
TEXTSIZE	THEN	TO	TOP
TRAN	TRANSACTION	TRIGGER	TRUNCATE
TSEQUAL	UNION	UNIQUE	UPDATE
UPDATETEXT	USE	USER	VALUES
VARYING	VIEW	WAITFOR	WHEN
WHERE	WHILE	WITH	WRITETEXT

Table A-3: MySQL Keywords

ACTION	ADD	AFTER	AGGREGATE
ALL	ALTER	AND	AS
ASC	AUTO_INCREMENT	AVG	AVG_ROW_LENGTH
BETWEEN	BIGINT	BINARY	BIT
BLOB	BOOL	BOTH	BY
CASCADE	CASE	CHANGE	CHAR
CHARACTER	CHECK	CHECKSUM	COLUMN
COLUMNS	COMMENT	CONSTRAINT	CREATE
CROSS	CURRENT_DATE	CURRENT_TIME	CURRENT_TIMESTAMP
DATA	DATABASE	DATABASEs	DATE
DATETIME	DAY	DAY_HOUR	DAY_MINUTE
DAY_SECOND	DAYOFMONTH	DAYOFWEEK	DAYOFYEAR
DEC	DECIMAL	DEFAULT	DELAY_KEY_WRITE
DELAYED	DELETE	DESC	DESCRIBE
DISTINCT	DISTINCTROW	DOUBLE	DROP
ELSE	ENCLOSED	END	ENUM
ESCAPE	ESCAPED	EXISTS	EXPLAIN
FIELDS	FILE	FIRST	FLOAT
FLOAT4	FLOAT8	FLUSH	FOR
FOREIGN	FROM	FULL	FUNCTION
GLOBAL	GRANT	GRANTS	GROUP
HAVING	HEAP	HIGH_PRIORITY	HOSTS
HOUR	HOUR_MINUTE	HOUR_SECOND	IDENTIFIED
IF	IGNORE	IN	INDEX
INFILE	INNER	INSERT	INSERT_ID
INT	INT1	INT2	INT3
INT4	INT8	INTEGER	INTERVAL
INTO	IS	ISAM	JOIN
KEY	KEYS	KILL	LAST_INSERT_ID
LEADING	LEFT	LENGTH	LIKE
LIMIT	LINES	LOAD	LOCAL
LOCK	LOGS	LONG	LONGBLOB
LONGTEXT	LOW_PRIORITY	MATCH	MAX
MAX_ROWS	MEDIUMBLOB	MEDIUMINT	MEDIUMTEXT
MIDDLEINT	MIN_ROWS	MINUTE	MINUTE_SECOND
MODIFY	MONTH	MONTHNAME	MYISAM
NATURAL	NO	NOT	NULL
NUMERIC	ON	OPTIMIZE	OPTION
OPTIONALLY	OR	ORDER	OUTER
OUTFILE	PACK_KEYS	PARTIAL	PASSWORD
PRECISION	PRIMARY	PRIVILEGES	PROCEDURE

Table A-3: MySQL Keywords (continued)

PROCESS	PROCESSLIST	READ	REAL
REFERENCES	REGEXP	RELOAD	RENAME
REPLACE	RESTRICT	RETURNS	REVOKE
RLIKE	ROW	ROWS	SECOND
SELECT	SET	SHOW	SHUTDOWN
SMALLINT	SONAME	SQL_BIG_RESULT	SQL_BIG_SELECTS
SQL_BIG_TABLES	SQL_LOG_OFF	SQL_LOG_UPDATE	SQL_LOW_ PRIORITY_ UPDATES
SQL_SELECT_LIMIT	SQL_SMALL_ RESULT	SQL_WARNINGS	STARTING
STATUS	STRAIGHT_JOIN	STRING	SQL_SMALL_ RESULT
TABLES	TEMPORARY	TERMINATED	TEXT
THEN	TIME	TIMESTAMP	TINYBLOB
TINYINT	TINYTEXT	TO	TRAILING
TYPE	UNIQUE	UNLOCK	UNSIGNED
UPDATE	USAGE	USE	USING
VALUES	VARBINARY	VARCHAR	VARIABLES
VARYING	WHEN	WITH	WRITE
ZEROFILL			

Table A-4: Oracle Keywords

ACCESS	ADD	ALL	ALTER
AND	ANY	ARRAY	AS
ACS	AUDIT	AUTHID	AVG
BEGIN	BETWEEN	BINARY INTEGER	BODY
BOOLEAN	BULK	BY	CHAR
CHAR_BASE	CHECK	CLOSE	CLUSTER
COLLECT	COLUMN	COMMENT	COMMIT
COMPRESS	CONNECT	CONSTANT	CREATE
CURRENT	CURRVAL	CURSOR	DATE
DAY	DECLARE	DECIMAL	DEFAULT
DELETE	DESC	DISTINCT	DO
DROP	ELSE	ELSIF	END
EXCEPTION	EXCLUSIVE	EXECUTE	EXISTS
EXIT	EXTENDS	FALSE	FETCH
FILE	FLOAT	FOR	FORALL
FROM	FUNCTION	GOTO	GRANT
GROUP	HAVING	HEAP	HOUR
IDENTIFIED	IF	IMMEDIATE	IN
INCREMENT	INDEX	INDICATOR	INITIAL
INSERT	INTEGER	INTERFACE	INTERSECT
INTERVAL	INTO	IS	ISOLATION

Table A-4: Oracle Keywords (continued)

JAVA	LEVEL	LIKE	LIMITED
LOCK	LONG	LOOP	MAX
MAXEXTENTS	MIN	MINUS	MINUTE
MLSLABEL	MOD	MODE	MODIFY
MONTH	NATURAL	NATURALN	NEW
NEXTVAL	NOAUDIT	NOCOMPRESS	NOCOPY
NOT	NOWAIT	NULL	NUMBER
NUMBER_BASE	OCIROWID	OF	OFFLINE
ON	ONLINE	OPAQUE	OPEN
OPERATOR	OPTION	OR	ORDER
ORGANIZATION	OTHERS	OUT	PACKAGE
PARTITION	PCTFREE	PLS_INTEGER	POSITIVE
POSITIVEN	PRAGMA	PRIOR	PRIVATE
PRIVILEGES	PROCEDURE	PUBLIC	RAISE
RANGE	RAW	REAL	RECORD
REF	RELEASE	RENAME	RESOURCE
RETURN	REVERSE	REVOKE	ROLLBACK
ROW	ROWS	ROWID	ROWLABEL
ROWNUM	ROWTYPE	SAVEPOINT	SECOND
SELECT	SEPERATE	SESSION	SET
SHARE	SIZE	SMALLINT	SPACE
SQL	SQLCODE	SQLERRM	START
STDDEV	SUBTYPE	SUCCESSFUL	SUM
SYNONYM	SYSDATE	TABLE	THEN
TIME	TIMESTAMP	TO	TRIGGER
TRUE	TYPE	UID	UNION
UNIQUE	UPDATE	USE	USER
VALIDATE	VALUES	VARCHAR	VARCHAR2
VARIANCE	VIEW	WHEN	WHENEVER
WHERE	WHILE	WITH	WORK
WRITE	YEAR	ZONE	

Table A-5: PostgreSQL Keywords

ABORT	ADD	ALL	ALLOCATE
ALTER	ANALYZE	AND	ANY
ARE	AS	ASC	ASSERTION
AT	AUTHORIZATION	AVG	BEGIN
BETWEEN	BINARY	BIT	BIT_LENGTH
BOTH	BY	CASCADE	CASCADED
CASE	CAST	CATALOG	CHAR
CHAR_LENGTH	CHARACTER	CHARACTER_LENGTH	CHECK
CLOSE	CLUSTER	COALESCE	COLLATE

COLLATION	COLUMN	COMMIT	CONNECT
CONNECTION	CONSTRAINT	CONTINUE	CONVERT
COPY	CORRESPONDING	COUNT	CREATE
CROSS	CURRENT	CURRENT_DATE	CURRENT_SESSION
CURRENT_TIME	CURRENT_TIMESTAMP	CURRENT_USER	CURSOR
DATE	DEALLOCATE	DEC	DECIMAL
DECLARE	DEFAULT	DELETE	DESC
DESCRIBE	DESCRIPTOR	DIAGNOSTICS	DISCONNECT
DISTINCT	DO	DOMAIN	DROP
ELSE	END	ESCAPE	EXCEPT
EXCEPTION	EXEC	EXECUTE	EXISTS
EXPLAIN	EXTEND	EXTERNAL	EXTRACT
FALSE	FETCH	FIRST	FLOAT
FOR	FOREIGN	FOUND	FROM
FULL	GET	GLOBAL	GO
GOTO	GRANT	GROUP	HAVING
IDENTITY	IN	INDICATOR	INNER
INPUT	INSERT	INTERSECT	INTERVAL
INTO	IS	JOIN	LAST
LEADING	LEFT	LIKE	LISTEN
LOAD	LOCAL	LOCK	LOWER
MAX	MIN	MODULE	MOVE
NAMES	NATIONAL	NATURAL	NCHAR
NEW	NO	NONE	NOT
NOTIFY	NULL	NULLIF	NUMERIC
OCTET_LENGTH	OFFSET	ON	OPEN
OR	ORDER	OUTER	OUTPUT
OVERLAPS	PARTIAL	POSITION	PRECISION
PREPARE	PRESERVE	PRIMARY	PRIVILEGES
PROCEDURE	PUBLIC	REFERENCES	RESET
REVOKE	RIGHT	ROLLBACK	ROWS
SCHEMA	SECTION	SELECT	SESSION
SESSION_USER	SET	SETOF	SHOW
SIZE	SOME	SQL	SQLCODE
SQLERROR	SQLSTATE	SUBSTRING	SUBSTRING
SYSTEM_USER	TABLE	TEMPORARY	THEN
TO	TRAILING	TRANSACTION	TRANSLATE
TRANSLATION	TRIM	TRUE	UNION
UNIQUE	UNKNOWN	UNLISTEN	UNTIL
UPDATE	UPPER	USAGE	USER
USING	VACUUM	VALUE	VALUES
VARCHAR	VARYING	VERBOSE	VIEW
WHEN	WHENEVER	WHERE	WITH
WORK	WRITE		

Keywords

Index

Symbols

+ addition arithmetic operator, 121
= assignment operator, 121
* asterisk, 25
@ at symbol, 61
& bitwise AND operator, 122
^ bitwise exclusive OR operator, 122
| bitwise OR operator, 122
: colon, 84
/ division arithmetic operator, 121
' ' double apostrophe, 22
| | double-pipe mark, 46, 170
double-pound sign, 61, 68
" " double quotation marks, 22
= equal to comparison operator, 122
=* equal-asterisk, 135
> greater than operator, 122
>= greater than or equal to operator, 122
< less than operator, 122
<= less than or equal to operator, 122
% modula arithmetic operator, 121
* multiplication arithmetic operator, 121
!= not equal to operator, 122
<> not equal to operator, 122
!> not greater than operator, 122
!< not less than operator, 122
+ outer join operator, 25
+ plus sign, 46, 170
+* plus-asterisk, 135
# pound sign, 61, 68
' ' single quotation marks, 21, 22
- subtraction arithmetic operator, 121
+ unary operator, 123
- unary operator, 123
~ unary operator, 123
_ underscore, 66

A

abbreviations, using consistently, 20
ABSOLUTE operation (FETCH
    statement), 104
access privileges (see privileges)
ADD keyword (PostgreSQL), 36
adding
    columns (PostgreSQL), 36
    records/rows, 115
addition (+) arithmetic operator, 121
aggregate functions, 144, 164–166
ALL clause, DISCONNECT statement
    and, 95
ALL logical operator, 123
alphabetical reference of
        statements, 30–162
    list in table, 28–30
ALTER PROCEDURE statement, 30
ALTER TABLE statement, 32
    multiple clauses issued in (MySQL), 34
ALTER TRIGGER statement, 36
ALTER VIEW statement, 38
altering
    procedures, 30
    tables, 32
    triggers, 36
    views, 38
American National Standards Institute
        (ANSI), 2
AND CHAIN keyword, 45
AND logical operator, 123

anomalies, 155
ANSI (American National Standards Institute), 2
ANSI joins, 25
ANSI standards, 5
ANSI style of joins, 135
ANY logical operator, 123
ANY option (GRANT statement, Oracle), 109
arithmetic operators, 121
AS keyword, assignment operator and, 121
ascending indexes, creating (PostgreSQL), 59
assignment (=) operator, 121
asterisks
    asterisk (*), SQL Server and, 25
    equal-asterisk (=*), 135
    plus-asterisk (+*), 135
at symbol (@) specifying stored procedure input parameters (SQL Server), 61
atomic values, 10
Authorization ID, 10
    function for currently active, 166
AVG aggregate function, 144
AVG function, 164

B

base tables, 24
    (see also tables)
BEGIN TRANSACTION statement, 156
    vs. START TRANSACTION statement and SET TRANSACTION statement, 156
BETWEEN logical operator, 123
binding styles, 7
BIT_LENGTH function, 168
BITMAP indexes (Oracle), 57
bitwise AND (&) operator, 122
bitwise exclusive OR (^) operator, 122
bitwise OR (|) operator, 122
blank spaces, LIKE operator and, 119
BLOBs, MySQL datatypes for, 14
boolean comparison operators, 122
built-in scalar functions, 166

C

CALL statement, 39
Cantor, Georg, 9
CASE function, 40
case of strings, changing, 172
case sensitivity
    LIKE operator and, 118
    naming conventions and, 19

CAST function, 42
    vs. CONVERT function with SQL Server, 171
    vs. CREATE FUNCTION statement, 50
categories of syntax for SQL statements, 19–23
changes committed to databases, DROP TABLE statement and (Oracle), 101
character literals, 21
character sets, 10
    translating, 171
character strings
    converting, 171
    extracting one from another, 173
    leading spaces, removing from, 174
    trailing characters, removing from, 174
CHARACTER_LENGTH function (MySQL, PostgreSQL), 168
CHARINDEX function (SQL Server), 169
CHAR_LENGTH function, 168
CLOSE CURSOR statement, 43
closing server-side cursors, 43
clustered indexes, 56
    as defined in Oracle vs. SQL Server, 58
clusters created with Oracle-specific command, 57
Codd, E.F., 2
    Twelve Principles of Relational Databases, 7, 8
collations, 10
colon (:) prefacing OLD/NEW pseudo-tables, 84
column lists, 87
columns, 1, 10
    ALTER TABLE statement and, 33
        Oracle, 35
        PostgreSQL, 36
    calculated, indexes created on (SQL Server), 56
    multiple
        building indexes upon (MySQL), 57
        comma indicating, 67
        multiple actions to (Oracle), 36
    renaming (MySQL), 34
    retrieving, 132–151
comma
    identifying multiple roles with, 152
    indicating multiple column definitions with, 67
    specifying multiple access privileges with, 105
    SQL and, 21
commands (see statements)

overloading, 55
returning multiple via TABLE datatype
(SQL Server), 52
scalar, 166–170
string, 170–175
terminating processing of, 124
types of, 164–175
user-defined, 163

G

global temporary tables, 68
GRANT statement, 105
contained in CREATE SCHEMA
statement, 65
revoking privileges and, 126
greater than (>) operator, 122
greater than or equal to (>=)
operator, 122
GREATEST function (MySQL), 165
GROUP BY clause (SELECT
statement), 144
SQL Server, 148
groups, revoking privileges of, 125
guidelines for assigning names, 19

H

HAVING clause, 145
aggregate functions and, 166
hierarchical queries, 150
host operating system, function for
currently active user, 166
host-DBMS user, 64

I

identifiers, 19–21
identity rules, 20
IF-THEN-ELSE functionality provided by
CASE function, 40
IN logical operator, 123
indexes
ascending
creating (PostgreSQL), 59
vs. descending (Oracle), 57
BITMAP (Oracle), 57
building upon multiple columns
(MySQL), 57
clustered, as defined in Oracle vs.
SQL Server, 58
creating, 55
dropping, 98
partitioned (Oracle), 58
space required for (SQL Server), 57
spanning several columns, 60
unique (PostgreSQL), 59
INIT.ORA file, 50

inner joins, 136
input parameters
altering, 31
for stored procedures (SQL Server), 61
INSENSITIVE option (SQL Server), 90
INSERT privilege (GRANT statement), 105
INSERT statement, 115
CREATE TRIGGER statement and, 81
LIKE operator and, 118
operators and, 120
INSTR function (Oracle), 169
Intermediate-level conformance, 3
International Standards Organization
(ISO), 2
interval literals (Oracle), 21
INTO clause (Oracle), 40
ISNULL() function (SQL Server), 144
ISO (International Standards
Organization), 2
isolation levels, 154

J

JOIN clause, 25
SELECT statement and, 135
joins, 25, 135–138
NULL values and, 19
Julian calendar, 14

K

keys, 1
keywords, 23
in MySQL, 200
in Oracle, 201
in PostgreSQL, 202
in SQL Server, 199
in SQL99 standard, 197

L

language extensions by vendor
(lists), 175–193
LAST operation (FETCH statement), 103
LEAST function (MySQL), 165
left (outer) joins, 136
length of a column, 57
LENGTHB function (Oracle), 168
less than (<) operator, 122
less than or equal to (<=) operator, 122
levels of conformance, 3
LIKE logical operator, 123
LIKE operator, 118
list item separator, 21
literal values (literals), 21
LOCATE function (MySQL), 169
locks, releasing opened, 44
logical operators, 122

users
    current, functions for, 166
    privileges for
        accessing/using database
            objects, 105
        revoking, 125
    roles, creating for, 63
    specifying user for server, 47
users (data access), 10

V

values
    average of, computing, 164
    minimum/maximum, finding, 165
    sum of, computing, 164
varrays, 76
vector aggregates, 144
vendor implementations, 1, 2
    supplemental features packages
        and, 3–5
vendors
    functions supported by, alphabetical
        listings of, 175–193
    support for SQL99 standard, 28
vendor-specific datatypes, 10–12
views
    altering, 38
    creating, 86

dropping, 102
indexes on (SQL Server), 56
modifications to, allowing
    (SQL Server), 38
operators and, 120
recompiling (Oracle), 38
triggers on, 38
virtual tables (see views)

W

WHERE clause (SELECT statement), 24,
    138–144
    comparison operators and, 122
    DELETE statement and, 92
    vs. HAVING clause, 145, 146
    joins and, 25
    logical operators and, 122
    UPDATE statement and, 159
wildcard characters, search conditions
    and, 144
wildcard operators, LIKE operator
    and, 118
WORK keyword
    Oracle, 46
    PostgreSQL, 46
work tables, 24

About the Author

Kevin Kline is the team leader for Information Architecture within Shared Information Services at Deloitte & Touche LLP. Kevin and his team perform data and infrastructure architecture in support of major knowledge management and transaction processing systems for Deloitte's Client Service Technology organization. Kevin is also the author of *Transact-SQL Programming* (O'Reilly, 1999) (*http://www.oreilly.com/catalog/wintrnssql/*) and numerous magazine articles on Microsoft SQL Server. When he's not pulling his hair out over work issues, Kevin likes to romance his wife, play with his three kids, tinker with his '66 Chevy pickup, and garden.

Other than being Kevin's brother, **Daniel Kline** is an Assistant Professor of English at the University of Alaska, Anchorage, where he specializes in medieval literature, literary and cultural theory, and computer-assisted pedagogy. He completed his Ph.D. at Indiana University, Bloomington, and in addition to numerous scholarly presentations, Dan recently has published academic essays in *Literary and Linguistic Computing*, *Philological Quarterly*, *Chaucer Review*, and *Essays in Medieval Studies*. When he's not spending time with his wife and two boys, Dan frets over his pet project, the Electronic Canterbury Tales (*http://cwolf.uaa.alaska.edu/~afdtk/ext_main.htm*). Dan can be reached at *afdtk@ uaa.alaska.edu*.

Colophon

Our look is the result of reader comments, our own experimentation, and feedback from distribution channels. Distinctive covers complement our distinctive approach to technical topics, breathing personality and life into potentially dry subjects.

The animal on the cover of *SQL in a Nutshell* is a chameleon. There are approximately 85 species of chameleons existing in the world today. They are mostly indigenous to Africa, although there are a few species found in Asia and in Europe. Most are tree dwellers. The chameleon is relatively small; the average adult size is between 6 inches and 12 inches. It lives mostly on insects, and uses its long tongue to capture its prey. Indeed, the tongue is a critical tool. It can stretch up to 1.5 times the lizard's body length, and there is an adhesive pad on the end, which the insects are trapped on. There are several other characteristics common to all species of chameleons. For example, its eyes are large and protruding, and the lizard can see 360 degrees around without moving its head or body. Its toes are on either side of its feet, usually with three on one side and two on the other. This is ideal for moving quickly and efficiently through tree branches.

Chameleons are best known for their ability to change their appearance to adapt to their physical environment. Actually, several types of reptiles can change their skin color, but the chameleon is far and away the most accomplished. This skill, which is moderated by the nervous system, obviously is invaluable for hunting prey and avoiding predators, and also helps to stablize body temperature. The extent of this camouflage capability is related to the gender, age, and species of the lizard.

Mary Sheehan was the production editor and proofreader for *SQL in a Nutshell*, and Jeffrey Holcomb was the copyeditor. Emily Quill and Colleen Gorman provided quality control. Linley Dolby provided production assistance. Brenda Miller wrote the index.

Ellie Volckhausen designed the cover of this book, based on a series design by Edie Freedman. The cover image is a 19th-century engraving from the Dover Pictorial Archive. Emma Colby produced the cover layout with QuarkXPress 4.1 using Adobe's ITC Garamond font.

Melanie Wang designed the interior layout based on a series design by Nancy Priest. The text and heading fonts are ITC Garamond Light and Garamond Book. The illustrations that appear in the book were produced by Robert Romano using Macromedia FreeHand 8 and Adobe Photoshop 5. This colophon was written by Mary Sheehan.

Whenever possible, our books use a durable and flexible lay-flat binding. If the page count exceeds this binding's limit, perfect binding is used.

O'Reilly & Associates, Inc.
101 Morris Street
Sebastopol, CA 95472-9902
1-800-998-9938

Visit us online at:
www.oreilly.com
order@oreilly.com

O'REILLY WOULD LIKE TO HEAR FROM YOU

Which book did this card come from?

_____

Where did you buy this book?
- ❏ Bookstore
- ❏ Direct from O'Reilly
- ❏ Bundled with hardware/software
- ❏ Other _____
- ❏ Computer Store
- ❏ Class/seminar

What operating system do you use?
- ❏ UNIX
- ❏ Windows NT
- ❏ Other _____
- ❏ Macintosh
- ❏ PC (Windows/DOS)

What is your job description?
- ❏ System Administrator
- ❏ Network Administrator
- ❏ Web Developer
- ❏ Other _____
- ❏ Programmer
- ❏ Educator/Teacher

❏ Please send me O'Reilly's catalog, containing a complete listing of O'Reilly books and software.

Name _____   Company/Organization _____

Address _____

City _____ State _____   Zip/Postal Code _____ Country _____

Telephone _____   Internet or other email address (specify network) _____

Nineteenth century wood engraving
of a bear from the O'Reilly &
Associates Nutshell Handbook®
Using & Managing UUCP.

POST CARD

BUSINESS REPLY MAIL
FIRST CLASS MAIL   PERMIT NO. 80   SEBASTOPOL, CA

Postage will be paid by addressee

O'Reilly & Associates, Inc.
101 Morris Street
Sebastopol, CA 95472-9902